Racist Murder
and Pressure Group Politics

Dedicated to those founts of pride and joy

Robert and Sarah Hodkinson of Holyport
and Max Dennis of Pensacola

Institute for the Study of Civil Society
London

First published September 2000

© The Institute for the Study of Civil Society 2000
email: books@civil-society.org.uk

ISBN 1-903 386-05 5

Typeset by the Institute for the Study of Civil Society
in New Century Schoolbook

Printed in Great Britain by
The Cromwell Press
Trowbridge, Wiltshire

Contents

The Authors

Norman Dennis was born in 1929 in Sunderland, one of the four sons of a tram-car driver. He was educated at Green Terrace Elementary School and the Bede Collegiate Boys' School. He won a place at Corpus Christi, Oxford, but chose to go to the London School of Economics, where he was awarded a First Class Honours in Economics. He was Reader in Social Studies at the University of Newcastle upon Tyne, where George Erdos and Ahmed Al-Shahi were his long-time colleagues and friends. He has been a Rockefeller Fellow, Ford Fellow, Fellow of the Center for Advanced Study in the Behavioral Sciences at Palo Alto, Leverhulme Fellow, and Visiting Fellow at the University of Newcastle upon Tyne. He is currently Director of Community Studies at the Institute for the Study of Civil Society.

With Professor A.H. Halsey he is author of *English Ethical Socialism,* Clarendon Press, 1988. The Institute for the Study of Civil Society (ISCS) is the current publisher of his *Families Without Fatherhood* (with George Erdos), Third Edition, ISCS, 2000; *Rising Crime and the Dismembered Family*, ISCS, 1993 and *The Invention of Permanent Poverty*, ISCS, 1997. He edited and with Detective Superintendent Ray Mallon contributed two chapters to *Zero Tolerance: Policing a Free Society,* ISCS, 1997, and contributed 'Beautiful Theories, Brutal Facts: the welfare state and sexual liberation' to *Welfare, Work and Poverty* (edited by David Smith), ISCS, 2000. He is also well known for his study of a Yorkshire coal-mining town, *Coal Is Our Life* (with Cliff Slaughter and Fernando Henriques), Eyre and Spottiswood, 1956, and two participant-observation studies of bureaucracy and politics as they affected the working-class district of his birth, Millfield, Sunderland, *People and Planning*, Faber and Faber, 1970, and *Public Participation and Planners' Blight*, 1972.

He has been a Sunderland city councillor and is active in his ward Labour party. He is currently studying the question of what constitutes effective and appropriate policing in a free society when it experiences a rapid rise in the frequency of crime and sub-criminal disorder. He is also studying the struggle between the bureaucratic, political, academic and media advocates of drug, educational and family permissiveness in Zürich and one of their most important opponents, a Zürich citizen's organisation called the VPM.

George Erdos was born in 1946 in Hungary, and spent his formative years there. He left in 1964. He finished his secondary education in Germany. He then studied psychology at the universities of Frankfurt,

New Hampshire, Bar-Ilan, Mainz and Cambridge. He settled in England and took British citizenship. He is currently lecturer in psychology at the University of Newcastle upon Tyne. In the 1980s he worked on the Educational Opportunities programme of the state of New Jersey. Its basis was that, in the course of studying for and by obtaining a university degree, the African-American male would assimilate his conduct to that of the American white middle-class male and be enabled to enjoy success in American terms. Although the programme was targeted at African-American men, it was actually utilised with enthusiasm by African-American women. Changes rapidly taking place at that time in the culture and conduct of white middle-class men stimulated Dr Erdos's interest in the role of the colour, class and culture (including the weakening of all cultures towards a state of what Emile Durkheim called *anomie*, the absence of cultural controls) in English and American society. He is an adherent of ethical socialism, in the sense given the term in *English Ethical Socialism*. He experienced communism directly, and through his German relatives he experienced fascism indirectly. He saw that in times of disorder people can be brought to abandon their civil liberties for the sake of security.

Ahmed Al-Shahi is a British citizen of Kurdish origin. He received his university education in Baghdad. He came to England in 1959, where he completed his postgraduate training in social anthropology, first at the University of London, and then at Oxford University. He taught social anthropology at the University of Khartoum and at the University of Newcastle upon Tyne. In the course of his research in northern Sudan, particularly among the Shaygiyya tribe, he experienced at first hand a society of rich ethnic, cultural and religious diversity.

Among his publications are *Wisdom from the Nile* (with F.C.T. Moore), Oxford, 1978; *Islam in the Modern World* (co-editor with Denis MacEoin), Croom Helm, 1983; *Themes from Northern Sudan*, Ithaca, 1986 and *The Diversity of the Muslim Community* (editor), Ithaca, 1987. He is currently attached to the Middle East Centre at St. Antony's College, Oxford, where he teaches the anthropology of the Middle East. He continues his research and writing on the role of knowledge, tolerance, and institutional structures in striking the right balance between integration, the maintenance of cultural identity, and mutual accommodation in the special circumstances of each society.

Foreword

Racist Murder and Pressure Group Politics dissects the Macpherson report and questions its approach. Race has become an issue surrounded by raw sensitivities and the authors, Ahmed Al-Shahi, Norman Dennis and George Erdos, have shown great courage in tackling it without fear or favour—in the best tradition of university scholarship.

This book is published as a companion volume to *Institutional Racism and the Police: Fact or Fiction*, which contains a range of views as an aid to public debate. In that book, John Grieve of the Metropolitan Police and Mike O'Brien, a Home Office Minister, describe their reactions to the Macpherson report, while Lord Skidelsky and Michael Ignatieff challenge Macpherson's claim that the Metropolitan Police were guilty of 'institutional racism'.

David G. Green

Authors' Note

Since the achievement of universal suffrage, English democracy has been a system, in world-historical terms, of relatively open discussion, respect for the views of unpopular minorities and weak external controls on conduct. If the internalisation of the values appropriate to it fails, then civil liberties are threatened—on the one side by the growth of crime and private violence, and on the other by the growth of governmental intervention to contain them. Displaying the correct set of beliefs then becomes more important than collecting and weighing evidence.

The Macpherson report shows with compelling clarity how 'evidence' in these circumstances is elicited, evaluated and presented. The authors applaud the benevolence of the report's intentions. But it is their shared view that even the best cause is in danger of serving the worst interests if its supporters grow reckless in their attributions of guilt and careless in their acceptance of what constitutes evidence of it.

Preface

Over seven years have passed since Stephen Lawrence was murdered. He is remembered and mourned. But the passage of time is blunting the memory of the plain chronology of the tragedy and its ramifications. The purpose of this Preface is simply to set out the sequence of the main events.

The First Few Minutes

Stephen Lawrence was murdered on the night of Thursday 22 April 1993. Stephen Lawrence and Duwayne Brooks were waiting with three other people for a bus home. Restless, the two friends walked away from the stop to get a better view of any available bus. While they were moving back towards the bus stop, separated by a few yards, a white gang appeared. Seeing Stephen closest to them, and shouting 'What, what! Nigger!', they rushed across the road, and Stephen was stabbed twice by the leading thug. Stephen was a fine athlete. Fatally wounded, he was able to run up the road with Duwayne before collapsing to the ground.

There was a telephone kiosk immediately across the road from where Stephen fell, and Duwayne Brooks' 999 call is logged as being received at 10.43 p.m. A local couple making their way home from a prayer meeting at the Roman Catholic church nearby had seen Stephen fall. They crossed the road and began to attend to and comfort him as best they could. An off-duty police constable and his wife were passing in their car. They stopped and went to Stephen's assistance.

The first few minutes that elapsed between the arrival of the police on the murder scene and the departure of the ambulance loom large in the racist charges against the police. First, the inadequacy of the first aid administered by the on-duty police was allegedly due to their racism. The police officers, Mrs Lawrence said, 'did not want to get their hands dirty with a black man's blood'. Second, racism was the explanation for the casualness of the police at the scene in not searching for the suspects and not ensuring that evidence was preserved.[1] Third, the police's alleged inappropriate treatment at the murder scene of Stephen's friend, Duwayne Brooks, is one of the six proofs adduced by the Macpherson report that the officers concerned with investigating the murder were racist.[2]

Then, at 10.50 p.m., seven minutes after the 999 call had been received by the British Telecom operator, the first police car arrived. The ambulance arrived at 10.54. The ambulance left the scene at 11.03, and it reached the hospital three minutes later. Duwayne

Brooks was taken to the hospital in a police car that accompanied the ambulance. The medical team desperately attempted to resuscitate Stephen, but failed. His death certificate was signed at 11.17 p.m.

When the chairman of the Commission for Racial Equality, Herman Ouseley, heard early on 23 April 1993 of the previous night's murder he telephoned the Metropolitan Police Commissioner, Paul Condon, to say this was a racist crime, and it was imperative that it should be investigated as a racist crime. The Metropolitan Police Commissioner passed Herman Ouseley's message to Detective Chief Superintendent Ilsley, the senior officer in the area where the murder had been committed.

At 2.30 p.m. on that Friday afternoon a press conference was held in Woolwich police station, where the major figures were Neville Lawrence and DCS Ilsley. DCS Ilsley immediately said that it appeared to be a racial murder, 'outrageous and senseless'. The local MP said he was seeking meetings with government ministers. Neville Lawrence said that he would bring back hanging for such crimes. DCS Ilsley then attended an emergency meeting of the Greenwich council police consultative committee, which was attended also by the local MP and the MP for the neighbouring constituency. Councillors, council workers, race-relations officials and representatives of various ethnic groups aired the grievances that black people had against the police.

The First Vital Hours

While the ambulance was still at the scene of the murder, a vanload of officers from the Territorial Support Group (TSG) arrived and started to tour the neighbouring streets. More TSG vans arrived in the next hour. Other police officers were called to the scene from their homes. Dogs and powerful lamps were brought in to search the road along which the attackers had escaped.

At 12.30 a.m. Detective Superintendent Crampton was called from his bed to take charge of the investigation for the first three days, after which he had to return to his own current case. He worked continuously on the case for more than 18 hours, returning home for a break at 7 p.m. on Friday 23 April.

At 6.30 a.m. on Friday 23 April, having interviewed Duwayne Brooks and visited the murder scene, DS Crampton discussed the case with DCS Ilsley. That morning DCS Ilsley began to assemble a team of officers. In size it came closer to meeting Metropolitan Police Service (MPS) guidelines than most MPS murder investigations. By Friday midday the first information had been entered into the computerised Home Office Large Major Enquiry System (Holmes). The newly assembled team, which quickly grew to be about 25 strong, had to cope with the usual inconveniences and confusion attendant upon first setting up an incident room. The computer network had to be reconnected, enlarged, cleared of the data from the previous investigation and made to function.

In a phone call made to the police at 1.50 p.m., David Norris and Neil Acourt were named by an anonymous informant. They were described as members of a knife-carrying and bullying gang that might have been involved in the stabbing of the night before. Other anonymous messages, received through various channels in the course of the day, contained accusations that the Acourts and their gang had stabbed other people to death in the past, white and black, and were responsible now for the death of Stephen Lawrence.

An informant came to Eltham police station on Friday evening and identified himself. He was another who named the Acourt gang as the murderers of two local youths, Stacey Benefield (a white man) and Rohit Duggal. The informant said that he suspected that the Acourts, David Norris, and two other youths had killed Stephen Lawrence the night before. An anonymous woman phoned at 9 p.m. The notes of the conversation say that she accused two boys known as the Krays of murdering Stacey Benefield, and said that they might be involved in the murder of Stephen Lawrence.

The First Investigation, The Aborted Trial And The Barker Review

DS Crampton decided over the course of the weekend that the information that had accumulated did not yet form a body of evidence that would justify the arrest of the suspects. As planned, DS Crampton was replaced by a new Senior Investigation Officer on Monday 26 April. The new SIO, DS Weeden, continued to pursue DS Crampton's policy, namely, to gather evidence before arresting the suspects, rather than arresting the suspects and then gathering evidence.

A fortnight of intensive police work followed, some of which could be easily criticised as bungled. (It was to be mercilessly lampooned by counsel for the Lawrences at the Macpherson inquiry.) The Senior Investigating Officer, DS Weeden, conducted a review of the evidence on the afternoon of Thursday, 6 May.

The Lawrence case was by now an international *cause célèbre*. That same afternoon, 6 May, the Lawrences were being received by Nelson Mandela in his suite at the Atheneum Hotel in Piccadilly. Nelson Mandela said that 'the Lawrences' tragedy is our tragedy'. He commented on the brutality of the murder. They were used to such brutality in South Africa, he told the press, 'where black lives are cheap'. Doreen Lawrence said that she was sure that the police knew who her son's killers were, but had not arrested them. What is more, the police were patronising the Lawrences. 'They're not dealing with illiterate blacks. We're educated.' Why was it that a leader of a foreign country was expressing sympathy with the Lawrences, she asked, 'while our own government has expressed no sympathy at all?'

DS Weeden's decision of 6 May was that he now did have enough evidence to arrest some of the suspects. Warrants were issued for the arrest of the Acourt brothers, Gary Dobson and David Norris. The first three were arrested on 7 May, Norris on 9 May. Luke Knight was arrested on 3 June.

Intensive investigations preceded and followed the arrests of the suspects. But the police had not collected enough evidence to satisfy the Crown Prosecution Service (CPS). The long-awaited forensic evidence proved negative. On 28 July 1993, therefore, formal notices were issued that there would be no committal and no trial at that time. The case was still open. Although investigations did not cease, this marked the end of what came to be known as the first investigation into the murder of Stephen Lawrence.

The reasons for the failure of the first investigation, and the lessons to be learned from it, were reviewed in an internal inquiry for the MPS by DCS Barker. The results of the Barker review were produced on 1 November 1993. The conclusion was that although it was deeply regrettable that evidence that was strong enough to go before the court had not been uncovered, 'all lines of inquiry had been correctly pursued'.

The Second Investigation And The Failure Of The Private Trial

The first murder investigation continued its efforts to no avail. On 5 April 1994 the CPS for the second time announced that it had reached 'the unavoidable conclusion ... that there was no prospect of a jury convicting anyone on the evidence available'.[3] In June 1994 the decision was taken to reinvigorate the inquiry into the murder of Stephen Lawrence. DS Mellish was put in charge, as Senior Investigation Officer, of what became known as the second investigation. He was conspicuously backed by the personal presence at the launch of the second investigation by Assistant Commissioner Ian Johnston. The dwindling numbers of the team from the first investigation was raised to 15, and, in Cathcart's words, 'resources in money and specialist support were suddenly available on a scale more often seen in anti-terrorist investigations than a civil murder'.[4] The Lawrences were later to put on record their appreciation of the way in which DS Mellish had conducted the second investigation, and Macpherson says that 'Mr Mellish did all that he could during his time as SIO'.[5] The innovation in the second investigation best known to the public was the secret videotaping of the hate-filled idle leisure of members of the Acourt gang in the flat of one of its members.

The Lawrences (on the advice of their lawyers) decided that the evidence from the second investigation was strong enough to ensure that a private prosecution for murder would be successful. This was against the advice of the police. In the police's view, the evidence was too weak; and, of course, if anyone were to be acquitted on the weak evidence, he would be freed from the threat of being prosecuted again, even if strong evidence were subsequently to be brought to light. In DS Mellish's judgement, the videotapes produced 'not one iota' of evidence of murder and would not be admitted, and that 'a half-reasonable defence barrister' would 'make mincemeat' of Duwayne Brooks' identification evidence.[6] Once the Lawrences had made their decision to prosecute the suspects privately, however, they received the full co-operation of the police in preparing their case.

Two years to the day after the murder, on 22 April 1995, proceedings were started at Greenwich Magistrates Court against four of the main suspects, namely, the Acourts, Norris and Knight, and they were immediately arrested. The committal trial began at Belmarsh Magistrates' Court on 23 August 1995. Dobson was arrested on 28 August, and was committed for trial half way through the main committal proceedings. The magistrate found that there was enough evidence to commit Neil Acourt, Luke Knight and Gary Dobson for trial.

The private prosecution began at the Old Bailey on 17 April 1996. The judge ruled that Duwayne Brooks' identification evidence relating to Acourt and Knight (which was linked to the evidence against Dobson) was tainted. He instructed the jury that in the circumstance it had no alternative. It must bring in a verdict of not guilty. All three defendants were duly pronounced not guilty and discharged.

Assistant Commissioner Johnston issued a statement that Scotland Yard would go on looking 'forever' for evidence that would convict the murderers of Stephen Lawrence.[7]

The Inquest and The Kent Report

The inquest had been convened and adjourned in December 1993. It had been postponed on several occasions in 1994. It was then deferred again until after the conclusion of the Lawrences' private prosecution of the Acourts, Knight and Dobson in April 1996. It finally took place over four days in February 1997. The images of the conduct of the five suspects at the inquest, now young men, no longer underage teenagers, are well known. 'Do you know a woman called Michelle Casserley?' 'I claim privilege.' 'Where were you living at the time?' 'I claim privilege.'

'Are you Mr Norris?' 'I claim privilege.' It was the same answer from all of them, to nearly all questions. On Friday 14 February 1997, the day after the inquest closed, the *Daily Mail* produced photographs of the Acourts, Norris, Knight and Dobson, and under the two-inch headline 'Murderers' challenged the men to sue the newspaper.

The coroner granted Doreen Lawrence's request to make a statement at the inquest. In it she said that the suspects at the private trial had been acquitted because the Crown Court had been staged. The purpose of the rigged acquittal was to make a clear statement to the black community that their lives were worth nothing. The system of British justice, she said, supported any white person who wished to commit murder against any black person. Her son had been stereotyped by the police as a criminal and a gang member because he was black. 'Our crime was living in a country where the justice system supports racist murderers against innocent people.'

The Lawrences announced on 13 February 1997 that they had decided to take their case to the Police Complaints Authority (PCA). The family's complaints lay in six main areas: the failure to administer first aid to Stephen; the management of the murder scene; police liaison with the family; the conduct of the murder investigation; separately, the lack of commitment by the police because it was a black and not a white youth who had been murdered; and possible corruption or collusion.[8]

The PCA mounted a full external examination of these complaints. The investigation, undertaken for the PCA by Kent Constabulary under Deputy Chief Constable Ayling, began in March 1997. The evidence that was to constitute the full 400-page report was made available to the Macpherson inquiry. A brief version of the report was made public as command paper Cm 3822 on 15 December 1997.

The Kent investigation had found, the report said, that the police's initial response had been 'prompt and professional' and that the management of the murder scene was 'of a high standard'. Overall, however, the Kent report identified in the first investigation of the murder of Stephen Lawrence a 'large number of oversights and omissions which resulted in the murder investigation failing to operate to an acceptable standard'. The second investigation of the murder was described as being 'successful in some respects'.[9] But the intensive complaint investigation, undertaken by a deputy chief constable and with the full-time commitment of a detective chief superintendent, two inspectors, a sergeant, six detective constables, and a Holmes specialist over period of nine months, had not produced, said the Kent report, *'any evidence to support allegations of racist conduct by police officers'*.[10]

The next day, 16 December 1997, the main headline of the *Daily Mail* was, 'Lawrence: the damning facts', and the publicity for the report was similar in the other national newspapers.

The Macpherson Inquiry

In June 1997, shortly after Labour's victory in the general election, the setting up of what was to become the Macpherson inquiry was announced in the House of Commons by the new Home Secretary, Jack Straw. Its remit was to inquire into matters arising from the death of Stephen Lawrence. In particular, what lessons could be learned for the investigation and prosecution of racially motivated crimes? The first preliminary hearing took place at Woolwich on 8 November 1997. The inquiry, which Macpherson estimated would have cost in excess of £3 million, took place in three parts.

After some initial postponements, Part I proper commenced on 16 March 1998. This took the form of formal hearings at Hannibal House, Elephant and Castle, in which the police officers involved in the Lawrence investigation were called as 'witnesses' and were examined and cross-examined by legal counsel. Other witnesses, including Mr and Mrs Lawrence, were also called and examined and cross-examined by counsel. These proceedings looked in this and other ways something like an English court of law, including hearings described as being 'in chambers'.[11]

From the evidence from these hearings, at the organisational level Macpherson did not find any official policies, sanctioned rules or permitted practices that encouraged or condoned racism. Even at the level of the conduct of individual police officers, Macpherson said, 'we have not heard evidence of overt racism or discrimination, unless it can be said that the use of inappropriate expressions such as "coloured" or "negro" fall into this category'.[12]

When the inquiry was over, Macpherson and his colleagues 'grappled with the problem'. They took into account 'all that they had heard and read'. They came up with the following concept of chronic organisational failure:

> *The collective failure of an organisation to provide an appropriate and professional service to people because of their colour, culture or ethnic origin. It can be seen or detected in processes, attitudes and behaviour which amount to discrimination through unwitting prejudice, ignorance, thoughtlessness and racist stereotyping which disadvantage minority ethnic people.* It persists because of the failure of the organisation openly and adequately to recognise and address its existence and causes by policy, example and leadership. Without recognition and action to eliminate such racism it can prevail as part of the ethos or culture of the organisation. It is a corrosive disease.[13]

The language of infection replaced the language of conduct: Macpherson applied this notion of endemic organisational failure retrospectively to the Stephen Lawrence investigation.

The second part of the inquiry also took place in Hannibal House, in late September and early October 1998. It took the form of oral evidence from certain of the 148 organisations and individuals ('those best placed to implement any recommendations') who had responded to public invitations (for example, through advertisements placed in various newspapers) to make written submissions 'about their concerns in respect of racially motivated crime, and ideas about the future handling of such cases'.[14]

The proceedings of Part II did not resemble those of a court of law. Contributors were questioned by Sir William and his three advisers. Among those questioned were the Commissioner of the Metropolitan Police Service, Sir Paul Condon.

Part III of the inquiry took the form of meetings in public at Ealing, Tower Hamlets, Manchester, Bradford, Bristol and Birmingham during the course of October and November 1998. The purpose of these meetings in public was not fact-finding in the broad sense. It was, Macpherson said, to 'test the temperature of opinion outside South East London'.[15]

Macpherson concluded from Parts II and III of the inquiry that the chronic organisational failure defined above (the concept was soon to be universally known by Macpherson's term for it, 'institutional racism') was not confined to the police. 'It is clear that other agencies including for example those dealing with housing and education also suffer from the disease.'[16]

The report, published as command paper Cm 4262 in February 1999, was received with general acclaim.

Norman Dennis

Summary

The public inquiry set up under the chairmanship of Sir William Macpherson sometimes had the appearance of a judicial proceeding, but in many crucial respects it departed from practices which have traditionally been regarded as essential in English law. Rules of evidence were modified and witnesses were harassed, both by the members of the inquiry team and by the crowd in the public gallery. Representatives of the Metropolitan Police were asked to 'confess' to charges of racism, even if only in their private thoughts. They were even asked to testify to the existence of the racist thoughts of other people. It is part neither of the English judicial process nor of English public inquiries to put people on trial for their thoughts. The proceedings bore some resemblance to the Stalinist show trials of the 1930s.

However, no evidence of racism on the part of the police was ever produced. There was no attempt to show that the Metropolitan Police Service was racist in the sense of being formally structured to put members of ethnic minorities at a disadvantage. Nor was any evidence produced that individual officers dealing with the murder of Stephen Lawrence had displayed racism, unless one includes the use of words like 'coloured' which are currently out of favour with professional race relations lobbyists. No evidence was produced to indicate that the police would have handled the investigation differently had the victim been white.

In spite of this, the Macpherson report found the Metropolitan Police, and British society generally, guilty of 'institutional' or 'unwitting' racism. This claim was justified by referring to 'other bodies of evidence' to that collected at the public inquiry, including a list of publications consulted which in many cases had nothing to do with the Lawrence case, and sometimes nothing to do with the UK at all.

Some of the Macpherson report's proofs of racism were circular and self-reinforcing. To question whether the murder of Stephen Lawrence was a purely racist crime was, in itself, adduced as evidence of racism. This was despite the fact that the suspects had been accused of violent offences against white people and were heard, in tape recordings made of their private conversations, to express violent hatred against white people. The tape recordings were quoted selectively, and this crucial fact does not appear in the Macpherson report.

The Macpherson inquiry, unable to find evidence of racism, produced a definition of racism that at first glance absolved it from producing any. It switched attention, in one direction, away from racist conduct and towards organisational failure. The ineffectiveness of the police had (purportedly) been demonstrated. That ineffectiveness concerned *a racist crime. Therefore the ineffectiveness was due to police racism. It switched attention, in the other direction, away from observable conduct, words or gestures and towards the police officer's 'unwitting' thoughts and conduct. But how could the Macpherson inquiry know what was in an officer's unconscious mind—except through the failure of the police to be effective in the investigation of a racist crime? This definition puts charges of racism outside the boundaries of proof or rebuttal.*

The Macpherson report has had a detrimental impact on policing and crime, particularly in London. Police morale has been undermined. Certain procedures which impact disproportionately on ethnic groups, like stop and search, have been scaled down. The crime rate has risen. Nevertheless, the Macpherson report has been received with almost uncritical approval by pundits, politicians and academics. It is still routinely described as having 'proved' that the police and British society are racist.

Introduction

Mrs Lawrence's Experience Of Racism

At the time of the Macpherson inquiry Mrs Doreen Lawrence was aged 46, and she had lived in England since she was nine. In her statement to the inquiry she said:

> I personally have never had any racism directed at me. There was always something I felt on the outskirts but nobody ever directly approached me and was racist towards me. ... Because of how we lived as a family we got on with people. Our immediate next-door neighbour were a white family and we got on with them very well. The children were the same age as my children. We lived in each other's houses and we had no problems.[1]

Yet Mrs Lawrence is now the best-known victim of police racism, just as her son is now the best-known victim of racist criminality that this country has every seen.

The Macpherson Report's Evidence And Findings

The Mass of 'Evidence'

In Part I of the proceedings of the Macpherson inquiry, held in Hannibal House, Elephant and Castle, police officers, in effect the accused, were pitted against their accusers for 59 days.

All had their lawyers. There were lawyers for the Lawrences, for Stephen Lawrence's friend Duwayne Brooks, for the Metropolitan Police Service, for the police superintendents, for police officers of lower rank, for the Commission for Racial Equality, for Greenwich Borough Council, for the Crown Prosecution Service. There were QCs, other leading barristers, junior barristers, solicitors.

Twelve thousand pages of transcript were amassed. One thousand pages of submission came from counsel for the parties they represented. The 400-page report from the Kent Police Service, 'that damning assessment of the performance of the Met',[2] had not been made public, but the lawyers relied heavily upon it.

Eighty-eight witnesses gave evidence.

In Part II of the inquiry 100 people and organisations gave evidence. In Part III public meetings were held in Ealing, Manchester, Tower Hamlets, Bradford, Bristol and Birmingham.[3]

Macpherson selected from this massive body of material what was considered the most telling evidence on police racism.

Macpherson's Findings on Police Racism

The good intentions of police officers

Inconsistent with findings of police racism, Macpherson refers to the 'good intentions' of the officers involved in family liaison with the Lawrences.[4]

The exoneration of officers as individuals

Inconsistent with findings of police racism, there are clear exonerations of police officers of racist conduct whenever concrete, evidential matters are at stake. On the issue of the poor quality of the first aid administered to Stephen Lawrence, for example, Macpherson writes that:

> There was no indication given to us during her long cross-examination that PC Bethel would have acted differently if the person on the pavement had been white.[5]

> We gained a favourable impression of PC Geddis. He was after all the good Samaritan ... Mrs Lawrence passed on her thanks to PC Geddis. We have no hesitation in saying there was no racist motivation in PC Geddis's failure of first aid.[6]

> There is no indication that he [PC Gleason] was consciously affected by the fact that Stephen Lawrence was black, and that Mr Brooks was black.[7]

> ... we are sure that any deficiency ... was caused by lack of training rather than lack of will to help.[8]

Macpherson's insistence on the police racism it did not find

The Macpherson report expresses its anxiety that it should not be misunderstood.

Was the report to be understood as saying that the policies of the Metropolitan Police Service were racist? No. 'It is vital for us to stress', Macpherson says, 'that neither academic debate nor the evidence presented to us leads us to say or conclude that an accusation that institutional racism exists in the MPS implies that the policies of the MPS are racist. No such evidence is before us. Indeed the contrary is true'.[9]

Nor was Macpherson saying 'or implying' that every officer was 'guilty of racism'. 'No such sweeping suggestion can be or should be made.'[10]

Nor was Macpherson saying that he had found any evidence of 'overt' racist conduct. 'In this Inquiry we have not heard evidence of overt racism or discrimination, unless it can be said that the use of inappropriate expressions ... fall into this category.'[11]

Was it to be understood as saying that the police investigation had failed because of racism? No, Macpherson was not saying that the police investigation had failed because of racism. Macpherson says: 'We do not accept that'.[12]

Brian Cathcart, former deputy editor of the *Independent on Sunday*, who attended the inquiry throughout, and whose book *The Case of Stephen Lawrence* cannot be described as critical of Macpherson, wrote that 'as the inquiry moved towards its close it was still the case that no evidence had been produced of a single act of deliberate, malicious racism by a single officer'. Nor had there been shown, he continues, that racism in any form had been the primary cause, or even one of several primary causes, of the failure of the Stephen Lawrence investigation to produce a conviction.[13]

The otherwise damaging report by the Kent Police Service team for the Police Complaints Authority 'found no evidence to support the allegation of racist conduct by any Metropolitan police officer involved in the investigation of the murder of Stephen Lawrence'.[14]

One searches in vain, indeed, throughout the Macpherson report and its appendices for evidence that any of the actions or statements of any officer was racist.

Yet the Macpherson report is now very widely quoted as the document that does contain the evidence that shows that not only the Metropolitan Police Service, not only all British police services, but all English institutions are 'riddled with racism'.

How did this come about?

1

The Main Issues

Stephen Lawrence's Death

The Stephen Lawrence affair is first and foremost—beyond comparison with any other issue—about the loss of Stephen Lawrence's life; the loss to his family of a son and brother; the loss to his other relatives and to his friends; and the loss to the country of an exemplary young citizen. No decent person wants it to be thought by anybody that, to the slightest degree or in any way, he or she is not wholeheartedly in sympathy with those who suffer from his loss, especially Doreen and Neville Lawrence.

The Murderers

Secondly it is about his murderers. No decent person sides with, or wants it to be thought by anybody at all, in the slightest degree, or in any way, that he or she is siding with them. That wish and this anxiety reaches to the main suspects. Knowing their way of life, no decent person sides with, or wants it to be thought that he or she is siding with them.

It is about murderers, and about the defects of the strong institutions of the media and the state (especially education and welfare) that produced them. It is about the strength of the murderers' nihilistic gang culture. It is also about, therefore, the weak or moribund social institutions of family, religion, other voluntary associations, and neighbourhoods.

Not long ago the use of knives in private quarrels or obsessions was as a matter of fact very unusual. As a matter of culture it was defined as something men from some countries might resort to in certain circumstances, but not English men in English civilian life. (Even in countries in which it is used to settle disputes and petty quarrels, the knife is looked down upon as the resort of ruffians and brigands.) English culture had for long succeeded in inculcating an abhorrence of any violent use of knives. The murderous use of knives in private life, and above all the murderous use of knives on a complete stranger, a kind of running amok, was for centuries almost unknown. William Cobbett gives an account of the anti-knife English culture in action in

4

1817. He was at Barnett Fair, and saw a quarrel going on between a butcher and a West-country grazier. The butcher, 'though vastly superior in point of size', reached for a knife. The grazier ran off, and came back with a stout ash stick. He knocked the knife from the butcher's hand, and then struck the butcher to ground. 'Draw thy knife wo't!' Such 'amongst Englishmen' was the abhorrence of fighting with a knife, Cobbett remarks, 'that not a soul attempted to interfere, and nobody seemed to pity the Butcher so unmercifully beaten'.[1] Hundreds of thousands of boys, as boy scouts, were once routinely armed by their parents with deadly sheath knives to wear on their belt, and sometimes with a second to stick in their stocking. Because their misuse was such a remote possibility and rare occurrence, parents and public accepted this state of affairs with perfect equanimity. As we write, flowers are being laid outside Sunderland railway station, where after a quarrel in the local Burger King yet another young man was stabbed to death.

Stephen Lawrence cannot be brought back to life. The main questions for public policy are, therefore, how had English society come to produce the young men who had killed him (that they used knives was incidental); was English society producing more of them than in the past; and if it was, what were the causes and ramifying consequences?

Racist Criminality

Thirdly, the tragedy was about the very important fact that the murderers' perception of Stephen Lawrence's race selected him for death. No decent person is a racist. Very few people want to be suspected of being racist.

When someone is chosen as the victim of a crime simply because he is hated or despised as being old, or a gypsy, or bourgeois, or an African-American, or homosexual, or a protestant, or a catholic, the single criminal incident threatens the whole category of which the victim is a member. That is what makes so special this reason for committing a crime, or appealing to prejudice in politics.

Since 1990, the Attorney General of the United States has been required to collect data 'about crimes that manifest evidence of prejudice'. Considerations of prejudice are restricted in the Act to the four categories of race, religion, sexual orientation and 'ethnicity'. The last takes into account only 'Hispanic' ethnicity as against any other ethnicity.[2] Some states of the USA have made selecting the victim of a crime because of prejudice a crime in its own right. The Louisiana criminal code, for example, now adds to the penalties for certain crimes, including murder, a penalty for the hate element. For the listed misdemeanours and felonies the additional hate penalty ranges up to a fine of $5,000 plus five years imprisonment with hard labour. The prison sentence for hate cannot be served concurrently. It has to be served in addition to the sentence for the underlying offence.[3]

But in this country it was not until 1993 that Her Majesty's Inspectorate of Constabulary required police forces nationally to add the 'ethnicity' of the people they searched to records kept under the Police and Criminal Evidence Act of 1984. The Home Office system of 'ethnic' monitoring dates back only to 1996. The Crime and Disorder Act 1998 then created the offences of racially aggravated assault, criminal damage and harassment. It also created racially aggravated offences against public order.

There are also, of course, 'kindness' crimes. Here the perpetrator selects as his or her victim the most virtuous of his fellow-citizens. His *modus operandi* (not his motive) is to appeal to passing pedestrians or motorists for help. It is the one who identifies himself as kind enough and civic-minded enough to stop who is attacked or robbed. This crime is destructive not only of the security of one category of citizen. It is destructive of the still more basic quality of trust, and between all citizens. If any civilians hesitated in coming to the assistance of Stephen Lawrence, the blame might or might not have lain partly with their prejudice; but it certainly lay partly with corrosive influence of such criminals. So far, however, there has been no suggestion that additional penalties should be borne for kindness crimes.

Police Racism

Fourthly, there was the important fact that none of Stephen Lawrence's murderers has been convicted. It is possible to take the view that because there is an additional threat and offence to society in the commission of a hate crime, the failure to convict hate criminals is particularly unacceptable. The Queen's Counsel who appeared for the Macpherson inquiry took this view. He said that it is repellant that anybody who commits a murder should get away with it. That 'anyone who murders for racist motives and should escape is *doubly* repellant'.[4] The failure to apprehend Stephen Lawrence's murderers, on these grounds, was twice as serious as, say, the failure to convict the murderers of PC Keith Blakelock, the Metropolitan policeman who was hacked to death by rioters on the Broadwater Farm estate in 1985.

This raises the issues of the effectiveness of the system for collecting evidence on the murder and of the personnel who worked within the system (largely a police matter); the way in which the evidence was brought before the courts (largely the concern of the Crown Prosecution Service); and the way in which the courts dealt with it (largely a matter for judges and juries). In so far as any of the systems or staff failed, in what ways and why were they defective? Was anyone concerned affected, and if anyone, to what degree was it due to ignorance of standard procedures; was it due to slackness in carrying them out; was it due to corrupt protection of one or more of the suspects; and to what degree was it due to their own racist approach to a racist crime?

The terms of reference of the Macpherson inquiry directed it to look at 'matters arising'—that is to say all important matters arising—from the death of Stephen Lawrence. It was also instructed to look particularly at lessons that could be learned for the ways in which racist *crimes* should be investigated and prosecuted.[5] As it turned out, it concentrated on the role of police officers. In concentrating on the police, it concentrated also on *police* racism as a principal explanation for the failure to convict any of Stephen Lawrence's murderers. In some sense it concentrated on the racism 'generally', somehow 'deep dyed', of all officers of all ranks serving in the MPS.

Macpherson says that, 'as the committal and trial papers show', the case against the five subjects for the racist *crime* was 'weak'. Whether the irony was lost we cannot tell, but in the end the 'true purpose or reason', as Macpherson put it, for which the youths who were suspected of the racist *murder* were called before the inquiry was to see if their evidence would convict the police of racism in the *investigation* of it.[6] Ironically, too, while Macpherson was able to 'infer' freely the guilt of the police officers suspected of racism, the rules of British justice forced the report to make clear that *no* inference was allowed to come from the inquiry as to the guilt of the racists suspected of murder.[7]

Under this fourth heading, there were in addition several important issues that were not connected directly or at all with the effectiveness of the police in the collection of evidence, but that were connected with the issue of police racism.

One of these important issues was the way in which Stephen Lawrence's injuries were treated by the police at the scene of the murder. His mother read a statement at the inquest into Stephen's death. She stated as a fact that the police officers present 'just stood there' while her son bled to death. 'I suppose once a policeman always a policeman who protects their own and not the black community.'[8]

Edmund Lawson QC, counsel for the Macpherson inquiry, said that it had to consider 'whether first aid was *denied* by the police because *"they did not want to dirty their hands with a black man's blood"*, as Mrs Lawrence asked after the inquest'.[9] That was a careless way of stating the inquiry's task, for there was not the single question only of *why* police officers at the scene 'denied' first aid to Stephen Lawrence.

There was also the previous and crucial question of *whether* they did 'deny' him first aid—an even stronger allegation than Mrs Lawrence's that they had 'just stood there', for 'denial' of first aid implies wilful callousness.

Another of these important issues, partly but not entirely a matter of the efficient collection of evidence, was the way in which police officers conducted themselves towards Duwayne Brooks, the other victim of the attack on Stephen Lawrence, and towards other witnesses or potential witnesses. This can be broadly described, without in any way diminishing its importance in this or any other all sphere of life, as the issue of 'sympathy', 'sensitivity' and, generally, 'politeness'. Dr Robin Oakley is quoted as saying that what is required in the police service is an 'occupational culture' that is sensitive to minority 'experience'.[10] Within the over-riding consideration of the police's role in applying those rules that apply equally to all, namely, the laws of the land, made by a democratically-elected parliament, there is no reason to restrict sensitivity to personality, culture and experience, only to the contacts between police officers and 'minorities'. As much politeness as is possible, given the situation, and for as long as possible, is a desideratum in all contacts between police officers and their fellow-citizens and others.

Remedies

Fifthly, there is the issue of what remedies ought to be applied to defects discovered. What should desirably be done, and what can practically be done, to stop other such murders? (In relation to any specific social problem, there are means of practically solving *that* problem which are ethically unavailable because of their ramification into areas of social life. In relation to any specific social problem there are, conversely, ethically desirable outcomes for the achievement of which there are insufficient efficacious means.) What both should be done that also can be done about the cultural conditions surrounding the murderers, and boys and men like them? Included among the cultural conditions here is, crucially, the *absence* of cultural constraints—what Emile Durkheim called elements of *anomie*.[11]

The Acourt brothers are supposed to have called themselves the Krays. The Kray twins, notorious East End thugs and tribal philanthropists, were in their heyday fêted as such by figures who were or had been at the peaks of aristocratic and political English life. 'From low to high doth dissolution climb, /And sinks from high to low ...'[12]

What should and can be done about securing the capture and conviction of racist murderers? In January 1997 a black musician and son of a Ghanaian diplomat, Michael Menson, was taunted, abused, robbed and deliberately doused with white spirit and left to burn to death on a January morning in a London street. As in the Lawrence case, the police had early information that pointed to suspects; as in the Lawrence case there were early police mistakes. But after the inquest in this post-Lawrence case, Deputy Assistant Commissioner John Grieve's Racial and Violent Crime Task Force took over the investigation. Mario Pereira was sentenced to life imprisonment for murder. Harry Constantinou received a 12-year sentence for manslaughter. A third attacker, Ozguy Cevak, who had taken Turkish citizenship after the murder, was tried and jailed in northern Cyprus for 14 years for manslaughter. Within the circle of their friends the three made no secret of the killing, and John Grieve described it therefore not only as a hate crime, but also as a 'boast crime'. Police surveillance had recorded Pereira telling an acquaintance, Hussein Abdullah, who was jailed for perverting the course of justice, that he had said, 'He's a nigger. Let's burn him'.[13]

The very least that a Task Force such as John Grieve's can ensure is that not less than equal resources are put into the investigation of crimes palpably affecting the basic sense of security of a wide stratum of the population as are put into crimes impinging mainly on the welfare of the victim only.

What should and can be done about any racism defined and approved by the law of the land, or the rules governing the practices of public bodies and voluntary associations? What both should and can be done about overt racism, about covert racism, in states, public bodies and voluntary associations whose laws and rules universally ban both? What, specifically, should be done that can be done about any individual or subcultural racism in the MPS, an institution which, *as an institution*, has neither a single rule nor a single approved procedure which condones it in any way? What can and should be done to make all police officers rigorous in their professional politeness—polite to people who are not to the slightest degree polite to them, as well as to those who are?

Passion And Proportion

All social situations are a complex amalgam of facts (many of them unascertainable) and values (most of them contestable). Some political commentators, therefore, have emphasised the importance of a person's location on the continuum formed by those people, at one extreme, who fully recognise this, to those, at the other, who totally ignore it. For Max Weber, for example, one's position on this continuum was far more important in its practical consequences than one's position on the continuum from 'left' to 'right'. He identified three pre-eminent qualities of an admirable social activist. The first, certainly, is passionate devotion to his or her cause, to the god—or demon—who is his overlord. But the second is realism. The admirable activist's passion is no 'sterile excitation'. He is passionately devoted to pursuing an end that is realisable, by means that are efficacious. Weber calls this 'matter-of-factness'. The third is, if it is possible to say so, even more important. For Weber 'the *decisive* psychological quality' of the admirable activist is a sense of proportion. To place less important issues above more important issues, to mix up the crucial with the trivial is, for Weber, the essence of irresponsibility. For Weber there are 'only two kinds of deadly sin' in social policy. One is the sin of irresponsibility. The other is the closely related sin of lack of objectivity.[14]

2

The Methods of Inquiry
used by Macpherson

Not everyone believes that it is possible to arrive at one version of 'the facts of the case' that is superior to other versions. Postmodernism, for example, holds that one person's account of 'the facts' is just as good as anybody else's. Most people in most societies, however, have taken the view that better and worse versions of 'the facts of the case' do exist. What are judged better- or worse-based facts depends on the extent to which procedures have been followed which are approved at the time by the people making the judgement. (Being better-based relative to other claims to the truth is not the same as being truer. Superior method is no guarantee of superior result. A factual description based on what are thought to be the well-based methods can be false; and a factual description based on what are thought to be poor methods can be correct—a good one-off guess, or a sound intuitive reading of the situation by someone with consistent 'good judgement'.)

One proof of factual truth is its enunciation in or by some authoritative source. This authority is very often some religious treatise, or some religious functionary or charismatic religious innovator. For example, for some people Darwin's theory of evolution cannot be true, because they know for certain from the Hebrew and Christian Old Testament, from the Word of God Himself, that God created the different species separately at the beginning of earthly time.[1]

Where the successful activities of many people over long periods of time have depended upon the veracity of a certain version of the facts, then 'what everybody knows to be true' is a persuasive argument for accepting this version oneself and expecting other people to do so. This is the appeal to common sense and common knowledge. Common sense is, however, hospitable to errors that do not adversely affect the activities of their time. It was once harmless common sense that the sun went round the earth. The common sense of particular groups can be particularly hospitable to errors that, if believed by other people, are beneficial to the group that propagates them.

Another way to prove that something is true about a specific local event is to expose various competing versions of the facts to several people who themselves have no particular reason for hoping that one version rather than another will be accepted as the correct one. They have no particular interest either way. For example, the facts of such a case were once what '12 good men and true' declared them to be. Like common sense this method of determining what is true is acknowledged by nearly everyone as extremely rough and ready. But it is better than very many of the possible alternatives. Both common sense and the jury are quite different from what, in the here-and-now, 'many people' think is true about something they have no reason to have studied—establishing the truth by show of hands.

Another widespread and major claim to truth is that 'scientific method' has been followed in trying to establish the facts and regularly observed associations between facts.

Different criteria for judging how well-based a given alleged 'statement of fact' is, can and do co-exist in the same society. In any specific situation several criteria of truth might be in operation, and often will be. In a court case, for example, there will be claims to truth based now on authority, now on science, now on the jury's verdict. The same person can be satisfied at one time or with one topic with one criterion or, at another time, or with another topic, with another criterion.

The Macpherson inquiry was concerned with a number of factual matters. What the facts actually were was fiercely contested by different individuals and different sets of people. The better or worse bases of at least some of these sets of facts were capable, *prima facie*, of being established by the use of something resembling scientific method. This was particularly the case with disputed facts in an area which increased in salience throughout the period of the Macpherson inquiry, and which ended in the public as the main 'findings' of the inquiry. These were the facts about the existence, the degree, and the character of the 'racism' of police constables, sergeants, and higher officers of the Metropolitan Police Service who had been involved with the investigation of the Stephen Lawrence murder and liaison with the Lawrence family.

To people who are not post-modernists, it would appear that the way to arrive at the best version of the facts was *not* to depend on the assertions of principled believers in an endemic and universal English racism which has severe consequences generally in the lives of members of ethnic minorities. (Portentous personal tragedies are a different matter.) Still less was it to depend on the assertions of principled opponents of the police.

It was best to make use of the closest approach to scientific method that the situation allowed. At the very least a conclusion would follow only from a quasi-scientific thought experiment designed to answer the question: '*in the given situation* was *this or that* black person treated worse than a white person would have been treated by *this or that* police officer, given the police officer's distinctive but legally and professionally permitted temperament, social experience, cultural affiliation, and so forth?' (With few exceptions, in present-day Britain anybody's 'cultural affiliation' is shorthand for his or her personal mélange of cultural traits gathered from many quarters, heavily qualified with an anomic disbelief in the legitimacy of cultural controls of any sort.)

The mode of arriving at the truth adopted by the Macpherson inquiry, however, was not scientific collection of data; and it would be difficult to point to any trace of an attempt to undertake even the kind of thought experiment described above.

The Macpherson 'Court'

In Part I of his three-stage inquiry, within the framework laid down by Lord Salmon for the conduct of Tribunals of Inquiry,[2] Sir William claimed flexibility for himself in controlling the procedures —on the authority of a few words spoken in a public lecture. Sir Richard Scott had said that 'the golden rule was' (that is, this is what Sir Richard thought the golden rule ought to be) that procedures 'to achieve fairness' should be 'tailored to suit the circumstances of each inquiry'.[3] What did Sir William's flexible approach create?

Superficially, the Macpherson inquiry resembled in many ways an English court trial. There was more than a score of barristers, many of them QCs. Witnesses were examined and cross-examined.

But there were no defendants and no jury. Assisted by three advisers, Sir William alone was responsible for assessing the degree and nature of the truth, of the exaggerations and of the lies contained in the statements put before him. His three advisers were the Rt. Reverend Dr John Sentamu, Bishop of Stepney; Dr Richard Stone, a general practitioner and chairman of the Jewish Council for Racial Equality; and Mr Tom Cook, a retired senior police officer.

The five youths suspected of stabbing Stephen Lawrence to death had secured a High Court ruling before appearing before the inquiry. It ensured that they could not be asked any questions linking them with the murder. Macpherson says that the court's ruling, which enabled the five suspects to appear before him at his inquiry with attitudes that were 'arrogant and dismissive', was 'plainly correct'.[4] When more is brought into the equation than moral outrage, the most righteous person can discover that the constraints of due process lie upon him or her as well as upon the police, and the criminal gallingly remains free. The circumspection of the policeman and the formality of the judge can both look to the victim or his family as inexcusable inefficiency (or worse) in the pursuit of 'justice'. (And both can be, indeed, the cause of inefficiency, or the excuse for it.) But the judge's problem and the police officer's is in many respects the same. What exonerates the judge from blame for letting the criminals go free also exonerates the police officer.

In the vast majority of the cases in what was, in effect, a trial, there was no suggestion of anyone having committed a crime or tort. Apart from the suspects, the main exception was the allegation of police corruption and collusion in acting in the interests of David Norris, the suspect who was the son of a prominent south-east London criminal. No proof was produced at any of the inquiries leading up to Macpherson's, and the Macpherson inquiry produced none.[5]

The Macpherson inquiry was nearly all about the proficiency of police officers' professional conduct and the purity of police officers' private thoughts. What those 'witnesses' who were 'defendants' in all but name had to face was in most cases an amorphous mass of accusations, ranging from the most heinous and disgusting racism, to the inappropriateness of their body language in stressful encounters, the former being sometimes deduced from the latter.

On the particular subject of racism, Macpherson applied the civil standard of proof of what the facts are, 'namely, that we are satisfied upon a balance of probability that any conclusion that we reach is justified'. He applied as the standard of 'legitimate inference' that which can 'fairly and as a matter of "common sense *not law*" be drawn from the evidence'. His authorities for adopting such a method of 'establishing' the extent and degree of racism in the actions and feelings of police officers are the civil law and the *obiter dicta* of Lord Justice May and Mr Justice Mummery. Mr Justice Mummery's methodology is quoted in full. 'The process of inference is itself a matter of applying common sense and judgement to facts, and assessing the probabilities on this issue of whether racial grounds were an effective cause of the acts complained of or not. The assessment of *the parties and their witnesses when they give evidence* also form an important part of the process of inference.'[6]

The Abstraction Of Abject Apologies[7]

In a criminal court the accused is not there so that he can be compelled to confess his crimes; still less so that he can confess his sins; much less again so that he can disclose the sins of his subordinates. English law expelled those abhorrent ideas long ago.[8] But confession was the spirit of much of the Macpherson proceedings, partly due to the effect of the 'truth and reconciliation' proceedings in post-apartheid South Africa. This was especially clear in the interruption by one of Sir William's three advisers, Dr Richard Stone, of Sir Paul Condon's evidence in Part II of the inquiry. 'It seems to me, Sir Paul', he said, 'that the door is open. It is like when Winnie Mandela was challenged in the Truth Commission in South Africa by Desmond Tutu to acknowledge that she had done wrong ...' Sir Paul might well have been taken aback by his being put in the same category as a convicted kidnapper, and his relationship to racist attitudes and conduct in the Metropolitan Police in the same category as Winnie Mandela's relationship to the Mandela United Football Club and the murderers of Stompie Seipei. Dr Stone continued: 'She just did it and suddenly a whole burden of weight, of sort of challenge and friction melted away ... I say to you now, just say, "Yes, I acknowledge *institutional* racism in the police" ... Could you do that today?'[9]

Yet Sir Paul had commenced his testimony with an apology to the Lawrences for the failures of his organisation. He had added a further apology to Duwayne Brooks. He had then made 'a series' of other 'confessions'.[10] None of that had satisfied the inquiry.

The insistence, not on establishing that a specific offence had been committed, but on the contumacious unbeliever's own *confession* of his or her fault, is not the only quasi-religious feature of the proceedings. Errors and the use of tabooed words are condemned as 'anathema', that is to say, a thing or person damned; or a solemn ecclesiastical condemnation of a teaching judged to be gravely opposed to accepted church doctrine.

Cross-examination of many officers was 'undoubtedly robust and searching'. But, Macpherson writes, it was of 'central importance' that the Commissioner of the Metropolitan Police and his officers should 'recognise and accept' the 'fact', and publicly declare, that their own conduct, including their conduct under cross-examination, was the cause of dissatisfaction with and *justified* hostility to the police. Failure of the police to publicly declare their guilt could only be a reflection of their 'lack of understanding' of 'the essential problem and its depth'.[11] 'The essential problem' was racism of a scope and form to which the inquiry attached the term *institutional*. The police had to agree that racism did exist in that scope and that form; and their acceptance of the term 'institutional' was mandatory.

In the event, Sir William's flexible procedures meant that he was indeed able to obtain what he calls 'abject' public apologies from the Assistant Commissioner and eventually from the Commissioner of the Metropolitan Police Service for the existence of racism as described by Macpherson, and labelled 'institutional' racism by him.[12]

The extreme political excrescence of this phenomenon of abject confession were the Stalinist show trials of 1936. Arthur Koestler explored its motivational roots in his novel, *Darkness at Noon*. The self-denunciations of stalwarts of the Russian Revolution made no sense, he argued, except as the sacrifice of their lives (and their 'integrity' in the banal sense) in the interests of an impeccably good cause. 'I have pleaded guilty to having pursued every ... *objectively harmful* policy', Rubashov tells his interrogator at the end of his false 'confession'. 'Isn't that enough for you?' He did not see (yet) how it could serve the Party 'that her members have to grovel in the dust before all the world'. Gletkin's answer is that whatever the 'facts', the Party's aims are the correct ones. 'Your task is simple ... to gild the Right, to blacken the Wrong.' The opposition must be shown to be not merely mistaken, but 'contemptible'.[13]

The Taaffes

The inquiry did not restrict itself to the thoughts of police officers only. Conor Taaffe was a passer-by who had gone to Stephen's assistance. He and his wife had seen a television programme a week or two before about the St John's Ambulance Brigade, and they thought that Stephen was already in the recovery position. Conor Taaffe prayed by Stephen's side. At home he washed Stephen's blood from his hands and poured the water containing it at the foot of a rose tree, as an act of piety to Stephen's memory. Mrs Taaffe had comforted Stephen with the words, 'You are loved, you are loved'.[14] Macpherson says that their actions deserved 'nothing but praise'.[15]

But when the Taaffes had first been asked by Duwayne Brooks to help, they had hesitated for a moment, weighing up the scene: one youth on the ground, another youth asking them to go over to him. Whether the youths were white or black, at 10.30 p.m. on the open street, what sensible person, white or black, would not consider that it might be a trap?

At the Macpherson inquiry Conor Taaffe was asked about his hesitation by Ian Macdonald QC, Duwayne Brooks' barrister:

Macdonald: Was that because they were two young black men?

Taaffe: I would say that was *part* of my assessment, yes.

As evidence of the racism of the Taaffes this was flimsy enough. Of course they had hesitated because they were two young black men. That is what they were on that occasion. Why would the answer have been different if they had been two young white men? 'You hesitated, Mr Taaffe. Was that because they were two young white men?' 'I would say that was part of the assessment, yes. I would not have hesitated if it had been someone from the prayer meeting I had just attended who was asking for help.'

Cathcart describes this as one of its 'important moments', because of what it showed about English racism in general. Cathcart comments:

> The lesson was plain, ordinary people, even good people, can have such thoughts; *what matters is that they do*. Recognize a racist *thought* for what it is and you can set it to one side; fail to recognize it and it can more easily influence your actions.[16]

The general comment that thoughts affect actions is, of course, true. But Cathcart adds: 'Such ideas are hardly revolutionary'. By writing that, he reveals either that all he means is 'hardly new', which is true; or that he has suffered a momentary lapse in memory about, or that there is a hiatus in, his own knowledge of the revolutionary left and right in modern times. One of the distinguishing marks of secular revolutionary régimes has been, as it has often been in dominant religious régimes, that they have sought to subject those thoughts *that cannot be shown to have affected discernable conduct* to scrutiny in *public* inquiries. Conduct is deduced from the thoughts, not thoughts from the conduct.

J.L. Talmon examined the roots in the French Revolution of the early 1790s of what he called 'totalitarian democracy'. The Jacobins, he writes, did not depend only on coercion. They depended on confession. Inside the Jacobin clubs there went on openly 'an unceasing process of *self*-cleansing and *self*-purification'. What was true and what was moral was known to the 'enlightened and infallible' few. To deviate *in thought* from what was true and good was a not an error but a crime, and revolutionary exaltation flowed from recognising and repudiating criminal thoughts within one's own mind, and joining unsullied the ranks of the 'apostles of virtue'.[17]

Trial By Pressure Group

In Part II of the inquiry the Macpherson 'evidence' consisted of written and oral representations of advocates, authors, and advocacy groups. 'It should be stressed that the Inquiry itself had few documents', Macpherson says. 'All the vast documentation came from others.'[18] A great deal depended, therefore, on whom those documents happened to come from. In the world-view of most of those submitting documents, looming large was a belief in the universality, profundity and destructiveness of police racism, and of English racism generally. It was in the nature of the case that the inquiry would hear from the pressure groups who believed there was widespread and seriously damaging racism in the police and elsewhere in English society, and for whom therefore it was a burning issue. He was much less likely to hear from the dispersed private individuals who believed there was not, and who therefore had no personal reason to press their view on anyone.

Catharsis

In contrasting it with other types of inquiry, Sir William characterises his own in striking and original terms, Some inquiries are, to him, 'simply' concerned with establishing 'what happened and why'. Inquiries of another type, he writes, concentrate on 'discipline'. He gives as an example the inquiry by the Kent Police Service (it immediately preceding his own) into how the Metropolitan Police handled the investigation of the murder of Stephen Lawrence.[19] His inquiry, by contrast with these, while involving 'analysis' of what 'may' have gone wrong (as distinct from simply what happened and why?), also involved 'catharsis'.[20]

He returns to this concept more than once. Brian Cathcart says that the inquiry was always 'tense and ill-tempered', which is hardly a description of a cathartic situation.[21] But Sir William's own assessment was that he 'hoped and believed' that catharsis is what Part I of his inquiry achieved. Without searching cross-examination of the police, he writes, this catharsis might never have been achieved.[22]

'Catharsis' means, of course, the purifying of the emotions, or the relieving of emotional tensions, especially by art. The concept was applied originally by Aristotle to the effect of tragic drama on the audience. It means the alleviation of irrational fears, problems and complexes by bringing them to consciousness or giving them expression. It therefore does not mean the unbiased collection of relevant information and its objective assessment. It means very nearly the opposite.

But if it *had* achieved this primary objective, cathartic release for the Lawrences, the Macpherson inquiry would have been entitled to feel that it had achieved one of its primary declared objectives. Who would begrudge the Lawrences' themselves this meagre solace?

It was so far from doing so, however, that in due course the Lawrences took steps to sue 42 of the police officers involved in the case, including the Commissioner of the Metropolitan Police Service, Sir Paul Condon, for £500,000.[23]

The Macpherson report, which is full of praise for itself, also says that 'nobody listening to the whole case could with justification allege any unfairness in the procedure and conduct of the inquiry'.[24] There is one passage where for one moment it looks as though the report has fallen from its high standards of self-congratulation. 'In the first century AD Philo wrote, "When a judge tries a case he must remember that he is himself on trial."'[25] It turns out, however that the report is applying that to the police service, not to the proceedings of the inquiry. Throughout the report, furthermore, its version of the truth is presented as better-based than anybody else's. No independent observer, however, is obliged to accept either of these elements in the highly favourable judgement by the inquiry on its own performance.

3

The Crowd in Hannibal House

Before their work and prestige was largely superseded in the late 1960s by that of the 'critical' philosophers of the Frankfurt School and various other 'new' sociologies like 'ethnomethodology' or the well-meaning anarchism of writers like Ivan Illich,[1] sociologists had been interested in what they called 'social morphology'. This was an attempt to distinguish the various forms in which social life expressed itself, and to give names to these forms. Generally the names were those in common use for phenomena with which ordinary people, being social beings, were quite familiar.

Thus there are some kinds of group where people are related to one another face-to-face over long periods in achieving together many different objectives. In these groups there exists a certain shared and substantially agreed view of the facts that are true and are relevant to their existence and, in value terms, an agreed view of how people ought to act within the framework of these facts. They feel loyal to other members, and give them preference over members of other groups. They feel loyal, indeed, to 'the group as such', and respond emotionally to symbols of the group's solidarity. Members of such a group who deviate in their beliefs or their actions from this shared view of earthly existence (including their conception, if any, of the 'divine' or the 'sacred' in human existence) and how to behave appropriately, are punished and may be expelled from it. Sociologists called such a group a 'community'. To the extent that members of what had been a community begin to deviate from the shared view; to the extent that force increasingly replaces consent; to the extent that loyalty evaporates, to that extent it ceases to be a 'community'.

The members of the disintegrating or disintegrated community might then pursue their own private interests in isolation (always a short-lived adaptation), or enter into other types of relationship with one another, and with other people. One way in which the members of the former community can be related to one another or to new people is by each following his or her own self-interest. In the pursuit of the particular, limited activity which interests them all, or in relation to which their diverse personal interests interlock, they obey rules that apply to all members, and recognise as convenient rules which require certain things of certain members and other things of other members. Sociologists called such groups 'associations'.

One of the easiest ways to unite people is to mobilise their hatred for others. It is infinitely more difficult to unite them on the basis of constructive proposals. This unity of having an enemy in common gives rise to various kinds of sociological formation. In the short term there is the specialised and transitory hatred of 'the lynch mob'. There is the longer-term unity of hating communists, or hating capitalists, or hating protestants, or hating catholics, or hating blacks, or 'hating whitey'.[2] People hate others for a host of diverse and private motives of pride and power, of fear of loss, of hope of gain, of resentment, of revenge. Communities produce their own mobs and movements, and movements can develop into communities. But mobs, movements and amorphous, loose bodies of shared hatreds are themselves not communities in the sociological sense; they are almost the opposite of them.

One very important association is the large group of people who live in the same territorial area, and are in agreement that certain people can use physical force to protect the group from outsiders and punish members of their own group, including themselves, who break its rules, called in the case of this association the laws of the land. Sociologists gave the name 'a state' to such a large territorially-based group, in so far as one identifiable person, or one set of people, has been conceded a monopoly of the authority to use violence to secure the compliance of everyone within its jurisdiction, regardless of their other personal characteristics or other group affiliations or loyalties.[3]

'Authority', 'institution', 'culture', 'mass society', *'anomie'*, 'the *mores*' 'fashion', 'custom'—the study of all these social units and social processes (and of many more), was the staple of the old sociologists. So was the subsidiary and clarifying work of definition. Most such sociologists agreed with Thomas Hobbes, that words are the counters of wise men but the money of fools.[4] They insisted, that is, that what the name described was what was really important, not the particular label chosen by and agreed among sociologists for it.

One of the social phenomena so studied and defined was 'the crowd'.[5] A peculiarity of the Macpherson inquiry was the existence of crowd behaviour. Here are some examples that illustrate this point.

Many people seem to believe that the Kent Investigating Officer's report for the Police Complaints Authority resulted in a blanket condemnation of the investigation by the Metropolitan Police Service of the murder.[6] Much of the Lawrence family's criticism was focused on the police's inefficiency on the night of Stephen's death. This inefficiency was so gross, it was alleged, that it must have been due to the racist indifference—or worse—of the police to the racist killing of a black man.

The Kent team traced everyone who was present and who could conceivably have any memories of, or observations to contribute to the first night's events.[7] Its conclusion, like the much-criticised internal inquiry by the MPS before it, was that the police's first actions at the scene were 'prompt and professional'.

Nineteen officers spent a year in the study by the Kent Police Service of Mr and Mrs Lawrence's submission to the Police Complaints Authority. But in the Macpherson inquiry the influence of such careful investigations (which might still be shown to be erroneous in whole or in part, of course, as the result of other careful investigations) was diminished, and the influence of the crowd was able to make itself felt.

The Kent investigation had given the Metropolitan Police Service a clean bill of health on its performance on the first night after the murder. The barrister representing the Lawrences, Michael Mansfield QC, had no such intention. He and his team attacked the cleared police officers (to use Cathcart's words) with 'extraordinary ferocity'.[8]

The Crowd And Mrs Lawrence

For much of the time the public gallery was solidly and noisily anti-police, thanks mainly (according to Cathcart's observations) to the recruiting efforts of the family's supporters.

Doreen Lawrence's statement to the inquiry formed the basis for many of the accusations against the police. The public gallery was therefore packed when the time came in June 1998 for her to be a 'witness'. Jeremy Gompertz QC, a barrister for accused police officers, began by assuring her that it was not his purpose to criticise her, and that he would be questioning her only on matters of fact and not opinion.

The first matter he raised was whether the Lawrences had delayed passing information to the police. 'Much detail about this was put to Doreen, but to cheers from the gallery she swatted it all aside', writes Cathcart. When Gompertz began to question her about the accusation that there had been no police activity at the scene immediately after the murder, Mrs Lawrence asked, 'Am I on trial or something here? ... For me to be questioned in this way, I do not appreciate it'.

'By now', Cathcart writes, 'there was uproar, cheering and applause from the public gallery ... Gompertz was being howled down.'

Gompertz appealed to Sir William. Sir William replied, 'I should indicate, *and I am sure the public will accept*, that I understand Mr Gompertz's position, but I think your [Gompertz's] discretion should be exercised in favour of not asking further questions'.[9]

On one occasion Sir William had to suspend a Part II session because of crowd behaviour. When the five main suspects were appearing before the inquiry about 100 people had failed to gain admission to the chamber. Some of them had remained below, chanting 'Let us in! Let us in!' At one point the crowd, with members of the Nation of Islam to the fore, surged forward. One or two officers used their CS sprays. (A police spokeswoman said that a chief inspector had been knocked to the floor and kicked by seven or eight people.) Some of the Nation of Islam men burst into the room where the hearing was being held, shouting, 'This is a sham!' Sir William suspended the session. In a typical crowd scenario, Doreen Lawrence took a microphone, and she assumed responsibility for restoring order by appealing to her supporters to be calm—though not without saying to the crowd that 'since the time of our son's murder the police attitude to our family and people in the black community has been disgraceful'.

The police were later accused of over-reacting and failing to listen to the 'warnings that had been given'.[10]

The Crowd And Inspector Groves

In questioning Inspector Steven Groves Michael Mansfield QC asked why Groves had used the word 'fight' in relation to the stabbing of Stephen Lawrence. Groves said he believed that when he was first called to the scene by radio a fight had been mentioned. (Someone had been assaulted. It would not have been extraordinary for it have been reported as a 'fight'.)

'Mr Groves, I suggest to you very clearly, this is one of your assumptions *because he was a black victim*. Is it not so?'

'No, sir. You are accusing me of being a racist now and that is not true. I would like it noted that I do not think it is fair either.'

The 'evidence' for Grove's 'racism' would not have stood for one moment in a court of law. But it will satisfy a crowd.

Mansfield asked about the passage in Groves' Kent interview in which he used the word 'coloured'.

Groves answered, 'I am in sort of quandary here... *He* is a white man; *that* is a coloured woman. What else can I say? I have to make some description...'

The use of such a word, Macpherson says, is 'now well known to be offensive'. Yet a number of officers used this word, one officer saw no difficulty with the word 'Negro', and 'some did not even during their evidence seem to understand that they were offensive and should not be used'.[11]

Anthony Richmond's standard academic book on race—his anti-racist book—published by Penguin in 1955 was entitled *The Colour*

Problem.[12] In the phrase 'colour prejudice', 'prejudice', not 'colour' is pejorative. The *Macpherson* report *defines* racism as discrimination against people because of their *'colour'*.[13] By what mental gymnastics does *Macpherson*, that being so, find the noun inoffensive and the adjective offensive?

Did Mansfield and Sir William not know that one of the main black civil rights organisations in the United States is still called the National Association for the Advancement of *Colored* People (NAACP)? Did they not know that in France *'de couleur'* and *'noir'* (or 'black') are interchangeable? What, in this country, would a survey of usage reveal? It could well find that some people prefer 'coloured' to 'black' because of a mistaken but innocent belief that 'coloured' is a term only of description not disparagement, while 'black' is possibly pejorative. The offence of people who use the word coloured is, at worst, that they are not up-to-date with, in the time frame of language, the rapid switches of respectable usage from Negro, to coloured, to black, to African, Afro-Caribbean or African-American. 'Coloured' is not self-evidently intended to offend or shock, unlike other terms of centuries-old racist insult or depreciation which have fairly easily been excluded from ordinary conversation (unlike the obscenities and blasphemies, for long tabooed as offensive, that have now commonly entered public discourse *because* they are offensive through the diligent efforts of our intellectual and artistic élites). The hero in the World War Two film *The Dam Busters* is told that his dog 'Nigger' has died. When *The Dam Busters* was shown on television in December 1999 the dog's name was edited out. (Perhaps because broadcasting abusive words likely to stir up hatred of any group of persons defined by the ethnic or national origin is an offence under the Public Order Act of 1986.)

Cathcart describes Inspector Groves' response as his 'floundering' over the use of the word 'coloured'. Why, in the cold light of day, rather than in the charged crowd atmosphere of the inquiry, should Cathcart perceive Groves' answer as 'floundering'? As an editorial journalist, Cathcart's job was to institutionally enforce the fine-tuned linguistic code of the *Independent on Sunday* on what words, hitherto neutral and in common use, this or that set of campaigners had decided their constituency will take offence at from now on. That people in other occupations are not as sophisticated and linguistically flexible as Cathcart is, is no proof of their ill-will.

Nelson Mandela, still in 1994, used the term 'Negro' freely as a term of neutral description.[14] Passengers travelling by United Airlines in 1999 received complimentary Harry London chocolate bars, on the wrappers of which the work of United *Negro* College Fund (UNCF) is applauded. The UNCF is an ancient and honourable charity established to assist blacks to benefit from higher education.

Is the word 'Negro' to be edited out of the titles and text of the vast library of serious academic books by distinguished black scholars in America and elsewhere on the same principles, as embellished by Macpherson? Yet the examples suggest that in some cases the offence could be that of being in one's own estimation 'better informed' than Macpherson (even though, in this case, in England, wrong). Pity the poor working copper who is better read or who has travelled more alertly than a barrister, a judge, or a broadsheet journalist!

DC Steven Pye, Macpherson says, was also 'accustomed to referring to black people as "coloured"'. DC Pye said at the inquiry that he was not aware that this might be regarded by black people as insulting until he watched Mr Groves giving evidence'. He 'could not remember receiving any formal racism awareness training'. Macpherson does not, however, attribute any sort of racism to DC Pye on this or any other account.[15]

In spite of the slightness of the evidence *in the report* of the use of 'inappropriate language', and none at all of the use of 'offensive language', 'the use of inappropriate and offensive language appears in Macpherson's 'Conclusion and Summary' as one of the six 'areas that are affected by racism'.[16]

During the police evidence, and particularly when Mansfield was in action, laughter and groans would greet such answers from police officers. This would not normally be allowed in a court of law. In order to protect Inspector Groves from the gallery crowd (and, though he perhaps did not think of it in this way, from the crowd influences that could be affecting the performances of all the witnesses, all the barristers and the judgement of all the assessors) counsel for the MPS, Jeremy Gompertz QC, rose to complain about 'constant interruption and background noise' from the gallery.

Though he said that his warning was 'crystal clear', Sir William's intervention could scarcely be described as full-hearted. If the laughing did not stop, he said, he would clear the gallery. He reminded Mansfield that he was not addressing a jury. Inspector Groves did not need to be 'pilloried'—(slight pause)—'*unnecessarily*'.[17] The pillory in its literal sense is essentially an instrument of control by a crowd. What had being figuratively 'pilloried', necessarily or not, to do with ascertaining the facts of the case?

The Crowd And Detective Sergeant Bevan

Detective Sergeant John Bevan was questioned by Edmund Lawson QC on why the search of the home of one of the suspects, David Norris, had been 'cursory'.

Bevan: ... the property was a mansion ... a very, very expensive property, very expensively decorated... I obviously made a decision at the time that the extent of my search was an adequate one, whether it be for the fact that David Norris used the address as a temporary basis, which might have been indicated by the fact that he wasn't there.

Lawson: Mr Bevan, forgive me. That might be taken to suggest that if you have a posh house you are not going to be the victim of a proper search, whereas if you live in a grubby council flat you will have it torn apart.

'By now disbelief and laughter had gripped the public gallery', and it was in vain that Bevan tried to explain further.[18] What 'evidence' had Lawson produced? That Sergeant Bevan's views of *his* mandate under the law, and *his* (realistic) views of the sort of trouble he could get into from the courts if he exceeded his authority, or from his superiors if he upset someone with social influence, or even his reasonable exercise of discretion given the situation as he knew it, were proof that the Metropolitan Police was not only racist, but that there was one law for the rich and another for the poor? That, indeed, Sergeant Bevan had somehow been shown to be someone who 'tears apart' council flats on the same legal mandate and administrative instructions that would have him touching his cap to the squire? In this exchange, where did gathering evidence end, and pleasing the crowd begin?

The Crowd And Sir Paul Condon

Sir Paul Condon versus the crowd and Sir William Macpherson

In phase two of the Macpherson inquiry there were no barristers. The chairman and his three advisers asked the questions. When Sir Paul Condon appeared to give his evidence, he said that there *was* racism in the police service. There *could be* unconscious racism.

Sir William was not happy with Sir Paul's confession. There was a small but *significant* difference, he said, between acknowledging that such features 'can' exist and acknowledging that they 'do' exist.

There was a 'discernible difference', Sir William said, between the approach of the Association of Chief Police Officers (ACPO) and the somewhat less 'positive' approach of Sir Paul. For ACPO had not only discerned 'unconscious' racism in the police service. It had discerned that 'institutional' racism was also '*inherent* in the *wider* society'. The Macpherson report does not refer to any of the evidence that ACPO had on 'unconscious' police racism and the 'inherent' 'institutional' racism of English 'society'. None is given, either, which enables the reader to consult its sources, or judge the quality of its own expertise in any of these matters.[19]

Sir William put the proposition to Sir Paul that the reluctance to accept the racial motive was a 'collective' failure of the MPS. (Again, the 'crime' was that of not having the correct thoughts.)

Did he accept that that might amount to institutional racism?

No, said Sir Paul, because most people then would accept that as a declaration that all MPS officers were racist.

Sir William commented that it would be his 'approach' that 'it'—institutional racism—did exist.

If this *had* been a court, rather than just having something of the appearance of one, could a judge have properly come so close to announcing at this stage, while a key witness (or defendant) was being examined that he had already reached his 'verdict', were he the jury, of 'guilty'?

Sir Paul Condon versus the crowd and Mr Tom Cook

One of Macpherson's three advisers, Tom Cook, then asked if Sir Paul would 'accept the *premise*' that 'unconscious' racism by individual officers was 'widespread'. The inquiry's terms of reference were to inquire into the Stephen Lawrence tragedy from the time of his murder onwards, particularly for lessons it threw up for the police investigation, and for the public prosecution, of racially motivated crimes. The fact that the terms of reference refers to 'racially motived *crimes*' may be taken as meaning that it had already be established as a premise, prior to the inquiry, that the murder of Stephen Lawrence had been racially motivated. It cannot be taken as meaning that it had been established as a premise prior to the inquiry that the *police investigation* of Stephen Lawrence's murder had been racially motivated. That was for the inquiry to investigate as a possibility and establish on the evidence, not for Sir Paul to accept as a datum.

As for Sir Paul being asked to say what went on in the 'unconscious' of other Metropolitan Police officers, did Mr Cook know what had gone on in the 'unconscious' of his officers when he was Deputy Chief Constable for West Yorkshire? What would he have said if he had been expected to know? How would he have gone about it if he had been instructed to find out?

No, came Sir Paul's courteous reply, not if you say 'widespread'.

Sir Paul Condon versus the crowd and Dr Stone

'You have heard me say ...', Sir Paul said in the course of being interrogated. But he was interrupted by Dr Richard Stone. 'You have told us ten times you are not in denial ... I say to you now, just say, "Yes, I *acknowledge* institutional racism in the police ..."'

'It was an approach that pleased the public gallery', writes Cathcart, 'and the pressure on the Commissioner was intense. Sir William chipped in: "You have been given the challenge, or the question, Sir Paul. What is your answer?"'

His answer was that it would be very easy to please the panel. It would be easy to please the people in the public gallery—'this audience', as he called them. It would be easy, also, to gain the favour of 'superficial media coverage'. But he would not do what would please any of them, because it would be 'dishonest'.

Over the uproar from the gallery, Sir William called for quiet and moved the discussion into other areas.[20]

Sir Paul's stand attracted critical headlines. But whose judgement, freed from the enthusiasm of a righteous crowd, would conclude that Sir Paul's opinion, reasoning, and sense of reality and responsibility were inferior to those expressed in the 'uproar from the gallery' or by the 'Sack Condon' campaign; or to the amateur-Freudian appeal of Mr Cook; or to the semi-religious appeal of Dr Stone?

Sir Paul Condon versus the crowd and Bishop Sentamu

Another of Sir William's advisers, Bishop Sentamu, asked Sir Paul about 'inappropriate language' by officers that 'often' went unchecked by their superiors. (The use of the word 'coloured' as 'inappropriate language' featured frequently in the inquiry.) Did the Commissioner not *see* that this is what many people understood as *institutional* racism?

It is much easier for us to formulate the apt reply at leisure than it was for Sir Paul to formulate them impromptu from the witness stand: 'With the greatest respect, your grace, Sir Paul, not you, will have to answer for the future figures. You can use any word, your grace, for whatever good religious reason, or for any good reason of social policy you may have, to describe any state of affairs you choose. If it reverses the ordinary meaning of the term, however, do not expect Sir Paul, with his obligations, to use it in your new sense. Such words are bullets, and Sir Paul is wisely reluctant to give them to anti-police individuals and pressure groups as ammunition to fire at police officers.'

Excluding pickpocketing there were 127 street crimes in total in the entire Metropolitan Police district in 1929. Between April 1998 and March 1999 excluding pickpocketing there were 31,600. Taking only one type of street crime, and taking only one part of the Metropolitan Police district, there were more than 200 snatches of the single item, watches, in central London in 1999. Is that enormous failure attributable principally to the failure of the churches in doing their job, or principally to the failure of the police service in doing its job?[21]

The reply that Sir Paul actually gave was that Bishop Sentamu was free to use the term 'institutional'. He was not. He had to think 'practically and constructively about the future'.

The Gullible Scepticism Of Special Interest Groups And Those They Succeed In Influencing

Sir Paul was concerned that criminals of whatever ethnicity should not be gratuitously emboldened to commit crimes, and his officers not unjustifiably discouraged from preventing them from doing so.

What 'the future' did hold soon revealed itself. In August 1998, while the inquiry was going on, there were 27,300 searches by the MPS. In August 1999, six months after Macpherson reported, the figure was down to 13,600. In Plumstead, as it happened one of the pilot sites selected before the murder of Stephen Lawrence, the figure was down from 745 to 417.[22] 'The fall in searches does not reflect a strategic move towards using the power [of stop and search] more efficiency. Rather, it seems to stem more from a mixture of insecurity, low morale and cynicism.' The only group for which both recorded searches and arrests fell consistently across the MPS area over the year was the black group.[23] Marian FitzGerald notes that 'the Macpherson inquiry undoubtedly had a significantly inhibiting effect; and this emerged strongly from my own interviews as well as those conducted by Mark Kilgallon'. The graph of crime trends in the MPS area shows a sharp upturn of 'street crimes' from the time of the publication of the Macpherson report, from 2,800 a month to over 3,500 a month. The number of 'drug crimes' fell from 2,800 a month to 2,250 a month.[24] Robberies are reported by the victims, and more robberies means more reports of robberies. Drug offences are only uncovered by the police, and fewer reported drug offences means simply more actual drug offences remaining undetected.

The fall in the number of stop and search incidents, moreover, has not resulted in a more favourable attitude of the public towards the police. The baby, says FitzGerald, appears to have been thrown out with the bath water.[25]

Sir Paul had then to say, in December 1999, that he was investing an extra £5 million to try to cope with the situation, but that 'there had been so far no signs of the tide abating'.[26]

The Home Office crime figures that were issued in January 2000 showed that nationally the number of crimes had increased 2.2 per cent to 5.2 million in the year October 1998 to September 1999. That increase, the first in six years, was largely due to increases in two police areas, London and the West Midlands, the areas with the highest concentrations of ethnic minorities. In London the increase was nine per cent, in the West Midlands 16 per cent.

The number of reported robberies in the whole country had increased by 19 per cent in the year. The number of reported drug offences had decreased by nine per cent.[27]

Naturally, these figures do not disturb the current ant-racist consensus in the slightest. The chairman of the Commission for Racial Equality, Gurbux Singh, pronounced in the summer of 2000 that the claim that the Macpherson report had affected stop and search and through that the crime rate was 'demonstrable nonsense'. He refrained from demonstrating anything at all.[28] Advocacy groups and their representatives (in some cases paid) are now generally familiar with the weaknesses of all social statistics. One of the unintended effects of teaching statistics to students in social-affairs departments is that a historically unprecedented large number of people have been equipped with the tools that enable them to dismiss out of hand all figures but those they want to believe.

There *might* be defects in the statistics due to faulty definition of terms. In the case of the Home Office crime statistics definitions of what a particular 'crime' is change from time to time. In the FitzGerald figures, what has been counted as 'street crime'? Was what was counted as stop and search at the beginning of the period the same thing as was counted as stop and search at the end of the period? In the Home Office figures, what has been the effect of changing an episode for recording purposes from one 'crime' if a vandal smashes ten cars in a car park to an episode that for recording purposes becomes ten crimes? Paul Wiles, Director of Research Development and Statistics at the Home Office said of the 1998-99 figures, 'We do not know the extent of this effect'.[29] Of course there are known and as-yet unrealised difficulties of this sort, and they *might* be fatally damaging to the case that is being made. People who remain faithful, in the face of the best available figures, to the version of the facts that suits their own or their constituency's case, believe they are statistical sophisticates when they refer to defects. But they and those they succeed in persuading are in reality gullible sceptics. As Wiles said about the effects on the 1998-99 figures of the changes in definition introduced by the Home Office in April 1998, 'it is almost certain there has been a genuine upward trend'.[30]

There *might* be other explanations for FitzGerald's and the Home Office's figures than 'the Macpherson effect'. The Macpherson effect is most unlikely to be the only factor operating. Of course. 'Correlation is not causation', still less is sequence. The coincidence of the fall in one figure and the rise in the other might be due, not to the effect of the first on the second, but to some other factor altogether. Any social phenomenon, whether changes in police or changes in criminal activity, is an enormously complex pattern of causes and effects. 'The statistics have to be unwrapped.' Insurmountable ignorance has to be acknowledged.

The figures themselves *might* be wrong. There is always the possibility of the actual falsification of figures that in due course might be exposed. There is always the possibility of mistakes in the gathering of the data or in the simple arithmetic of processing them.

But that is a reason for working cautiously, critically and with an open mind on the 'best data' available. It is not a reason for sticking to data that seem for the time being on the best grounds available to have been superseded.

On influential programmes like radio's 'Today' or television's 'Newsnight', the representative of a *category* of the population which is, or which claims or is claimed to be, oppressed, deprived or victimised is at an advantage. He or she, rather than the empirical investigator, is aided and abetted by the style imposed on all participants by the nature of the medium. The radio or television audience is likely to identify with the 'victim', the individual 'hard case'. Sitting at the breakfast table or relaxing before going to bed, the long-term and remote consequences of different social world-views of facts, value and goals are not, just then, their business. Interviewers are unavoidably intellectual jacks-of-all-trades. They are therefore strongly attracted to universally applicable verbal formulations that give the appearance of expertise in any discussion. Interviewees operate within the context of a few minutes' exposure of a subject. It is easier to give the appearance of having demolished a case in a few sentences than the appearance of having established one, especially when the interviewer's own sympathies lie with the altruistic *aims* of the special-interest group concerned. The empirical investigator can very easily be made to look, indeed, as if he or she has demolished his or her own case by 'admitting' that the figures are not immaculate and the deductions not irrefutable. Certainly *sufficient doubt* can be thrown on statistics or other data by parties with a vested interest, emotional or financial, in the public not accepting them as a better-based version of the facts than the pressure group's own.[31]

But the *intellectual's* obligation is to be sceptical about what are currently the best-based figures in order to be prepared to be critical of *them*. It is not to do as the pressure group does, which is say, in effect, 'The best-based figures, too, are defective, and *might* turn out to be worse than my own, therefore I will stick to the version of the facts that I am now using'. That is not what superficially and momentarily it might appear to be: 'scientific open mindedness' about the possibility that any given version of the facts might turn out to have been wrong.

It is always to be 'sceptical' of every other past, present and possible future version of the facts in order never to be sceptical about one's own. It is pseudo-scepticism mobilised in the interests of *never* having to shift from the version of the facts upon which the pressure group's reason for existing depends.

4

Mr and Mrs Lawrence's Treatment at the Hospital as Evidence of Police Racism

It is crucially important to be clear on what we are not saying, as well as what we are saying.

We are not saying that the standards of proof used in a criminal trial are appropriate to cases of internal discipline or abuse of public office. We decisively do not take that view.

We are not saying that corruption and abuse of power is not an endemic *potentiality* in any police service. Internationally, the culture and the effectiveness of controls differ widely between police forces. Money, sex, drugs and the abuse of power can all exercise a powerful attraction on police officers whose daily work is an exercise of authority, and brings them necessarily into close proximity with criminals. That such potentialities can become realities was demonstrated once more in the exposure in February 2000 of corruption within the MPS's East Dulwich crime squad.[1]

We are not saying that the officers concerned in the Stephen Lawrence case behaved efficiently. The investigation undertaken by the Kent Police Service for the Police Complaints Authority had many serious criticisms of the investigation. How unusually inefficient it was is another matter on which neither Kent nor Macpherson provide any information.

We are not saying that the conduct of the officers concerned was always governed by a high degree of sensitivity and politeness. One question not asked by Macpherson is, were they less sensitive and polite than usual? The crucial question not asked by Macpherson is, would they have conducted themselves with more sensitivity and politeness towards white people from the same stratum of society behaving in the same way towards them?

We are not making a comment on the amount or nature of police racism in the Lawrence case, or among officers of the Metropolitan Police.

We are only looking at *the quality of the evidence* Macpherson *produces* to make its case (within the latitude it allows itself, and which we would certainly allow, of 'reasonable inference') that police racism was a major cause of police failure in the Lawrence case.

'A central and vital issue which permeated the inquiry', Macpherson states, 'has been the issue of racism.' The 'chilling condemnation' made specifically by Doreen Lawrence, not only of the police but of the whole system of English justice, had 'sounded through all the months' of the inquiry's consideration of the evidence.

> Mr and Mrs Lawrence allege and fervently believe that their colour, culture and ethnic origin, and that of their murdered son, have thoroughly affected the way that the case has been dealt with and pursued ...These allegations are plainly supported by many people, both black and white, in our Public Gallery and in the community at large.[2]

But it was the task of Macpherson to the examine the case in order to determine to what extent what the Lawrences fervently believed, and what many people in the public gallery plainly supported, was justified by Macpherson's findings on fact and the inferences it would draw from them.

If anyone thinks that the Macpherson report on police racism depends principally upon the evidence it collected on the racist conduct of police officers *in the Lawrence case* then he is mistaken. That has not stopped very senior and influential figures saying and perhaps believing that the Macpherson report proves *from the evidence of the Lawrence case* that the Metropolitan Police Service is 'riddled with racism'.

The Macpherson report makes it clear that it bases its conclusion of police racism *only partly, and to an undisclosed* extent, on its 'findings in the actual investigation'.

There are other bodies of evidence, Macpherson states, in which 'institutional' racism is 'primarily *apparent*'. These 'other bodies of evidence' were partly gathered, we assume, from 'publications seen by the inquiry'.[3] It would require a major research effort, if it were possible at all, to discover what Macpherson took from this vast body of literature of 171 items in the course of a life-time's study or over the period of the inquiry, and to assess its relevance for police racism in the Lawrence case. It would have been encouraging to know that as much was known about the books as how to spell all the authors' names. If this had been a university thesis, what would examiners not ideologically committed to the student's cause have made of it? Perhaps a *viva voce* would have helped.

Three things can be said about the list in general. The first is that, from our knowledge of particular items, it contains works of varied quality. The second is very obvious. It contains works that not only have no connection with the Lawrence case, but works that do not deal with this country at all. The Rodney King case in Los Angeles, for example, concerned the use of police violence in subduing a suspect.[4] What 'evidence' that is for English racism is indirect. It is even more indirect in relation to the Lawrence case, where no allegation was ever made by anyone that any officer used or threatened any violence at all. The third is that it is predominantly, if not overwhelmingly, work that has contributed to or is part of the present anti-racist consensus. None of the 171 items is earlier than 1967. The degree to which only 'fashionable' current opinions are considered is shown in the fact that the earliest book mentioned, which broke with the anti-racism of Martin Luther King, is listed *twice*, and in the fact that no fewer than 138 of the items post-date 1989.

The second 'body of evidence' is the countrywide under-reporting of racial incidents.

Another is the failure of police training 'as evidenced by Her Majesty's Inspector of Constabulary's Report, *Winning the Race* and the Police Training Council Report'.[5]

The fourth 'body of evidence' is the disparity—again, vaguely and without figures, 'countrywide'—in the stop and search figures. Marian FitzGerald's is the most thorough study ever completed on stop and search. Macpherson had nothing like it when it reached its conclusions that police racist initiatives explained the over-representation of black people. Macpherson's sources seem to have been the assertions made to the inquiry by advocates and advocacy groups in its visits to various places around the country. We are given no indication of the statistical foundation for these assertions. But FitzGerald's research shows that proportionately more black people are the subjects of stop and search not because of the racist selection of the police, but because the police are responding to information *from third parties*. To the extent that there is racial prejudice, it is that of the third parties reporting suspicious activities or crimes more frequently when they concern black suspects than they do when the identical suspicious activities or crimes concern white suspects. 'If searches were limited only to information from third parties', she writes, 'the over-representation of black people would not diminish. Rather, it might actually increase.'[6]

These amorphous 'findings' of the Macpherson report, as evidence of the claimed 'inherence' of 'institutional' racism in British police services and other areas of British life, have very little to do with any *evidence* about police racism unearthed in 'The Stephen Lawrence Inquiry'. The function of the 'findings' on endemic and widespread racism in the United States and England is to enable the reader to *deduce* from them that police racism was an important element in what happened in Eltham, South-East London, in 1993.

The strongest of these three tenuous connections to the Lawrence murder investigation is that none of the officers concerned with it had received training in race relations.

The Macpherson evidence on the attitudes and conduct of the officers connected with the 'actual investigation' of the murder of Stephen Lawrence are the only ones that are relevant to the Macpherson findings on the racism *of some kind* of *those* officers. The findings relating to the police investigation of the Lawrence murder are those on:

(a) the treatment of Mr and Mrs Lawrence at the hospital on the night of the murder;

(b) the initial reaction to the victim and witness Duwayne Brooks;

(c) the family liaison;

(d) the failure of many officers to recognise Stephen's murder as a *purely* racially motivated crime;

and

(e) the lack of urgency and motivation in some areas of the investigation.[7]

Because the Macpherson report gives itself so much scope for 'inferring' police racism in the Lawrence affair from its 'evidence', it is instructive to go back to see what evidence it uses in establishing these five grounds.

The report says the treatment of Mr and Mrs Lawrence at the hospital on the night of the murder is its first reason for inferring racism—'institutional' racism—in the MPS. What this 'institutional' racism is will be discussed more fully later. But if the existence of this form of racism is to be inferred from the conduct of the police at the hospital, the existence of racism *of some kind or another* at the hospital would have had to be demonstrated in Macpherson's evidence.

Acting Inspector Little's Alleged Racism

Macpherson's discussion of the treatment of Mr and Mrs Lawrence at the hospital concerns mainly the conduct towards them of Ian Little, at the time a police sergeant at Plumstead, where he was Acting Inspector on the night of the murder.

Macpherson says that there is 'a fundamental conflict' between the evidence of Mr and Mrs Lawrence and that of Acting Inspector Little. Yet whose evidence is the more convincing, even as it is presented by Macpherson?

'Mrs Lawrence was distraught', the Macpherson report states, 'and *remembers little* about any police officers or police activity at the hospital while she was there. That is wholly understandable, and is in no sense any kind of criticism of her.' However, says Macpherson, 'Mr and Mrs Lawrence both deny that *any* officer spoke to them *at any time* during their stay at the hospital'.

As George Orwell said generally of those bereaved by hospital deaths, whoever they are, even a 'cruel detail too small to be told' can leave terrible memories behind.[8] This hospital death was especially difficult to bear. The Lawrences' complaint that no officer spoke to either of them must strike the impartial observer as one that is explicable only as a response to the extreme stress of the situation. For even if police officers had overlooked their presence as the key visitors to the hospital that night, and not had a word with the Lawrences, why did the Lawrences not have a word with a police officer?

The possibility is likely to occur to someone with no axe to grind, furthermore, that the reason in the case of at least some of the police officers could have been that they did not want to intrude immediately on parents so stricken with grief. Such reticence would have been an expression of respect rather than the opposite.

Mr and Mrs Lawrence, 'particularly Mr Lawrence', claimed that 'nothing was said at all' by Inspector Little to them and that Neville Lawrence 'never made any visit' to the resuscitation room in order formally to identify his son. Was the emphasis on 'never made any visit'? Or was it on 'in order to formally identify his son'—that the visit was made, but not for the purposes of identification, or of 'formal' identification?

At an early stage Ian Little claimed that he spoke to both Mr and Mrs Lawrence. 'Basically I identified myself to them and explained the situation, namely we've got a youth in the resuscitation room who has died and the indications were that he was their son, but we needed a confirmation.' Much later, when he was interviewed by the Kent Police Service he said that he did not recall actually speaking to *Mrs* Lawrence. In that interview a police officer had talked to Mr Lawrence. 'Certainly one of us said to him: "We've got a young lad in there. He is dead. We don't know who he is, but we would like to clarify that point. If it is not your son, then all well and good. But we do need to know. I am sure you would like to know as well".'

There follow Macpherson's 'inferences' from the use of these words (which he does not fully accept were used). *If* these were the words used, the report says, then the police's approach was '*grossly* insensitive and unsympathetic'. Ian Little agreed that in the circumstances Mr and Mrs Lawrence—like any other parents faced with such an emotionally devastating event—needed careful, delicate and sympathetic handling. But 'he did not seem to realise that the approach made by him (*if it happened*) was insensitive and clumsy and only capable of misinterpretation and difficulty'.

These words are *the most convincing 'proof' produced* by Macpherson of Acting Inspector Little's 'racism'. Yet the report does not definitely say that these words were actually used.

Macpherson might be trying to show that Acting Inspector Little is himself 'racist'. Or Macpherson might be trying to show that 'collective' (or, to use a term out of the same radical-revolutionary stable, 'structural') racism expressed itself through Acting Inspector Little's 'gross insensitivity'. If it is the latter, then it would mean that Macpherson's evidence does not come 'from the investigation', as the report claims, but from 'prior knowledge' of the racism of the Metropolitan Police Service and the society of which it is a part. The word for such 'knowledge' that is possessed before evidence is gathered is 'prejudice'.

But whether Macpherson is trying to prove the existence of 'collective' racism from the officer's racist conduct, or simply assuming that the officer's deceptively 'normal' conduct (including ineptness within the normal range) was 'really' racist because the institution is 'collectively' racist, it is incumbent upon Macpherson to show *something* racist or 'really' racist about what Acting Inspector Little, or some other officer at the hospital, did or said, or failed to do or say, to Mr and Mrs Lawrence at the hospital that night.

What if the words are considered only as evidence, not of the major offence of racism, but of the much milder offence of disrespect for bereaved parents? In a society that has shed nearly all rituals in relation to death, and left everyone to improvise for themselves, how many people would be immediately struck, without Macpherson's prompting, by the '*gross* insensitivity' of how this Acting Inspector fulfilled his difficult duty of asking a parent to identify a murdered son? How many would think it a little harsh to describe it even as 'bluff' or 'embarrassed'? What form of words would Sir William have chosen? Only a person for whom anything is grist for his grievance mill, or has been in prolonged contact with the way of thought of such people, could have considered that this was evidence of racism.

How do these passages from Macpherson constitute any evidence at all that Acting Inspector Little would not have behaved in exactly the same way and said exactly the same thing to a white father and mother? That he would have said better things to and done better things for white parents in these circumstances would be the *only* 'evidence' that he was racist.

The next scrap of 'evidence' of Ian Little's racist conduct at the hospital, whether as a marker of the institutional racism of the police service, or merely as a necessary emanation of it: 'it was apparent' that he had never undergone any course to assist him in his race relations awareness, an aspect of Macpherson's more general point about the countrywide weakness of race-awareness training as evidence for police racism. On this 'evidence' (whose natural home is in some utopia from the wilder shores of totalitarian social work) if someone has not taken the appropriate course on 'child abuse awareness' he is incestuous; if he has not taken the appropriate course on 'sexual preference awareness' he is a proven homophobe. If he has not taken a racial-awareness course he is a racist.

What other evidence is there of Ian Little's racism? It is that he considered that it was only a possibility, when he arrived at the scene, that this was a racist attack. He treated the matter, Macpherson says, simply as 'a murder'.

To the reader who has studied all Macpherson's views on 'treating everybody the same', the implication of the next comments on Ian Little are unclear. For Macpherson's ultimate conclusion is that the police ought *not* to treat everybody the same. They ought to treat at least witnesses and victims who are black, and perhaps black suspects, with special consideration. That Ian Little 'treated everybody the same' reads, however, like mitigation before sentence.

> He did say that 'everybody should be treated the same', and that he tried to be as sensitive as he could be with everybody irrespective of who they were. Although he had worked in multi-cultural societies and areas during his service and believed that he treated everybody in the same way his lack of sensitivity and his inaction, particularly at the hospital, betrayed conduct which demonstrates inability to deal properly with bereaved people, and those bereaved as a result of a terrible racist attack. He failed to deal with the family appropriately and professionally. *This was unwitting racism at work.*[9]

The Night Services Manager's Evidence

There then follows another passage that purports to present 'evidence' of police racism specifically on the night of the murder. It was the evidence of the Night Services Manager. Macpherson says it is 'necessary' to 'stress' her testimony 'as to what happened at the hospital'. (Macpherson does not say 'that night'.)

She remembers that the report initially reaching the hospital was that the victim has been attacked with an iron bar, and had head injuries. (This was roughly Duwayne Brooks' description at the scene of what had happened, rather than a stabbing.) *She recollected visits to the resuscitation room 'by a number of members of the family'.* She remembered prayers being said and hymns being sung. But she had 'no recollection of seeing or dealing with any police officers at the hospital'. She was not able to say anything, therefore, on the crucial matter of how police officers behaved towards Mr and Mrs Lawrence.

Macpherson comments on her evidence for its bearing on Acting Inspector Little's racism. Acting Inspector Little had said that he had spoken with Mr Lawrence and that Mr Lawrence had visited the resuscitation room. Mr Lawrence had said that neither of these things happened. Macpherson says 'it seems likely that [the visit to the resuscitation room] did take place in the company of Mr Little, and Mr Lawrence has *wholly and understandably forgotten* the short insensitive incident'.[10]

The text then changes to bold in the course of dealing with the Night Services Manager's evidence. In fact it is not at all testimony about how the police treated Mr and Mrs Lawrence in the hospital on the night of the murder.

The Night Services Manager had been asked about her experience in connection with the treatment of the victims of previous racist attacks. Except for their racism these attacks were totally unrelated to the Lawrence case. She told the inquiry that 'on occasion' (not 'always', not 'usually') she had 'felt a general sense of unease' about the police's approach. The police 'tended' to 'assume' (she said) that such attacks were drug related. Because they thought they were drug related, they tended to regard them as being less important than other assaults.

What, to use Macpherson's term, a 'witness' thinks unidentified members of some conspicuous body of people, none of who is present to answer the accusation, on unspecified dates have 'assumed' is not normally regarded as evidence (so strong that its importance must be stressed in bold print) against those accused members of the conspicuous group. It is normally regarded as having no relevance whatsoever to what somebody entirely different in the conspicuous group has 'assumed' or how somebody entirely different has behaved on an entirely other occasion. If it were not police officers whose conduct was being 'inferred' in this way, but some other conspicuous body of people, condemnation based on such reasoning would be identified in mild terms as prejudice, in stronger terms as bigotry.

Macpherson says that the witness did give *one* specific example of police racism on an occasion previous to the murder of Stephen Lawrence, 'namely the case of an Asian lady who had been subject to threats to kill and who had been doused with petrol'. Presumably because it was a specific example, its weakness as evidence of any sort was a little too apparent for it to escape comment. 'The difficulty of that evidence is that of course it is impossible to give a time or date for that incident, so that nobody can meet the allegation that the police did not view the incident with the same degree of seriousness as Miss Lavin.' If this witness's story, in bold print, was such weak evidence for any case of alleging racism against the police officer or officers who had dealt with the Asian lady, what was its possible relevance to the racism of the police officers dealing with the Lawrence case at the hospital? 'Miss Lavin was referring incidentally in this context mostly to her contact with junior ranks of police officers. Generally it was the more junior officers with whom she had to deal at the hospital.' So was that evidence that Ian Little, who was Acting Inspector, was *not* a racist?[11]

The word 'institutional' is not a magic incantation with the power to turn all assertions into proofs, so that they do not have to endure the tedious tests of what constitutes evidence.

5

The Initial Treatment of Duwayne Brooks as Evidence of Police Racism

That is the sum of Macpherson's evidence under heading (a). What of heading (b), the initial treatment of Duwayne Brooks? Duwayne Brooks was Stephen Lawrence's 18-year-old friend of long standing. Mrs Lawrence appears to have disapproved of him. She walked past him in the hospital without seeing him. 'We had been quite strict on being home in time in the beginning', Mrs Lawrence told the inquiry, 'but after the influence of Duwayne it was different. Duwayne was allowed to come and go as he pleased, and it didn't really matter what time he got home. I remember, Stephen was 14 when we first had this argument ...'[1]

How He Was Treated By The Police At The Scene Of The Murder

The police were alerted to Duwayne Brooks' 999 call at 10.43 p.m. The first police car arrived at 10.50 p.m. By 10.57 p.m. a Territorial Support Group vehicle was at the scene.[2] The ambulance arrived at about 10.55 p.m., left at 11.03 p.m., and arrived at Brook Hospital at 11.06 p.m.[3] 'How Duwayne Brooks was treated at the scene of the murder', therefore, covers the *12 or 13 minutes* from the arrival of the first police car at 10.50 p.m. until the departure of the ambulance.

In the first police car were two uniformed constables, Linda Bethel and Anthony Gleason. As he got out of the car PC Gleason radioed for back-up. He then went straight to Stephen and found a very faint pulse. Without moving the body, he checked for a wound, and found none. PC Linda Bethel, seeing blood, radioed to check the ambulance was on its way. She was told that it would be there in three or four minutes. She asked for another police car to be sent. Then she turned to Duwayne Brooks to find out what had happened. He answered a few questions, but he soon broke off, demanding to know why Stephen could not be taken to the hospital in a police car. Gleason left in the police car to ease the ambulance along its route. PC Joanne Smith then arrived in another police car. She and PC Linda Bethel, continued questioning Duwayne Brooks, who gave them some essential details. There is no controversy over this account.[4]

How Duwayne Brooks did behave at the scene (not how the police expected him to behave on the basis of any stereotype they might have held of 'how a black youth behaves') is best established from the statement he prepared for the Macpherson inquiry. When he knew that Stephen was injured, he says, he ran across to the phone box that was fortunately immediately in the vicinity of where Stephen finally fell. Duwayne Brooks dialled 999 and asked for an ambulance. 'We had an exchange about where I was. I knew where I was but looked at a printed card in the phone box. It was wrong.' As a result of the confusion over the printed card, he says, he became 'confused and frustrated'. He was shouting at the operator. 'I slammed the phone down on the shelf and left. I am told it is said that I kicked the box.' That was possible, he says, 'given how frustrated I was'.

Before the first police car arrived, a passing car stopped beside where Stephen was lying. It was an off-duty policeman, PC Geddis, and his wife Angela, returning from a prayer meeting. 'Mr Geddis asked what had happened and if I had called an ambulance, and I told him that we had been attacked'. Duwayne Brooks says that he 'was using the f-word', but not *at* PC Geddis. A couple, Conor and Louise Taaffe, had come out of another prayer meeting in a nearby church, and they were attending to Stephen. Duwayne Brooks's statement continues: 'Angela Geddis went and crouched by Steve... The Taaffes may have prayed... At some point either a woman or a man came and put a blanket on Steve'.

The first police car arrived. 'WPC Bethel came up and asked me who had done this... I said a group of six white boys. I then said, "Where is the fucking ambulance? I didn't call the police!"' PC Bethel told Mr Brooks that the ambulance was on its way.

Duwayne Brook's statement continues. 'I told her we were attacked, but I had got away. She asked me where the boys went and I pointed out the road... When I pointed to her where they had run, she did nothing... she didn't tell the other officers there or anyone else on her radio. She didn't ask what the name of the road was.'

'She asked me more than once where they had gone. The *second* time she asked I said something like "I fucking told you where they went, are you deaf? Why don't you go and look for them?"... She just kept saying calm down, which made me more frustrated her saying that and doing nothing for Steve. She asked what they looked like... She asked how did we get there. *I didn't answer that question*... She asked questions like "Who are they to you?"... She said, "Your friend is lying there and you don't know who those boys are!"... She was treating me like she was suspicious of me, not that she wanted to help.

When she asked *stupid questions* I kept saying where is the ambulance, I didn't call for you.'

He says, 'There they were talking rubbish to my ears and walking up and down and doing nothing... I became increasingly frustrated and loud and agitated'.

He asked PC Bethel and the other officers more than once why couldn't they put Stephen into a police car and drive him to hospital. They said they could not do that. 'They never gave a reason they just said I should calm down and "be sensible about it for your friend's sake". *I didn't answer those questions which I thought were stupid. I only answered her sensible questions.*'[5]

Later Duwayne Brooks told Detective Sergeant Crowley that he hated the police. In June 1993, when the conversation took place, he said that he wanted to 'take revenge on them, because they had arrived on the night of the murder before the ambulance men'. This statement is accepted by Duwayne Brooks as having been said by him.[6]

Duwayne Brooks praises 'one male uniformed officer'. 'He asked me if I was injured and if I needed to sit down. I said no I was fine.'

In his statement to the inquiry he objected to PC Gleason reporting later that he was 'virtually uncontrollable'. 'What did they want to control me for? They should have taken control of the situation and organised help for Steve and chasing the boys... I was not out of control or hysterical. I was perfectly capable of answering *sensible* questions.' He states he did so.

'The first time anyone made any use of the information that I gave them was when different police arrived... It [the newly-arrived police carrier] left in that direction [Dickson Road] almost straight away.' (The police carrier had started its search of the estate, on Duwayne Brooks's information, that is, within about 20 minutes of Stephen Lawrence being attacked.)

'I was very upset. I was *wound up by the officers.*'[7]

Given the plain words of Duwayne Brooks' statement ('she just kept saying calm down', 'they just said I should calm down and "be sensible about it for your friend's sake"') it comes as a surprise to see Macpherson's criticism of the police at the scene, that 'nobody appears properly to have tried to calm him down'.[8] If the emphasis is on the word 'tried', this statement is incorrect. If the emphasis is on 'properly' then we have merely the vague suggestion that the police constables present did have the ability to calm this person down, in these circumstances, during the time they were with him; and that they did not do 'properly' what they could have done 'properly' because of the fact that they were *in some sense* racists. Duwayne Brooks said later that he was anti-police, and that he had deliberately not called the police on the night of the murder.[9] Calming him down was, perhaps, easier said by Macpherson, long after the event, than done by the police officers dealing with him at the time.

PC Joanne Smith was called to the scene some time after 10.50 p.m. Her version of Duwayne Brooks' reception is that he said to her, 'Who called you fucking cunts anyway—pigs! I only called the fucking ambulance'.[10] Macpherson's comment is that PC Smith 'reported exactly what she had experienced in her short dealings with Mr Brooks'. But it had to be said, the report continues, that she should have shown 'much more interest in and sympathy for' him.[11] That is, if a police constable to whom the insults were addressed did react adversely in any way to being called a 'fucking cunt' and 'pig', her adverse reaction was because Duwayne Brooks was black, not because she was beings abused. In reporting 'exactly what she had experienced' from him she was ... 'stereotyping' him.[12]

What is Macpherson's 'evidence' of police racist conduct towards Duwayne Brooks in the four minutes before the ambulance arrived? The evidence is that the police officers concerned saw and described his conduct—the conduct that Duwayne Brooks gives his own full account of in his statement—in the way that they did. 'At the scene his conduct was described by ... PC Anthony Gleason as "highly excitable" and "virtually uncontrollable".'[13] In addition to reporting that Duwayne Brooks had verbally abused the women officers who were first on the scene with the words 'cunts' and 'pigs' (Mr Brooks said he had not used these words), PC Joanne Smith said that he was 'jumping up and down and being very aggressive'.

'Mr Brooks was the victim of racial stereotyping. By way of example, in her written statement made at the scene PC Bethel described Mr Brooks as "very distressed" and "very excitable and upset". In her answer to a 1994 questionnaire she said he was "aggressive, anti-police, distressed and unhelpful". To the Kent Police Service she said that Mr Brooks was "powerful and physically intimidating", and that his behaviour was "horrendous".' These descriptions of a particular person's behaviour and appearance on a particular occasion are, to Macpherson, evidence of 'racial stereotyping' and how it 'develops'.[14]

But, says Macpherson, what the police do not seem to have understood was that Mr Brooks simply was 'angry' at the scene of the murder, and 'justifiably' angry, and justifiably angry 'because he saw the arrival of the police as no substitute for the non-arrival of the ambulance, and to his mind the police seemed more interested in questioning him than attending to Stephen'. Duwayne Brooks was justifiably angry because the police arrived before the ambulance; how could anyone have come to write such a thing? (On his own evidence, he was angry because the police were there at all.) It is, furthermore, a misdescription of the situation to call the few minutes it necessarily took for it to travel without delay from Greenwich the 'non-arrival' of the ambulance.

The adverse reaction—the racist conduct of the police—was not that they subdued him, arrested him for a breach of the peace, or even shouted at him. No one says that they did any of these things. According to Macpherson, their adverse reaction was that, although they took him to the hospital in a police car, 'they left him to go into the hospital unaccompanied'.[15]

In addition to the way the officers described Mr Brooks' conduct, the fact that there was 'no evidence' *(sic)* that any officer 'tried properly to understand' that Duwayne Brooks's abuse of the police was *justified*. Mr Brooks 'needed close, careful and sensitive treatment'.

Who can tell, Macpherson asks, whether or not 'proper respect' and 'concern for Mr Brooks' status as a victim' would have helped to lead to evidence, should he have been used in a properly co-ordinated search of the estate?[16]

In fact, during their first few minutes the police were trying to find out who had done the attacking, and what kind of an attack it was. Macpherson's criticism of them is, and evidence of their racism, that they did not treat (the untouched) Duwayne Brooks *immediately* both as 'a *primary victim*', and as 'the victim of a *racist* attack'.

Macpherson concludes, 'We are *driven* to the conclusion that Mr Brooks was stereotyped as a young black man exhibiting unpleasant hostility and agitation... We believe that Mr Brooks' colour and such stereotyping played their part in the collective failure of those taking part to treat him ... according to his needs ...We have to conclude that *no* officer dealt properly at the scene with Mr Brooks.' Not even presumably, the one who Mr Brooks himself picked out for praise.[17] Did Macpherson weigh its use of the word 'driven'?

In discussing the conduct of the officers who arrived early at the murder scene Macpherson says more generally that Mr Brooks 'was also the *victim* of *all* that followed, including the conduct of the case and the treatment of himself *(sic)* as a witness and not as a victim.'[18]

This general statement is made in spite of the fact, acknowledged as such in clear terms by Macpherson, that in the private prosecution brought against Neil Acourt, Luke Knight and Gary Dobson (the trial was held at the Old Bailey in June 1996) all three were found not guilty. They can never stand trial again for the Stephen Lawrence murder. The 'not guilty' verdicts turned wholly on the finally undisputed fact—undisputed by Duwayne Brooks himself—that his evidence from identity parades held on 13 May 1993 and 3 June 1993 was hopelessly tainted. At the trial, Macpherson says, 'the evidence of Mr

Brooks was effectively destroyed by fair and logical cross-examination. There was nothing left to be put before the Court. Rightly the prosecution was abandoned'.[19]

On the topic of the collapse of the Lawrences' private prosecution Macpherson writes of the value of Duwayne Brooks as a witness:

> in our judgement anyone reading all the evidence put before Mr Justice Curtis will properly reach only one conclusion, namely (as Mr Justice Curtis put it), that 'where recognition or identification is concerned he simply does not know in ordinary parlance whether he is on his head or his heels'.[20]

There simply was no satisfactory evidence available. 'Where this is the position', Macpherson says, 'the Courts cannot change the law or the rules out of sympathy' for the victim's parents.[21]

By this time, however, Mrs Lawrence had adopted the world-view and the language of the strand in anti-racism that defines the black as permanent victim, and white society as a permanent conspiracy against him. In her statement to the coroner at the inquest on Stephen's death, held in February 1997, she interpreted the failure of the private prosecution as evidence that what had happened in the Crown Court had been 'staged'.[22] By acquitting the three suspects *because Duwayne Brooks' identification evidence was so defective*, the English judicial *system* (i.e. the whole set of institutions concerned with the law) was, according to Mrs Lawrence,

> making a clear statement saying to the black community that their lives are worth nothing and the justice system will *support* ... any white person who wishes to *commit* ... *murder* against any black person.[23]

Mrs Lawrence's statement to the coroner is published in full in the Macpherson report.[24]

The report praises senior officers in the Metropolitan Police Service for eventually accepting that police officers who had to deal with Duwayne Brooks during the first few minutes following the murder could have handled the situation better. 'Lengthy submissions set out the nature of his complaints. To a considerable extent, to the credit of the Metropolitan Police Service, they are accepted.' Assistant Commissioner Johnston had admitted that, although 'we did some things to try to help him', his assessment of how Mr Brooks was dealt with during the early stages was that he 'should have been dealt with much better'. 'These are understatements', Macpherson says, 'but they do at least demonstrate acceptance of fault.'[25]

It is not at all clear how far that passage in the Macpherson report is meant to imply that Assistant Commissioner Johnston accepted only the fault that the police officers could have done much better—a proposition that few could ever dispute in any situation whatsoever—or that it was also an admission by him that, beneath that fault, there lay the more fundamental one of racism. In the context it is easy to mistakenly read the passage as though it was Johnston's admission of racism; and that his admission was one more proof that racism was the explanation of the failure to convict Stephen Lawrence's killers.

There are two issues in connection with the overall investigation of the Stephen Lawrence murder. One is the competence of the police. On this issue Macpherson contributed nothing new. A year-long study by a score of police officers from Kent Police Service had combed through every aspect of the case, and the Kent Police Service report was critical of many features of the investigation and many officers. The second issue was whether racism had interfered with the investigation. The Kent Police Service had found no evidence of this.

The same two issues arose over the actions and attitudes of police officers in the 15 or 20 minutes or so (in the case of some officers less than 15 minutes) between their arrival on the scene and the departure of the ambulance. One was the issue of incompetence in administering first aid to Stephen Lawrence. The other was whether racism was the explanation for their incompetence.

Incompetence?

Michael Salih, one of the ambulance men at the scene, testified that he would not have advised anyone to move Stephen Lawrence. The report was of a head injury. Someone lying in that condition with a head injury should be left until professional help arrived.

Miss Helen Avery, on the other hand, who was 14 at the time, was amazed that no one was trying to staunch the flow of blood. Her knowledge of first aid told her that something should have been done.

Racism as the explanation?

Macpherson found Inspector Steven Groves guilty of racism because of what he had neglected to do in connection with first aid. He had simply left the scene because he believed there had been some sort of fight.

> We are forced to the conclusion that his attitude and dismissive conduct were contributed to, *if not wholly caused*, by *(sic)* unwitting but *clear racism*. He saw a young black man lying injured, and an obviously stressed and agitated young black man on the pavement nearby. It is plain to us all that ... his whole approach to what had happened was thus undermined by racist stereotyping ... he would not have been equally dismissive if the two young men involved had been white.[26]

All the others involved directly in the allegations of indifference and neglect in administering first aid were exonerated of the charge of being motivated by racism in that connection. 'We understand the reactions and strong feelings of Mr and Mrs Lawrence, but we are not persuaded that anyone involved in the immediate attention or lack of attention ... can rightly be accused of anything more than failure to heed to such training as had been given and an over-reliance on the imminent arrival of the ambulance.' 'We do not infer that their inaction was initiated or caused by overt *or* unwitting racism.'[27]

How He Was Treated By The Police At The Hospital

The ambulance arrived within a few minutes of being summoned by the 999 operator who, in spite of Duwayne Brooks' confused information, had worked out the location of the incident.

Once again, Duwayne Brooks' own account of how he behaved, and how he was treated by the police officers dealing with him will be used. 'I tried to get into the ambulance with Steve but the police officers would not let me. They said there was no space. I really wanted to be in the ambulance with Steve.' (According to Macpherson, it was the paramedics and not a police officer who told Mr Brooks he could not travel in the ambulance.)[28] He therefore 'agreed' to go in the police car. 'I told the driver to hurry up.' PC Joanne Smith later described Duwayne Brooks' behaviour in the police car as being highly excitable and particularly unco-operative. 'She found him to have been aggressive and shouting and swearing whilst she drove him to the hospital', writes Macpherson. 'Nobody should blame him for the things that he said at the scene and thereafter.'[29]

When he arrived at the hospital he walked behind the stretcher. 'One nurse asked me to go with her, but I said it's OK and walked off. I went into a waiting room. A policeman came up, and said he wanted to talk to me, to help my friend. I was most probably shouting and walking off. He told me his name.' (It was PC Gleason.) 'He said he needed a statement. ... *I kept walking off.* ... He kept saying "I need a statement, I need a statement".' At the hospital, he says, nobody asked if he was all right. Nobody asked whether he had been attacked. ('One nurse asked me to go with her, but I said I was OK and walked off.') He was, he says, 'offered no comfort'.[30]

An episode at the hospital throws light on the dangers of interpreting too much in racist terms. Mrs Lawrence had known Duwayne Brooks since he and Stephen had started secondary school. Duwayne's mother was friendly with Mrs Lawrence's brother. Yet, she reported, 'When I first came through the door I could see a black boy *standing in front of me*. I didn't recognise the black boy, but I now know it was Duwayne.'[31] We cannot help but wonder what Macpherson would have made of that if 'racism' could have been read into it.

That he was 'offered no comfort' by someone proficient in dealing with people shocked and agitated by participating in the appalling events of such an evening is one thing. To take that fact as evidence of racism is entirely another. Racism, and not lack of social skills, would be a reasonable explanation only if a white young man behaving identically would have been handled with more sympathy and patience.

Macpherson, however, was 'driven to the conclusion' that Duwayne Brooks' treatment by the police at the hospital was explicable by police racism, just as their treatment of him at the scene of the murder had been explicable by police racism. Macpherson repeats the same words:

> Mr Brooks was stereotyped as a young black man exhibiting unpleasant hostility and agitation ... We believe that Mr Brooks' colour and such stereotyping played their part in the collective failure of those taking part to treat him ... according to his needs.[32]

How He Was Treated At Plumstead Police Station

Duwayne Brooks, after being asked to wait in the police car parked at the hospital, and left waiting in it alone for some time, was driven to Plumstead police station in the early hours of the morning of 23 April 1993. The inquiry had little criticism of the police officers there, much less criticism of their racism. Why, if the MPS was 'collectively' racist was its 'collective' (or structural) racism, so to speak, raging at Eltham and 'switched off' at Plumstead? The officers there described Duwayne Brooks as 'very calm', 'remarkably together', 'truthful and helpful', 'perceptive' and 'intelligent', presumably because that was the way he seemed to them to be behaving. 'They treated him', Macpherson says, 'appropriately and professionally.'

As Marian FitzGerald reports (unsurprisingly) from her study of various London localities, some of the youths who are involved with the police 'actually initiate' aggression. In some areas, while 'the older generation welcomed police involvement', the police faced hostility irrespective of the ethnicity of the youths.[33] Adults in relation to children, and police officers in relation to all members of the general public, have to exercise the utmost restraint and skill. They must not reply in kind. But the relationship between adults and children, and between police and members of the public, is a two-way process. Any society in which the highest authorities in effect propagate the philosophical doctrine (it is not, and cannot conceivably be considered to be an empirical one) that the blame for less than ideal conduct always lies with the police officer is inviting, not to say inciting, ever worse behaviour from the people he or she is employed to control.

Macpherson notes that years later, that is, in his inquiry statement, Duwayne Brooks was to say that officers at the police station did not want to believe him, particularly when he said the attack was motivated by racism. 'We believe', says Macpherson magnanimously, 'that he may not have recalled the incident accurately [*for the inquiry*], since *at the time* and *thereafter* Mr Brooks made no complaint about his treatment.'[34]

In his own statement to the Macpherson inquiry Duwayne Brooks says, 'I wanted to start shouting and calling them idiots but couldn't, I was just too tired'. Detective Constable Cooper asked him if he wanted anyone with him. 'I said I didn't.' DC Cooper told him that if he wanted to go home and be interviewed later he could do so. 'I said. "No, now that am here I want to get it over with". DC Cooper said OK let's start from the beginning. He asked me questions and I answered them.'

The fact that it was a racist attack was established beyond doubt by the fact that one or more of Stephen Lawrence's attackers had shouted 'What, what! Nigger!' The police 'kept saying are you sure they said "What, what! Nigger!"' He remembered someone saying, 'You know what this means if you are telling the truth?'

Duwayne Brooks says repetitively, however, that he was not treated as a victim of crime. 'At no stage did any officer ask me if any of the white boys attacked me or touched me'; 'at no stage did any officer ask me if I had been attacked'; 'at no stage did any officer consult me about whether I wished to press charges.' What is likely to rise in the mind of anyone reading these parts of his statement is the question, 'Why did he not volunteer the information that he had been attacked, and that he did want to press charges?'

The fact that he did not raise these matters in the first few moments, or ever, was surely a plausible enough reason for everybody taking it for granted that they did not apply to him, especially as 'What, what! Nigger!', in the singular, not 'What, what! Niggers!', shouted at two men, was so central to his own eye-witness evidence.

How He Was Treated By The Police In Connection With The Welling Riot

The next body of evidence on the racist treatment of Duwayne Brooks concerns his part in a demonstration that was held a fortnight after the murder. Several thousand people took part, and there was a large police presence. The result was the 'Welling riot' of 8 May 1993. Nineteen police officers and demonstrators were injured, and shop windows were broken. Neville Lawrence said of Panther UK, the Anti-Nazi League and others who had taken part, 'We have no control over these groups who try to use us for political purposes'.[35] Operation Fewson, a large investigation only marginally connected with the

Stephen Lawrence murder, was set up by the police to identify those responsible for this serious riot from video evidence, still photography, and the statements of eye-witnesses. In his statement to the Macpherson inquiry Duwayne Brooks says that he went to protest against 'the way the police were handling' his friend's murder. He was charged with criminal damage to motor vehicles and violent disorder.

'In October I was arrested and charged with offences arising out of the demonstration ... I felt like the police and prosecution decided to get me to ruin my reputation—and the chance of any future prosecution of the murderers.' When the case came before Croydon Crown Court, it was stopped as an abuse of the processes of the court. 'The judge wasn't having any of it', Mr Brooks says in his statement.[36] The police came out of the incident badly on any reckoning of public image. But what was police racism, what was police resentment, and what was police efficiency or over-zealousness cannot be discerned from anything Macpherson has to say on the matter.

Macpherson says that sometimes, both during the inquiry and in submissions made on his behalf, Duwayne Brooks' case had been put 'too high', and that allegations that he was 'criminalised' and 'demonised' were 'inappropriate'.

But the report's overall finding is that 'lack of respect and sensitivity in handling him must reflect *"collective racism"* particularly among those who dealt with him on the night of the murder and at the hospital'.[37] (Again, why should 'collective' racism appear 'particularly' among these officers?) The Macpherson report says, 'We do not believe that a young white man *in a similar position* would have been dealt with in the same way'.[38]

Why did the report not say 'in a similar position *and acting in the same way*'? That is the test. Nothing but his change of conduct in Plumstead police station can explain the fact that there he was treated with what looks to the outsider as consideration and kindness. (The police officers were not to know that, according to his own account, he was by then simply too tired to 'shout at them and call them idiots'.)

'We hope and believe', says Macpherson, 'that the average police officer and the average member of the public will ... both understand and accept the distinction we draw between overt individual racism and the pernicious and persistent racism which we have described.'[39]

6

The Treatment of Mr and Mrs Lawrence
in Family Liaison
as Evidence of Police Racism

The treatment of the Lawrences by the MPS liaison officers is additional to, and separate from, the general issue of the Lawrences' anger at the failure of the police investigation to uncover evidence that would convict the murderers of their son. The failure of the police investigation as evidence of police racism suffuses the report, and is also dealt with under its own heading. Macpherson refers to 'the important topic of family liaison', and racism in family liaison is one of the main bodies of evidence to demonstrate the existence of racism in the MPS.

The Behaviour Of Officers Concerned With Family Liaison

As counsel for the Macpherson inquiry said in his opening statement, 'Sensitivity in dealing with a family traumatised by the sudden death of a son is obviously demanded, not only for reasons of common humanity but also, and practically, because the co-operation of the bereaved family is often required in the investigation'.[1]

Macpherson gives several examples of the attempts by the liaison officers to be friendly with and be of practical assistance to the Lawrences. The liaison officers managed to have the mortuary opened on the Saturday after the murder, so that the Lawrences would not have to wait until the Monday to view their son.[2] The Lawrences were given one of the officer's mobile phones to use, so that they could contact the liaison officers if they had anything to ask or report.[3] One of them delivered a birthday card to Georgina Lawrence who was away on an Outward Bound course. Mrs Lawrence said this was done because the officer 'wanted to be helpful'.

The Lawrences' solicitor, Imran Khan, says that, on the day of his first visit to the house, the liaison officers were 'nothing but supportive'.[4] He also says that the relations between the Lawrences and DCS Ilsley in family-liaison meetings were 'by and large cordial'.[5]

But 'despite the *good intentions* of the officers involved', the Macpherson report says, 'the liaison as a whole failed'.[6]

Whether there was lack of sensitivity is one question. If there was lack of sensitivity, whether it was due to racism is quite another.

Detective Sergeant John Bevan

Detective Sergeant Bevan told the Kent Police Service that he found it difficult to deal with Imran Khan. He had been surprised that it was thought that, from the very first moment, 'the *victims* needed legal representation'. He regarded Imran Khan as a barrier to communication.

Macpherson has no sympathy with DS Bevan's account of this, one of the difficulties he had had to face. 'It is not the business of DS Bevan', the report says, 'to criticise the arrival on the scene of a solicitor.' That is another aspect of the case that the liaison officers had simply to 'accept, cope with and respond to positively'.[7] The Macpherson report is often phrased in a curiously skewed way: it was not 'the arrival on the scene' of *a* solicitor that DS Bevan found difficult (he found that only 'surprising'). It was what *Imran Khan*, a particular solicitor, *did* at the scene.

Edmund Lawson's interrogation

In his opening statement on behalf of the inquiry, Edmund Lawson QC dealt with the question of family liaison. The 'so-called "family-liaison officers"—I do not use so-called in a derogatory manner', said Lawson without giving them any titles, were Bevan and Holden. They had been the subjects of public criticism by Mrs Lawrence. According to her they had been, Lawson said, 'unsupportive and very patronising'.

Lawson put three questions about the conduct of Linda Holden and John Bevan.

1. Had they been 'unsupportive and very patronising'?

2. If they had been was that because they had actually acted in an unsupportive way?

3. Or was it because Mrs Lawrence had simply misinterpreted supportive conduct? If it was, Lawson said, that 'might be just as bad'.

But it could not be 'just as bad' *as a criticism of the liaison officers*, the only point at issue. It cannot be 'just as bad' to behave well and be wrongly interpreted, as it is to behave badly and be correctly interpreted.

Edmund Lawson, and then the Macpherson report itself, accepted that DS Bevan's intentions were good, as were those of his colleague in family liaison, DC Linda Holden.[8] But however good the intentions, the family liaison had been a failure.

When asked for an explanation for the failure, DS Bevan said that he would 'love to have an answer to that'.

> I tried everything I could to communicate with the Lawrences. I wanted to be there for them. I have said in all the documentation to Kent and on statements that I want to be there for them today, and I wish I could be. There was a tremendous barrier to communication. ... I think they were being taken over—that is possibly a bad way of putting it—by lots of outside bodies who wanted to make their own statement through the Lawrences.[9]

The presence in the Lawrence home of radical anti-racists with their animus against the police from the very first day after the murder was the thing that, in his opinion, had had the biggest effect. 'Very, very soon after our initial meetings we were viewed with suspicion and mistrust.'[10]

But there was also the fact that his role was still that of a police officer. He had to be alert to any evidence that came his way in the course of carrying out his duties in liaison. Mrs Lawrence's feelings were, at any rate in retrospect, that, as black people were in the house, John Bevan's assumption was therefore that 'there must have been something criminal or whatever'.[11]

He had also to balance the desire of the family (or their Anti-Racist Alliance advisers) for information, against the need to keep lines of inquiry confidential. He was a liaison officer between the police service and the family, not the family's agent. He had told them that some suspects had been identified, and not much more than that.

He went on to deny that he had treated the Lawrences in an off-hand fashion. He denied that he had treated them badly because they were black.

Edward Lawson QC, during this interrogation, did not raise the possibility that the failures of family liaison were due to police racism. He raised only one possibility: that they were the consequence of defective training.[12]

Stephen Kamlish's interrogation

Stephen Kamlish was one of the counsel representing Mr and Mrs Lawrence at the Macpherson inquiry. This is the way in which the evidence against John Bevan was gathered, for Sir William to weigh in the report's conclusions:

Kamlish: Family liaison: firstly, to confirm a few matters, you had never done it before?

Bevan: That's correct.

Kamlish: You had not had any training?

Bevan: There is no training for family liaison, sir.

Kamlish: You had not seen the guidelines?

Bevan: I don't believe I had, no.

Kamlish: You had not done it before and you did not even look at the guidelines ... Don't you think that was something, with hindsight, you should have done?

Bevan: Using that lovely word 'hindsight' again, sir, quite possibly...

Kamlish: I want to put to you what is perceived by the Lawrences as your true motivation for doing this job ... it is all to do with self-gratification, is it not?[13]

Kamlish then produced a list of quotations from Bevan's statement to, and then his interview with, Kent Police Service during its investigation of the Lawrences' submissions to the Police Complaints Authority:

Cathcart describes what follows as the 'nub' of Kamlish's 'challenge' to DS Bevan:

John Bevan had said he had 'relished the opportunity' of a 'very demanding job'. He said that he believed that his 'caring, supportive' character would be 'an asset to that role'. One of his own 'greatest attributes', he had said, was that he could 'speak to different levels of people'. He believed that he could 'offer something to this role' that would be 'mutually beneficial' to the Lawrences and to him.

Later he had said that 'it would be a big feather in our cap' if he and Linda Holden could resolve the problems over the mortuary visit.

These were all, one would have thought, rather blameless remarks. At worst they were the sort of things that people are supposed to say in 'social-work' type jobs and job applications.

But Kamlish's suggestion to the inquiry was that Bevan was less interested in helping the Lawrences than in gratifying his own vanity.

Perhaps he was, perhaps he was not. Proof of vanity is not proof of racism, unwitting or not.

Yet Cathcart describes this as a 'devastating assault'. It was, Cathcart says, 'almost impossible for Bevan to answer'. That John Bevan was stunned by these accusations and insinuations in these circumstances, however, is scarcely surprising. What social-work type employee would not be open to them? But neither Kamlish's questions nor Bevan's answers threw any light at all on the issue of Bevan's *racism*.

Kamlish continued: 'You did not appreciate how they were seeing you: you only looked at it in terms of how they reacted to you. Do you understand?' John Bevan had on some occasion described Mrs Lawrence's behaviour towards him as 'aggressive'.

Kamlish: You described her in your interview as aggressive, this grieving mother, from day one, did you not?

Bevan: Mrs Lawrence did adopt an aggressive stance.

Kamlish: Was it aggressive for somebody whose son had just been murdered a day or two earlier in a racist attack, for her not to smile at you and not to talk to you. Is that 'aggression'?

Bevan: We can analyse all the words used throughout these interviews and we can pull them apart now, sir. What I felt is—I felt at the time and I feel now to some degree—that Mrs Lawrence's stance was aggressive.[14]

His use of the word 'aggression', he said, was not meant as a criticism. It was only a description of how she was dealing with him.

By a strange coincidence the identity of one of the key informants had been codenamed 'K', the protagonist of *The Trial*, and by another coincidence that was the initial of DS Bevan's interrogator, Kamlish.[15] DS Bevan might well have felt that he had strayed in a nightmare into the middle of Kafka's novel.

What was he being accused of? What did he have to defend himself against? How was it that he, a humble detective sergeant, was being questioned by barristers, in front of a High Court judge, an Anglican bishop, an ex-deputy chief constable, and an activist anti-racist GP, in the full glare of national publicity, about the semantics of standard job-application jargon? Is it impossible for a grieving mother to be 'aggressive'? Was vanity unknown among broadsheet journalists? Were barristers never patronising? ('You did not appreciate how they were seeing you: you only looked at it in terms of how they reacted to you. *Do you understand?*') What fatal word would ruin his career? What secret incantation would satisfy his interrogators and the panel of his judges?

K would not know for certain until after the Macpherson report was published and the answer was revealed. It was: 'I abjectly confess to being guilty of institutional racism'.

Detective Constable Linda Holden

The hat and gloves found near the scene

A hat and gloves were found at the scene of the murder. DC Linda Holden took the hat and gloves to Mr and Mrs Lawrence to ask if they were Stephen's. Linda Holden says that when they told her that they did not belong to Stephen, 'that was the end of the matter'. The report says that the evidence was *'palpable'* that no police officer ever thought that there was a 'shadow of suspicion' over Stephen. It says that it accepts Linda Holden's version. She had never suggested that Stephen Lawrence might have been involved in nefarious activity.

But the Lawrences took the question about the hat and gloves as a slur on their son's memory.

There are only two complaints dealt with by Macpherson, this, and the fact that the liaison officers, when they were at the Lawrences, wanted to know who was in the house also. In her statement read at the inquest in February 1997, Mrs Lawrence saw this as indicating that, because Stephen was black, he 'therefore must be a criminal and they set about investigating them and us'.[16]

The family was investigated, Mrs Lawrence said, because they had committed the 'crime of living in a racist country where the justice system *supports* racists murders'.[17]

Macpherson therefore accepts two sets of facts as being true. The first is no police officer thought, and no police officer suggested, that anything had happened except that questions had been put about whom the hat and gloves belonged to. The second fact was that the Lawrences had been offended by the questions.

How does the report deal with these two sets of what it accepts as facts? 'In the atmosphere of mistrust which existed', Macpherson says, 'it is perhaps not surprising that Mr and Mrs Lawrence's perceptions of the questions asked ... was that some kind of suggestion was being made against their dead son'.[18] No 'positive' suggestion had been made. But Mr and Mrs Lawrence had 'perceived' that a 'positive' suggestion had been made. Therefore the matter had not been dealt with properly. Therefore there was a racist element in the relationship.[19]

If Linda Holden had thought that the Lawrences would react in this way to her innocent act, perhaps she would have been more careful in preparing them with assurances that the questions were only to establish the ownership of the hat and gloves. Perhaps she should have had enough sense of how the Lawrences were reacting to such episodes to have given them careful assurances anyway.

Three things can be noted about this evidence of DS Bevan's and DC Holden's police racism.

The first is that the possibility of what, in all the circumstances, would be regarded as reasonably sensitive behaviour being responded to over-sensitively does not arise. The unstated but overriding assumption is that 'insensitive' conduct was anything that upset the Lawrences. 'The family of Stephen Lawrence' says the report, 'had to be taken ... as *they* chose to behave.'[20] The question of mutual adjustment does not arise. The police were obliged to adjust to however the Lawrences *or their advisers* chose to behave.

This observation in the particular case, that only the liaison officer, never a member of the family, could behave inappropriately, was then extended to apply as a generally applicable rule. 'It is the business of the police to ensure that they fit in with the ... *behaviour* of those to whom they are attached for family liaison purposes.'[21]

The second is that DS Bevan and DC Holden were taken off liaison duties at the end of May 1993. By that action the MPS showed that it made the feelings of the Lawrences paramount. The words and actions emanating from the personæ of DS Bevan and DC Holden were inappropriate or, however so sensitive, were being misinterpreted. Perhaps some other police liaison officer would be able to handle the situation more successfully.

Of course the problem would be insoluble by the police service if a large element of the difficulty were the simple fact that they were police officers. If the whole atmosphere was charged with an anti-police animus that preceded the murder of Stephen, and which had been introduced into the Lawrence dwelling by outside helpers, what degree and kind of police 'sensitivity' would have been required?

The third is that, even if we assume that Linda Holden was grossly insensitive, it would have to be shown that the same clumsiness would not have occurred with equal likelihood when dealing with a white family. There are no data to throw light on the question. But it is certain that it is not *obvious* that there would be a big difference. The burden of proof lay with Macpherson on this essential matter if the case for racism was to be made.

Detective Chief Superintendent Ilsley

At the end of May 1993 Detective Chief Superintendent Ilsley took over responsibility for the family liaison, but he had been in contact with the Lawrences already.

Folding the piece of paper

On 6 May 1993, after the meeting with Nelson Mandela, Mrs Lawrence was upset by an incident involving the behaviour of DCS Ilsley, who was at that time the senior detective in Number 3 Area of the MPS. The police already had the names from various sources of the five chief suspects, that is to say, the two Acourts, Norris, Knight and Dobson. But Mrs Lawrence took a piece of paper to the meeting with him on which she had written nothing but the following:

1. ZAK Pont

2. Nickname Blue Blonde hair age 20

3. Louie catonia

4. Dobson

5. Knox

6. Arecourts

The folding of this piece of paper features strongly in the issue of the family liaison, and there is a photograph of the piece of paper in the Macpherson report.[22] 'Louie catonia' might be a friend of the Acourts, Danny Caetano. Dobson is Gary Dobson. 'Knox' might be a misheard 'Norris'. The 'Arecourts' are obviously the Acourts. 'ZAC' might be Zachariah, but we have come across no name that resembles 'Zac Pont'.

After the meeting DCS Ilsley took the paper downstairs and the contents were entered into the information system. But during the meeting DSC Ilsley folded the note, and folded it again and again. 'I saw him fold the paper so small', Mrs Lawrence says in her statement to the inquiry six years later. 'I don't think I said anything because it was too much of a shock. He rolled the piece of paper up in the ball of his hand. I was so shocked when I saw that.'[23] When the meeting ended she said to Ilsley, 'You are not going to put that in the bin now?'[24]

The incident of the folded piece of paper had figured largely also in Mrs Lawrence's statement to the coroner at Stephen's inquest a year earlier, which the main report reproduces in its entirety.[25]

DCS Ilsley's affront to Mrs Lawrence on this occasion was a new obstacle to good relations being established between the police and the family.

The Lawrences had 'obviously been primed to ask questions'

DCS Ilsley was responsible for another incident that deeply rankled with Mrs Lawrence. In her statement to the inquiry Mrs Lawrence said:

> Basically we were seen as gullible simpletons. This is best shown by Ilsley's comment that I had obviously been primed to ask questions. Presumably there was no possibility of me being an intelligent black woman with thoughts of her own who is able to ask questions for herself.[26]

This incident, recorded in the appendices, is highlighted by Macpherson in two places in the report itself. Mrs Lawrence, who was studying for her BA in Humanities at the time, states that there were 'many incidents like this' where 'they patronised me as if I can't think for myself', but other examples are not given.[27]

Yet given the entourage of advisers around the Lawrences, including the highly active presence of the black rights solicitor, Imran Khan, Ilsley did not have to be a racist to think that the questions the police were being asked had been devised with the assistance of other people.

No doubt Detective Chief Superintendent Ilsley, when he was engaged in family liaison, could have behaved better. 'In this respect, as in others', as Lord Scarman said, 'the standard we apply to the police must be higher than the norms of behaviour prevalent in society as a whole.'[28] But the idea that normally no non-racist senior police officer would fold a piece of paper small, or assert his or her authority over a bereaved white working-class family who were giving him or her as much hassle as were the Lawrences, or even very little hassle, is the sheerest fantasy.

'Racism' is not needed at all to explain Ilsley's behaviour, and evidence *additional to that of the behaviour itself* would have had to be produced by Macpherson to show that he was racist, or that what he did or said were 'expressions' of his own 'unwitting' racism, or that he was the passive and personally guiltless carrier of the 'institutional' racism of the MPS.

Michael Mansfield's interrogation

Michael Mansfield QC, counsel for the Lawrences, asked DCS Ilsley what he understood by the meaning of the words racist and racism. Ilsley replied, 'People making derogatory remarks about people of different colour'. Mansfield asked if that was all Ilsley wanted to say about it. Ilsley replied that yes, there were other things to say. He would want to sit down and work them out. Mansfield acknowledged that such a question put to someone in the witness box might be a difficult one to answer quickly.

'There are a lot of things', Ilsley replied. 'Equal opportunities as well, sir.'

'Have you been aware of the more difficult kind of racism that sometimes appears within the police force?'

'No, I haven't.'

'Never?'

'Never, sir.'

Mansfield had thus made some statements of 'fact'. He had asked Ilsley one question about them.

The statements of 'fact' were

1. that there is another kind of racism in addition to that of verbal abuse and discrimination—'the more difficult' kind of racism;

2. that it appears 'sometimes', but not always;

3. that it appears sometimes in 'the police force'.

The sole question was, was DCS Ilsley *aware* of these 'facts'?

What is the value as 'evidence' of *racism* of the answer 'no'? In the circumstances 'no' is as polite a way as any of saying, 'What on earth do you mean, "the" form of racism that is "more difficult"? Tell me what you are referring to, and I shall do my best to give you an answer'.

What is supposed to have been demonstrated when someone has already said, clearly, that by racism he understands verbal abuse and inequalities of opportunity, but is now 'unaware', and has never been aware, that a 'more difficult kind of racism' 'sometimes appears' in the police force?

This is the application as farce of the skills appropriate to the investigation of concrete evidence about concrete events relevant to the breach of a specific law.

Cathcart writes that 'over time wider questioning brought out many signs of unreconstructed attitudes to race among police officers'. Among these, he says, 'none was more striking than Detective Chief Superintendent Ilsley'. It is this episode that he cites.[29]

Together with folding the paper small, and suggesting to Mrs Lawrence that someone from, say, the Anti-Racist Alliance (ARA), had briefed her, this is the 'evidence' of DCS Ilsley's racism.

Detective Superintendent Brian Weeden

In his evidence to the inquiry Detective Superintendent Weeden testified that he had created opportunities for the family to liaise with him, but the family had not responded to them. On 27 April 1993, five days after the murder, he had written to Mr and Mrs Lawrence telling them that Detective Sergeant Bevan and Detective Constable Holden were the liaison officers, but that if the Lawrences wanted to see him at any time all they needed to do was say so. On 30 April 1993 another family member let DS Weeden know that the family were going away for the weekend and did not want to be disturbed. He had then received a written note, he testified, that the family did not want to be disturbed for the next two days unless there were developments.[30]

DS Weeden said that he had tried to see the family at home but, as Macpherson put it, 'had failed to do so'. (DS Weeden's meaning was clearly that he had not been permitted by the Lawrences to do so.) He had also invited them to come to the incident room on their own, without Imran Khan, so that they could meet face to face. 'That invitation' Macpherson says, 'was turned down by Mr and Mrs Lawrence.' In DS Weeden's briefing note dated 13 July 1993, sent to the MPS Commissioner in preparation for a meeting with the All Party Parliamentary Group of Race and Community, he said that there had been 'many cancellations of meetings' by the Lawrence family after 6 May 1993.[31]

DS Weeden told the inquiry that he received two letters, two faxes and probably two telephone calls from Imran Khan asking that the family liaison should be through *him*, not the Lawrences themselves.

According to DS Weeden, he had phoned Khan's office on 28 April 1993 and spoken to one of the solicitors there, indicating that he would like to speak to Mr Khan. 'Mr Weeden believes that he made a considerable number of approaches and efforts', Macpherson says, 'but that there was little co-operation and communication to ensure that this was achieved.'[32]

On Tuesday, 7 September, when arrangements had been made for a family liaison meeting, the Lawrences and Imran Khan had gone instead to be interviewed by LBC radio. In his briefing note of 8 September 1993, prepared for the MPS Commissioner for a meeting with Peter Bottomley MP, DS Weeden wrote that the Lawrences and Imran Khan were making

> the usual untrue complaints about police failure, disinterest and prejudice. This diatribe was accompanied by threats to sue the police. ... Until recently the Senior Investigation Officer and his team have shown considerable understanding and forbearance in respect of the continuing irresponsible and damaging comments which have been made by the family and their representatives on radio, television and in print. However patience is now beginning to wear very thin in the face of frequently repeated slanderous remarks by the non-family group especially by Imran Khan.[33]

These briefing notes 'grated upon the ears of the members of the inquiry', Macpherson writes, 'since they show that Mr Weeden *lost patience* with the family, and in particular with Mr Khan'. Mr Weeden's intentions 'may have been good to start with'. But he was entirely at fault (in 'losing patience') because 'he *never took positive steps* to approach Mr Khan or indeed the family direct *(sic)* in order that a satisfactory meeting took place between them'.[34]

The evidence in favour of DS Weeden's version of events is strangely soft-pedalled. He in fact brought a libel action against a newspaper in connection with the publication of some of Imran Khan's remarks. Macpherson says that an award was *'apparently'* made in DS Weeden's favour.[35] Why does Macpherson not say whether it was or was not? Surely Macpherson knew, or could have found out.

Whatever might be said in criticism of DS Weeden, applying a standard that is probably impossibly high for Anglican bishops, his 'losing patience', after starting with 'good intentions', can only with the greatest distortion be turned into evidence of his *racism*.

The Situation Within Which The Family Liaison Had To Be Conducted

The Anti-Racist Alliance and other groups

The representative of the Greenwich Action Committee Against Racial Attacks described the state of affairs at the Lawrence home from the day after the murder as the ARA having 'already set up camp', and having started straight away to 'control' the Lawrences' communication with outside parties.[36]

A young activist with the ARA, Palma Black, had arrived at the Lawrence home on the afternoon of 23 April 1993. The ARA is a black-led group that exists, among other reasons, to provide help to black people by tapping into a network of black experts and professionals.

During the morning someone had contacted Palma Black at the Islington office of the ARA to tell her about the Lawrence case, including the fact that the MPS was holding a press conference that afternoon.

A plan of action was agreed between Palma Black and a colleague, Anne Kane. Anne Kane would go to the police press conference and introduce herself to Neville Lawrence. Palma Black would go to the Lawrence home. On the way she would pick up Vicki Morse, a black ARA supporter who was also a prominent Greenwich councillor. Before she left the Islington office Palma Black began to make the arrangements for finding a lawyer for the Lawrences.[37]

Palma Black and Councillor Vicki Morse went to the Lawrences'. They offered to help the Lawrences. Their advice was needed, they said, to handle the public aspects of the murder. In the days that followed, the Lawrences found that Palma Black was working full-time at their house, and often for very long hours.

On the second day after the murder, a Saturday, the Anti-Nazi League came to the house 'with some money they had collected'.

The Black Panthers also came on the Saturday.[38]

Imran Khan

In the Macpherson report Imran Khan gets a chapter to himself. 'His general experience was limited', the report says, 'and he had only been a solicitor for eighteen months.' He had some experience, however, of helping the victims of racist attacks, or the families of such victims. Palma Black had phoned him on the day after the murder and told him to announce himself as the ARA lawyer. 'Mr Khan was not at all happy to do that, since ... he was not in any sense their lawyer.' He went to the Lawrences' home on the Sunday following the murder.[39] After a few days, on 11 May 1993, Mr Khan wrote to various other organisations that had interested themselves in the case and had appeared at the Lawrences' house, indicating that 'their presence was not wanted at the family home'. 'The family's instruction' was that all communications must be directed through the ARA.[40]

The murder had been committed late on Thursday evening, 22 April 1993. DS Ian Crampton had been duty Senior Investigating Officer

(SIO) until the Monday, when he had to return to his normal duties. On Monday 26 April DS Brian Weeden took over as the regular SIO.

Imran Khan, who had seen the Lawrences for the first time on Sunday 25 April 1993, dictated a letter from his Ealing office to DS Weeden the next day, DS Weeden's first on the case.

He asked DS Weeden for answers to a series of questions, 'in writing', and 'as a matter of urgency'. Had any suspects been identified, arrested or interviewed? Had all the important witnesses been traced? There were other questions of this kind. He also asked whether the police *still* took the view, expressed by the police at their press conference the previous Friday, that this was a racist crime. Satisfactory answers would 'mitigate' the sufferings of the Lawrence family.

Imran Khan requested an answer by 'return of fax'.

Although the letter was dictated on the Monday, it was not sent by Khan's office until the Tuesday. The incident room received it at 8.44 a.m. Just after midday the incident room received another fax from Khan, asking for a reply to the first 'as a matter of urgency'. It also asked the police to comment on the rumour that Duwayne Brooks was regarded as a suspect. 'Clearly that is untenable to the Lawrences', Khan had written. Less than two hours and a half later, there was a telephone call from Khan's office. The caller said, 'We have sent you two faxes and are concerned that you have not replied'.

DS Weeden dictated a letter on that Tuesday. He said in it that the questions raised by Khan had been addressed by the family liaison officers. He understood that the Lawrences were happy with the liaison system (that by then had been in place for four days, since the morning after the murder). He hoped it would be useful both to the Lawrences and to Imran Khan. The police, he assured Khan, were conducting a 'vigorous and thorough investigation' into this 'grave and tragic case'.

The letter reached Imran Khan on the Thursday.

By then Imran Khan had written again, saying that this was his third letter, and he had not received an answer to any of them. If he did not receive a prompt reply he would have 'no alternative but to raise this matter with the Commissioner's office directly'. He complained that the liaison officers were providing no information.[41]

Imran Khan himself described all this as 'sniper fire'.[42]

Macpherson's comment is that it is 'unusual' (is it not almost unknown?) that requests should be made, not only 'so early in the investigation of a murder', but also in a 'somewhat peremptory manner'.[43] But it is 'the duty of the police' to be 'tolerant'.

DCS Ilsley provided the inquiry with what the report calls 'a catalogue' of Imran Khan's postponements and cancellations of meetings. Macpherson's language in commenting on Imran Khan is studiously uncritical. 'It can be said that Mr Khan *may* have allowed a *somewhat* cavalier attitude in connection with appointments ... ' It had to be uncritical to be consistent with its demand that in all circumstances the police be uncritical. It is the 'duty' of the police to 'ensure' good relations with the representatives of a bereaved family.[44]

Imran Khan, also, 'was *ready* to criticise' (that is, he did criticise) 'more than *might* be *expected*' (i.e. more than *had* ever *actually* been experienced before in these circumstances).

He was also 'more ready than might be expected to contact the media'. This also '*may* not have *assisted*' the relationship (as if it were mere failure of his good intentions to 'assist' the relationship) between him and the police.[45]

'As to his connection with Mr Brooks', Macpherson says,

> it is of significance that there was contact between Mr Brooks and Mr Khan during at least one of the identity parades attended by Mr Brooks ... Mr Westbrook [one of the witnesses of the murder] reports that Mr Brooks seemed to be giving a running account of the identity parade ... and when the call was finished Mr Brooks came back into the room and asked questions ... and he sought the addresses of witnesses. Mr Khan says he does not recollect having any telephone conversation with Mr Brooks. *We have no doubt there was such a conversation.* The connection between Mr Brooks and Mr Khan is a curious one.[46]

The distinction between stereotyping a person, and the opposite, which is responding not even to his known character, but to his actual behaviour, is quite lost on Macpherson. Yet the distinction is fundamental to the attribution of racism. DS Weeden, for example, is condemned for being 'infected' with racism of some sort, because (in Macpherson's typically nebulous but damning phraseology) 'he too readily allowed himself' to become 'involved in' the 'hostile *stereotyping*' of Imran Khan.

Macpherson may have succeeded in showing that senior police officers concerned were not 'tolerant' enough of requests couched in a 'somewhat peremptory manner' from a newly-admitted solicitor, or of Imran Khan's readiness, with his privileges as a solicitor, to criticise the police in the media, or (if they knew about them) of his 'curious' telephone calls. But to show that they were irritated is not to demonstrate that they are racists.

The press

The Lawrence family had immediate personal access to the press. Neville Lawrence had done plastering work in the homes of several journalists. On the morning after the murder he telephoned one of them, Nick Schoon of the *Independent*. Schoon came straight away, and was at the Lawrence home by about 10 a.m.

Schoon spoke mainly to Neville Lawrence. Neville went over a story he was to repeat at the press conference. Stephen, he said, had had high hopes of becoming an architect. He had never been in trouble. Like the rest of the family he had been law-abiding, unpolitical, and had had nothing to do with race matters. As Neville told Schoon, they were not the type to draw attention to themselves.

Later other reporters came.[47]

At the police press conference held on the afternoon following the murder, Anne Kane of the ARA briefed journalists on racism in the area. There had been three racist murders since May 1991 (Orvill Blair, by the man whose premises Blair had burgled, Rolan Adams and Rohit Duggal).[48] She was also able to tell the journalists that the offices of the racist British National Party (BNP) were at Welling, in the neighbouring borough of Bexley.

Twelve days after the murder the Lawrence family held a press conference of its own in Woolwich town hall (4 May 1993). The press conference had been arranged, Mrs Lawrence told the Macpherson inquiry, by the Anti-Racist Alliance.[49] The Lawrences were to meet Nelson Mandela two days later, and this gave it added journalistic interest. By now the message was quite different from Neville Lawrence's to Schoon. The Lawrences were no longer 'unpolitical', with 'nothing to do with race matters'.

At the press conference Mrs Lawrence argued that a form of ethnic cleansing was taking place in south London. 'If it was the other way round', she said, 'and a white boy had been killed by a gang of black men, they would have arrested half the black community in the area. But nothing has been done and there have been no arrests and the police won't tell us what is happening ... The black community and I cannot stand for this any longer. The killers are still out there and other black kids can't feel safe on the streets.'[50]

The local MPs

The local Conservative MP, Peter Bottomley, and the neighbouring Labour MP John Austin-Walker, soon took an interest in the Lawrence affair.

Peter Bottomley MP 'seems to have gone', the report says, to the Commissioner of the MPS, Sir Paul Condon, to report the Lawrences' complaints that they were not receiving enough information on what the police were doing, 'so the matter was reported to the highest places'.[51]

At this stage the lightening rod was the BNP offices. John Austin-Walker led a demonstration outside the Bexley civic office demanding that the BNP offices be closed by the local authority.

Both MPs called for government action on racist criminality. The question of police racism was not raised.[52] 'In these early days' writes Cathcart, 'the police were not the principal focus of anger.'[53]

The All-Party Parliamentary Group on Race and Community

By June 1993 the All-Party Parliamentary Group on Race and Community was involved. Baroness Seear wrote to the Commissioner of the MPS to register unease at the *'lack of sensitivity on behalf of the local constabulary towards the Lawrence family'*.[54]

President Nelson Mandela

A fortnight after the murder the Lawrences were invited to meet President Mandela (6 May 1993). She went to meet him, Mrs Lawrence says, because 'we saw him as a way to highlight the fact that the British government and the people in power here were not interested, and that nobody had come to visit us except the local MP'.

Nelson Mandela said to her that black life was cheap in South Africa.

Mrs Lawrence expressed her surprise that he thought it was different in this country. 'He didn't realise it was *still the same* [in England] as was happening there. He was quite concerned.' She complains, however, that 'nobody showed any interest in that'.[55]

'Family' liaison in this case was somewhat of a misnomer, for the police officers concerned, of modest rank, found themselves in the arena with the President of South Africa, the national broadsheet press, and English and American pressure groups. They had to work at the focus of attention, the Lawrence home; and any false move by any police officer was potentially an international scandal.

The Lawrences' Reaction To People Other Than The Police

The behaviour of the police officers in liaison with the family was 'manifestly inappropriate' in the sense that it manifestly failed in its objective of being satisfactory to the Lawrences. Whether there was any possibility that 'appropriate' behaviour could have been found by the police officers concerned or by anyone else cannot now be known.

Mrs Lawrence's complaint was that the police's handling of the family liaison upset her. In her statement to the inquiry she said:

> Weeden says that there were more solicitors for witnesses than for defendants. It is not surprising; the police upset Dwayne *(sic)*, they upset us, *they upset Jo Shepherd*, they upset us all. ... It was obviously necessary for us to have a solicitor, to act as a buffer between us and the people who were dealing so insensitively in our time of grief ... No black person can ever trust the police.[56]

Macpherson overlooks the fact that the impartial inclusion of Joseph Shepherd on Mrs Lawrence's short list complicates—to say the least

—the report's conclusion that the insensitivity of police officers was due to their racism. He is a white person.

The evidence submitted to the inquiry by Mrs Lawrence is a vivid record of her relations with different people in the aftermath of the murder of her son. It pictures the personalities and the situations that Linda Holden and John Bevan had to deal with, directly or indirectly, in their liaison with the family.

The local MPs

'Nobody had come to visit us', Mrs Lawrence says, 'except for the local MP, Peter Bottomley.' He visited her during the week following the murder, and Mrs Lawrence asked him, 'Does the Prime Minister know about my son?' 'He said: "Well, I don't think so". I said: "Why not?" and he couldn't answer.'[57]

The Anti-Racist Alliance

Mrs Lawrence's comment on the arrival of Palma Black of the ARA at the Lawrence home on the afternoon of the day following the murder is: 'How she got to our place I don't know. Nobody from our family would have contacted her'. On the Sunday another man came. 'He was frightening ... He was part of the ARA people with Palma and Marc Wadsworth.'[58]

Her relationship with Palma Black and Marc Wadsworth, she says, was that she did not know them, or anything about them. 'They were trying to reassure me that they were there to support. I remember seeing Palma forever using the phone, and I pointed out to her that it was our phone bill.'[59]

The ARA was eventually sent packing by the Lawrences. 'They said they were there for the family but they were there for the ARA', Mrs Lawrence told the Macpherson inquiry. 'They saw this as something to push themselves forward and to make themselves better known.'[60]

The behaviour of the Black Panthers was also inappropriate to the occasion of a bereavement. They had arrived at the Lawrences dressed in 'hoods and dark glasses'. Mrs Lawrence says that she had found them 'really frightening'.[61]

Imran Khan

The Lawrences' relationship with Imran Khan was always good. But according to Cathcart—his remark is not meant as criticism—even he was indirectly, for Doreen, the source of her humiliation. Doreen Lawrence, Cathcart writes, 'resented the way in which Imran Khan had been portrayed by some as a left-wing Svengali, (not least because that left her and her husband *appearing as dupes*').[62]

Duwayne Brooks' mother

On the morning after the murder Mrs Lawrence was being comforted by friends, including her white next-door neighbour. Duwayne Brooks' mother called, after having been with Duwayne in Plumstead police station. Mrs Brooks, like the white police, did not find the appropriate conduct for the occasion. 'I don't know why Duwayne's mum came round', Mrs Lawrence told the Macpherson inquiry. 'I presume she came around in sympathy but at the time it didn't come across like that.' The only thing that stuck in Mrs Lawrence's mind was that Mrs Brooks had told her that she was glad it wasn't Duwayne. 'And that was that' is Mrs Lawrence's bitter comment.[63]

Racism

Racism had not featured in the inquiry's opening statements on the two family liaison officers.

But racism loomed large in Macpherson's conclusions on them.

Mrs Lawrence was asked specifically during the inquiry whether she thought racism had played a part in the failure of the family liaison. 'Racism is something you can't always put your finger on', she replied. 'Racism is done in a way that is so subtle. It's how they talk to you ... It's just their whole attitude ... It was patronising the way they dealt with me and that came across as racist.'

Macpherson had accepted that over a range of issues the liaison officers had acted inappropriately simply because they had not gone far enough to correct the *wrong* interpretation that the Lawrences were putting on their conduct. The Lawrences were *wrong* in Macpherson's view in believing that they had been asked about the hat and gloves because Stephen was under suspicion. (The liaison officers, however, were wrong because *as liaison officers* they should have taken effective steps to ensure that that wrong impression did not arise.)

This was not the case when their conduct 'came across' (as Mrs Lawrence put it) as racism. If it came across to her as racism, it was racism.

These officers, Macpherson says, 'will forever deny that they are racist or that the colour, culture and ethnic origin of the Lawrence family played any part in the failure of family liaison'.[64]

But are they racists, Macpherson asks, and did the family's colour, culture or ethnic origin play a part in the way they related to the Lawrences?

Macpherson's answer is typically firm. The conclusion, the report says, is 'inescapable'. The inappropriate conduct and patronising attitudes of Linda Holden and John Bevan were the *'product'* of *'racism'*. Nothing could be firmer than that.

Detective Superintendent Brian Weeden 'too readily allowed himself, as his own briefing notes show, to become involved in the negative and hostile stereotyping of the family and Mr Khan. He *must* be said to have been *infected* by unwitting *racism* in this regard.'[65] Nothing could be firmer than that either.

But Macpherson produces no *evidence* that racism lay behind the inappropriate behaviour of these police officers. Macpherson's conclusion is therefore also typically fuzzy. For the plain statement that the conduct of the police in the family liaison with the Lawrences was *the product of racism* is wrapped in a sentence that says that their conduct was 'a *manifestation* of *unwitting* racism *at work*'.[66] These new phrases release the person who uses them from any obligation to show any evidence but the conduct itself. The cause is read back from the conduct; the fact of the conduct is proof of the cause.

Racism as a cause was not 'manifested', in the sense of being 'clearly shown', by anything these two officers, or any other officers concerned with the family liaison, said or did. Nothing they said or did could be *shown* to be racist at all.

But in its second meaning 'a manifestation' is 'the appearance of a ghost or spirit'. This is, in fact, the sense of Macpherson's passage on the police officers' racism in the family liaison. Without their knowledge even to this day, or ever, they were possessed by the invisible but ubiquitous miasma of disembodied 'racism', whose presence we cannot prove, but whose existence we can be sure of because of its results. Show that the inappropriate behaviour occurred; you have proven that its cause is racism. That is the logic of Macpherson's argument.

How many journalists have recognised that Macpherson is *not* saying that the officers who were in family liaison with the Lawrences, including Linda Holden and John Bevan, are racists in the ordinary sense of the term? How many journalists have recognised that such racism, racism that is 'at work', that 'manifests' itself, in the actions of for ever unwitting people, is a postulate that, as a 'cause', is independent of all evidence?

Handling Bereavement

On the subject of family liaison, Professor Simon Holdaway is quoted twice with approval by Macpherson. In both places Professor Holdaway refers to the 'negative' relations 'sustained' by the police. The first reference is to the police's relations with 'ethnic minorities' generally. The second is a specific reference to the police's relations with the Lawrences. Professor Holdaway says that the police 'create' the negative relationships with minorities.[67]

'Negative' here can only be a synonym for 'bad'. It is just a longer and vaguer word, with a bogus suggestion of science, mathematics, and nonjudgementalism. A bad relationship can be regretted by one or by both parties. It can be the fault of them both, or of one more than the other. But unless we join the flight from the English language, 'sustaining' a bad relationship means to strengthen or support it in that state, to keep it going continuously, to uphold it or to confirm it. There is the suggestion of malice aforethought. To say that someone is 'sustaining' a bad relationship is to identify him or her as the particularly unco-operative aggressor against the victim upon whom the injury of the bad relationship is wilfully inflicted.

But in dealing with this aspect of the Lawrence affair, neither Professor Holdaway nor Macpherson needed to ask why Mrs Lawrence was inconsolable. Mrs Lawrence was and remains the loving mother of a loving son lost in appalling circumstances.

One of her complaints against the police liaison officers was that they never asked her about Stephen *as a young child*.[68]

How to cope with the death of loved ones is a central human problem that nearly all cultures make provision for. Nearly all cultures produce their own specialists in consolation. Our increasingly anomic society is unusual in the degree to which it has discarded its provisions for bereavement, and leaves people to cope with death from their own emotional resources. The days when all neighbours' curtains would be drawn when someone in the street died; when passers-by would stop and doff their caps as a cortège passed on the road; when the appropriate words and gestures from each person on each encounter were known to all adults; and when the clergyman was a figure of respect, are fresh in living memory but are gone, whether beyond recall no one can tell.

Macpherson did not have to ask why the police were unable to console her. If neighbours and relatives have lost the culture, and bishops, judges, doctors and social workers do not have the skills of bereavement, why should the police be blamed as racists because in the Lawrence liaison they were incapable of replacing them all?

7

The Failure of Many Officers to Recognise Stephen Lawrence's Murder as a *Purely* Racially Motivated Crime as Evidence of Police Racism

Macpherson works on the theory that the failure to recognise and publicly state that the murder of Stephen Lawrence was a case of 'pure' racism is itself evidence of racism. This theory appears fourth in the list of the five bodies of evidence the report depends upon that are derived from Part I of the inquiry, namely, (a) the treatment of Mr and Mrs Lawrence at the hospital on the night of the murder; (b) the initial reaction to the victim and witness Duwayne Brooks; (c) the family liaison; (d) *the failure of many officers to recognise Stephen's murder as a racially motivated crime*; and (e) the lack of urgency and motivation in some areas of the investigation.[1] This criterion for establishing the existence of police racism appears again as one of the six 'areas' of evidence of 'unwitting' racism: 'At least five officers refused to accept that this was a *purely* racist murder'.[2]

Free-floating Aggression

The mentality of four of the five prime suspects and their circle is well-known. Wide publicity was given to the police surveillance video of them in Gary Dobson's flat in Footscray Road, recorded over a period of three weeks from 2 December 1994 onwards. Jamie Acourt does not appear on the video tapes. He was in custody awaiting trial for stabbing three white men in a Greenwich nightclub, penetrating the heart of one of them.[3]

The conversation is throughout ignorant, foul and violent. Here are Neil Acourt and Dave Norris discussing their attitudes to old white people. The television had shown that a syndicate had won a prize in the National Lottery:

Norris: Why on earth do old grannies want to play? They'll all die before ...

Acourt: At least they are white.

Norris: (*A little later*) See, if I was there, if I was one of the crowd, I tell you I would mug them.

Acourt: What, rob them?

Norris: If I was in a crowd, I tell you I'd fucking mug 'em, I'm telling you. For 500 grand ... !

Acourt: So would I, mate.

Norris: ... *I'd kill the cunts*. I'm telling you.

Acourt: You've got to wait till they cashed it, gone to the bank.[4]

Mugging here is the language of money. Killing is the language of hate.

The Macpherson report includes an account of Norris' violence, involving the use of a club, and of a screwdriver as a weapon. In the account it is less clear that it is against a white family walking in the park, but that is undoubtedly what it was. A powerfully-built black man actually came to Norris' rescue, thinking he was being of service to a young outnumbered victim.

Norris: ... I was walking over the park. Anyway, an old geezer comes up and was with wife and kids and that.
Anyway he was moaning about the dogs being over the field and he came up to me—and he was a big cunt, and he started going like ... *that*!
And he was going: 'I'll fucking take you on!'
I said 'Leave it out, I ain't going to hit you'.
All of a sudden he went bop on me jaw. So I just stood there—and I went to him ... Smack! Uppercut! and he went ... Crack!
All of a sudden I just flipped. I went and got me screwdriver and all that old lark and come running out and started like trying to do him, and I threw it.
And all of a sudden the geezer come and I went to get a club.
And he grabbed the club. (And he was like the daughter's husband or something, so it was his son-in-law.) ...
I went down the glove compartment, got me brother Ben's club. So I picked it up and started smacking him round the mouth and all of.
... I just kneed the cunt in the bollocks. ... he was a fucking grown man, he was about 40-odd. And his Gran'dad ... Smacko! ... and I was knocking the Gran'dad.

Martin: And then what? The nigger come along?

Norris: Yeah, a big nigger came along and said, 'Leave the fucking kid [i.e. Norris] alone, you silly cunt!'

(It is possible, and perhaps more likely, that Norris was insulting the civic-spirited black man, rather than the black man using this strange turn of phrase in what he said. *Norris*: "'Leave the kid alone!" The silly cunt!') But Norris and the two white men continued fighting. Norris says to one of the white men, 'Don't fucking come near me cunt 'cos I'm going to do you!' He concludes: 'Anyway he came round—like that—and as ... I went Smack!—about 50 times in his head. Dumb cunt!'[5]

In Sequence 50 of the videotapes Norris' violence is again directed at white people. 'If I was going to kill myself you know what I'd do? I'd go and kill every ... copper, every mug that I know, I'm telling ya.'[6]

Jamie Acourt was excluded permanently from his normal school in October 1991. Although he had nearly a year of compulsory schooling to complete at a special school for problem boys, he never attended. Three weeks after his expulsion he was cautioned by the police for threatening a woman with a stick. Cathcart does not say that she was a white woman; but it is highly likely that he would have mentioned her colour if she had been black.[7]

The thuggish violence of the suspects was therefore broader than their racism, as it is among other children and youths like them being produced by British society—in numbers unmatched for at least 150 years (the period over which numbers have been available), and perhaps unmatched ever in British history.[8]

The *Shields Gazette* carried a front-page story at the beginning of February 2000 about 'a neo-Nazi thug' and his friend.

> Jason Thompson was left badly bleeding when his throat was slashed during a savage knife attack in his own home. Doctors said that he only escaped with his life because the knife missed his main artery by millimetres. His 'white supremacist' attacker Stephen Coleman, 23, and his friend Richard Wingrove, 22, were seen joking and laughing only minutes after the attack.

The jury was told that Mr Thompson's throat was cut, he suffered stab wounds, a broken leg, two black eyes, and received treatment for other severe facial injuries. When police officers had asked the pair why they had attacked the defenceless Mr Thompson, they said *they disliked him because he was disabled*.[9] Mr Thompson, the disabled victim, was a white Middlesbrough-born machine operator working in South Shields.

Even when an attack is 'racist', it is sometimes impossible to overlook large elements of brutality for fun, not closely connected to racist sentiments. In November 1999, for example, two 14 year olds, a boy from an Italian family and his black friend, were sentenced for an attack in a Bedford park on a 26-year-old immigrant from Pakistan. The judge expressed sympathy for the families of the murderers, who 'appear to be decent, God-fearing people, who have done their best to bring you up properly'.[10]

The boys had beaten their victim to the ground. They had first stamped on his uncovered face. They had then put a wooden pallet over the victim's head before jumping on it so hard that his head was indented into the ground. Before they ran off they rammed pieces of wood down his throat and into his eyes.

One of the boys told his friends that the other was laughing so much that he had difficulty running away. Next day at school the boys thought they were in company where they could safely brag, 'We had a really wicked day yesterday. We had a mad day, we murdered someone'. (Among end-of-century schoolchildren 'wicked' meant 'highly enjoyable'.)

At a much lower level, senselessness and brutality is part of everyday experience. One of the authors was on his bicycle at Gateshead, returning from work one January evening, when three youths suddenly appeared. The first he knew of their presence was when one of them shouted 'baldy old c***!' and shoved him violently off his bicycle into the middle of the road, across the path of a car and a bus. It was sheer good fortune he was not killed or badly injured. They were taking out their aggression on him. If they had done it to a black man on a bicycle they would have shouted a racist insult, and it would have been then plainly a racist attack. It would have been recognised as such by the police.

But it is to be strongly doubted whether such an attack by these same youths would have been *'purely'* racist. Their racism is more plausibly to be accounted for in terms of their free-floating aggression. Their free-floating aggression, in turn, is to be accounted for, among other things, by reference to the richness of the messages they receive about, on the one hand, the centrality of their own entitlements to self-gratification and the severity of their own unjustified deprivation and the paucity of messages they receive about, on the other hand, their responsibility for their own lives, and the duties they owe to others.[11]

Putting 'racism' at the centre of the problem means that no attention needs be paid either to the power of institutions of the state, commerce, the media, politics and education that directly and indirectly inculcate the beliefs and values which have created the problems of the current situation, or to the weakness of the institutions that in the past kept them at bay. Violent disorder by 'the excluded' can then continue to be applauded. The dramatic increases in crime and drug-taking of the past 30 years can continue to be condoned as the admirable reactions of young people who have 'no stake in society'.

It is indeed sobering to read, for example, what George Orwell had to say about the trend in English culture in 1944. In his essay 'Raffles and Miss Blandish' he is merely comparing the work of some crime novelists: the gulf between 'the powerful taboos' of the one genre, represented by the work of E.W. Hornung and, masquerading as 'real life', the unremitting 'cruelty and corruption' of the other, represented by the work of James Hadley Chase.[12] The second genre nourishes the attitudes that 'make it possible for crime to flourish'. 'Such things as affection, friendship, good nature or even ordinary politeness simply do not enter. Nor, to any great extent does normal sexuality.' Any form of depravity is 'real life', and it is the artist's obligation to reflect it back to his or her audience. Any kind of elevated conduct is nostalgia for a golden age that never existed, and is not worth an artist's second thought.

Orwell writes that too much should not be read into this genre's growing popularity. Perhaps it was all due to the war. But if such books did acclimatise themselves to England, he said, 'there would be good grounds for dismay'.[13]

Macpherson's Initial Approach: The Murder Was Not 'Purely' Racist

At the beginning of the Macpherson inquiry whether the murder was 'purely' racist was not an issue that it raised. Judging from the content of its opening statement, the idea does not seem to have occurred to the inquiry at all.

By the time the report came to be written, however, Macpherson had decided the failure of a police officer to have operated on the assumption *from the beginning* that the murder was a *purely* racist murder was some sort of proof of some sort of racism.

Yet Macpherson, six years after it occurred, did not at first see it as *purely* racist murder. On their own argument, therefore, had the Macpherson people concerned with preparing and presenting early statements about the problem inadvertently proved themselves to be racists?

The details of the early days of the inquiry's views lie buried in dense Condenselt transcripts of the thick appendices. But the popular Macpherson report itself is careless in not removing all traces of the inquiry's original assumptions. It retains a passage that is damning to its subsequent emphasis, that the refusal to recognise the attack as *purely* racist was evidence of racism. Royston Westbrook, the report says:

> was a white man in his thirties who was on his way home after finishing the evening shift as a hospital support worker. He was at the bus stop with Stephen Lawrence, and witnessed the murder. As he got onto the bus which came almost at once he felt a shiver of apprehension when he thought to himself that *the attack seemed so motiveless that it might have been levelled at him if the two boys had not been there*.[14]

In his opening address, Edmund Lawson QC, counsel for the inquiry, listed a number of violent attacks in which the suspects in the Stephen Lawrence case were also suspects. Some of them were attacks on white victims.

Lee Pearson, a white youth, was stabbed in December 1991. When he was seen by the Macpherson inquiry team Pearson asserted that the Acourts had been part of the gang that had attacked him. He would not co-operate further with the police for fear of revenge being taken upon him.

In March 1993, a short time before the Lawrence murder, another white youth, Stacey Benefield, alleged that he had been stabbed in the chest. When he was first seen in hospital he refused to name those who were responsible. When he was seen by the police investigating the Lawrence murder, however, he 'asserted and confirmed', Lawson said, that he had been the subject of an attack by David Norris and Neil Acourt.

In May 1992 Terry and Darren Williams were set upon in the street *'for no apparent reason'* by Jamie Acourt, David Norris, and Luke Knight, three of the five Lawrence murder suspects. On the advice of the CPS the charges against them of wounding and possession of an offensive weapon were not pursued. (Lawson does not say whether the Williamses were black or white, a surprising omission in the circumstances.)[15]

In his opening speech counsel for the inquiry took the view that is implicit in the above account of the Pearson and Benefield stabbings, the South Shields case and the trivial Gateshead incident: that racism is neither the essence of the conduct of such white English youths, nor the root explanation for it.

Edmund Lawson QC said in his opening address that the attackers were 'violent thugs' who 'did not limit their gratuitously violent attacks to black victims'.[16] That is to say, the fact that the attack on Stephen Lawrence was racist was extremely important. But it was an aspect of the wider problem of the existence of clockwork-orange type savagery that also takes its prey from other groups and on other pretexts.

Racism is an aspect of the problem that Britain is producing youths of this character. It is not the central feature or main underlying cause of their conduct.

Nor was it an issue at the beginning of the inquiry that the police had not recognised Stephen Lawrence's death as a racist murder. At their press conference on 23 April 1993, the day after the murder, the police had described the murder as a racist killing. It was a racist murder and, counsel for the inquiry said, 'it was recognised as such by the police'.[17]

White thugs, who had attacked white men and women on one pretext or another on other occasions, had on this occasion killed a black man because he was black.

By the time the report came to be written, however, the doctrine was in full play that it was a *purely* racist attack. If officers had not recognised this from the beginning, this was evidence of their racism and the racism of the police service. It was no longer enough to say that is was simply a racist attack, without it being *purely* racist. Of the press conference of 23 April 1993 Macpherson writes,

> Mr Ilsley indicated, as we have seen on the recorded television films of this occasion, that it was an *outrage* that two black youths had been attacked totally unprovoked by white youths. The 'Daily Telegraph' of the following day seemed to suggest he had also indicated that it was a *purely* racist murder.[18]

Macpherson says that the *Daily Telegraph* was wrong. The recognition that the attack was *purely* racist was 'not reflected in the two recordings we have seen'. What is more, Detective Chief Superintendent Ilsley's briefing notes had said 'if asked re motive *believe* it was a racist attack'. This may suggest, the Macpherson report says in 1999 (as distinct from what its counsel said in 1998)

> a decision had been made that the announcement should not include, certainly at first blush, the important indication that this was *purely* a racist attack. There is no indication of the reason why the motive was not positively identified.[19]

Between Edmund Lawson QC's elaborate and dense opening statement for the inquiry and the final draft of the report, Macpherson developed the doctrine that *pure* racism should have been obvious to the police 28 hours after the murder, as it would have been obvious to Macpherson 28 hours after the murder—with the benefit of six months of statements from anti-racist experts, and then six years of hindsight.

The Switch To 'Pure' Racism

To demonstrate that some particular action or some pattern of conduct towards black people is racist, there must be some evidence that the black people have been treated worse than white people are treated in the same circumstances. The Macpherson inquiry ruled out from the earliest days its having to meet that requirement. There was not the time or resources. Instead, the inquiry would not necessarily require the same standard of proof with racism as was demanded in other matters. It was prepared to infer on reasonable grounds that because something might have happened because of racism, it had happened because of racism. Cathcart used the *parti pris* terms that this is what was 'promised' and this was what the inquiry was 'prepared to do'.

If the inference were not reasonable, however, what would be a promise to those who for one motive or another wanted to prove police racism, was a threat to those police officers who were innocent of it.[20]

The evidence for the racism of Detective Sergeant John Davidson

'The race issue remained elusive and intangible in the early days of the inquiry', Cathcart notes.[21] 'It was during the questioning of "OJ" Davidson ... that things began to change. This was one of the most explosive cross examinations of the inquiry.'[22]

The key exchange about race, when it came, was a relatively calm one. Mansfield asked Davidson whether anything in particular had struck him when he had first read the papers on the case. Davidson said he did not see the point in the question. What had struck him in particular, as it would strike anybody, was that it was a heinous murder.

'And?', asked Mansfield imperiously.

'Is there an "and", sir?'

'Yes, there is an "and" ... I am not going to take all day about it. I just wondered if it occurred to you that it was a *race* attack?'

Davidson replied that at the stage of reading the statements, he was aware that four or five white youths had attacked two black youths (he called both the whites and the blacks 'lads'). It had been reported that the attack had been accompanied by a racist shout.

But then, fatally for him and the MPS, he referred to the conclusions he himself had reached from the information that he himself had gathered in the course of the inquiry:

> From other information I gleaned during the inquiry I would say that the persons ... allegedly responsible were persons who would have killed anybody had they been there at the time. I do not think in my own mind that it was a race attack. I believe it was thugs attacking anyone, as they had done on previous occasions with other white lads. ... They were thugs who were out to kill, not particularly a black person but anybody ... not racism, *just pure, bloody-minded thuggery*.

Cathcart's comment is, that this appeared to put Davidson at odds with his superiors Crampton, Weeden and Ilsley.[23] (What is Cathcart saying or implying? That it is *insubordination* for a detective to come to his own conclusion on the evidence?)

It put Davidson, Cathcart continues, at odds, 'indeed with the national police policy laid down by ACPO'. The Association of Chief Police Officers (ACPO) *defined* a racial incident as '*any* incident which included an *allegation* of racial motivation made by *any* person'.[24]

The evidence from facts is thus superseded by the 'policy' of ACPO based on a definition. Davidson's full reply should have been, 'It is a racist (or racial) incident as defined, but it has the characteristic of having been carried out by thugs who would have attacked somebody else for non-racist reasons'.

Detective Sergeant Davidson had made plain that he placed far more significance on the free-floating aggression of the youths than on the fact that it sometimes discharged itself on black people. By doing so, Cathcart writes, 'Davidson had opened a can of worms. The question of racial motivation and racial classification became a recurring theme of the weeks that followed'.[25]

The evidence for the racism of Detective Constables Martin Hughes and Linda Holden

An attack is *defined* as racist by the police if anybody says it is. The attack on Stephen Lawrence was by that definition racist. *'Purely'* racist is a concept that appears only when the Macpherson report is published. The confusion of the Queen's Counsellors and Sir William's advisers on the issues involved was often contrasted with the clarity of the police constables. Here are two examples of this from the interrogation of Detective Constable Martin Hughes and Detective Constable Linda Holden.

Mansfield: Nobody could possibly say that this incident had nothing to do with colour, could they?

Hughes: I believe that the motive for Stephen's death had nothing to do with colour. I agree that it was a racist attack. Stephen Lawrence was killed in my opinion because he was there, not because he was black.

Mansfield: Many of us would like to know what the distinction is. If this is a racist attack, how has it nothing to do with colour?

Hughes: I'm not saying it wasn't a racist attack, sir. What I am saying is that the reason for the attack had nothing to do with Stephen's colour. The fact that he was black, and was there, was the reason in my opinion why he was killed. It is a racist attack because it is perceived as a racist attack.[26]

Linda Holden insisted only that the motivation of the attackers could not be established until it was known what was in their minds. This drew a series of questions from Mr Tom Cook. (Cathcart calls them 'trenchant' questions.)

Cook: If you are given a crime to investigate which involves three men who go into a post office and discharge a firearm, demand the money and run out with the money, what would you say the motive was?

Holden: A robbery, sir.

Cook: You are not inside the minds of the people committing it. ... There is no alternative evidence that points to another motivation, is there?

Holden: No, sir.

Cook: And there is not in this either.

Holden: I can only stick to the answers I have given.

But robbers are robbers for all sorts of reasons. Being robbers, they have their reasons for attacking a post office rather than other targets that will give them money or whatever psychological rewards they are seeking. The motivation of any of the robbers in being a robber, and the motivation for robbing money from a post office could only be established when it was known what was in his mind. He could be doing it also or even mainly to prove his own courage to himself or his friends or enemies; or to raise his prestige; or because he enjoyed the feeling of power that wielding a gun gives him. He could have chosen a post office because he was a disgruntled post office worker, or because robbing a post office seems to him to be 'harming' people even less than insurance fraud. Linda Holden was saying that white men who attack a black man do so for all sorts of reasons. How important it is that he was black is not the same in all cases; and how important it is in the given case can only be shown by the evidence. She had a far better intellectual or intuitive grasp of the argument than had Mr Cook.

The inability of "this group of officers" to accept the racial motive, the report found, "is a manifestation of their own flawed approach and their own unwitting collective racism".' The 'group of officers' referred to comprised 'as much as half of the First Investigation team'.[27]

Macpherson says that it was 'difficult to understand why so many detectives working on this case were not willing to accept' that the murder of Stephen Lawrence 'was a *purely* racist crime'.[28]

The reader will recall the passage from the surveillance video which records the suspects' foul rant against the old white women, which ends, *'I'd kill the cunts*. I'm telling you'.[29]

Although Macpherson reproduces part of the passage, that highly significant section, showing generalised aggression and hatred, *does not appear in the Macpherson report*. Macpherson shows only five lines from the transcript of the diatribe against the lottery winners, one of them blank, and one of them meaningless.

Norris: [line blank]

Acourt: Fifteen minutes.

Norris: Why on earth do old grannies (want to play) they'll all die (tomorrow).

Acourt: Good luck to them, fuck it.

Knight: At least they are white.[30]

As quoted by Macpherson it sounds as though the interlocutors, in genially obscene banter, are wishing 'good luck' to 'old grannies' *because they are 'white'*.

Evidence Versus Public Opinion

Macpherson's conclusion on the power of the criterion, the expression of the belief that the murder was not purely racist, to demonstrate that individuals are racist, is unambiguous. The fact that officers '*expressed* the view that they did not believe that the case was *purely* motivated by racism ... reflects *inherent racism* in the officers involved and in the police service'.[31] It 'clearly' was so. The 'perception' of 'all who heard evidence at this inquiry is inevitably' that the officers concerned were racists. 'DS Davidson and others have only themselves to blame' for the perception that 'they *were indeed* "institutionally racist".'[32]

Expression of the view that the attack was not purely racist, the report says, gave rise 'in the minds of the Lawrences' to the 'suspicion' that proper concentration was not brought to bear on the murder of their son. It 'did not encourage ... the black community to revise or review their opinions of police officers'.[33] It was, indeed, 'understandably anathema' to 'the black community'. It also 'offended' 'the white community'.

In Cathcart's opinion, this issue *more than any other on the question of race* exercised the inquiry team. Those who did not accept the Macpherson view, that the attack was *purely* racist, were 'obdurate'. Their position was 'untenable'.[34]

> It is clear that this was a racist crime committed by this *(sic)* group of white youths. They might *(sic)* have committed crimes against white people as well, but the facts of the case show with crystal clarity that this was *purely* a racist killing.
>
> As we have indicated before, the expressions used and the *determination* to water down the racist element of the killing offends Mr and Mrs Lawrence and the community, black and white.[35]

Why did Macpherson stress so often that people were *offended* by what the detectives thought? All that is relevant to people changing their minds on the facts is what the facts are. Macpherson says that the facts were 'crystal clear' and with crystal clarity they showed that it was a *purely* racist killing.

Macpherson is entitled to state that that is the inquiry's conclusion. Macpherson is entitled to hope that people will be persuaded by the case that is put. What if people objectively examining the facts think that Macpherson's facts are feeble and its conclusion ill-based? Is no one entitled to disagree with Macpherson?

What is as important: is anyone any less entitled to disagree with Macpherson on the facts because either 'the black community' or 'the white community' or even both together are 'offended' when he or she does so? Are the *facts* to be established by popular vote and by measuring their power not to give offence to 'the community'?

'The community' at least makes sense as a very misleading word for 'a set of people who share an opinion'. It may have been, it is very probable, that the vast majority of black people were offended if anyone said that the murder of Stephen Lawrence was not *'purely'* racist. But was any survey ever conducted *on that particular point* to enable Macpherson to state it as a fact? We have seen none.

What is the *white* 'community' in this context? It is a propaganda term for nothing but the opinion of the currently dominant anti-racist lobby, representing only a certain kind of anti-racism, that has vigorously and successfully pressed its case through the media, and on that 'quintessentially establishment personality',[36] Sir William Macpherson of Cluny.

8

The Lack of Police Urgency and Poor Police Motivation in Some Areas of the Investigation as Evidence of Police Racism

Macpherson's Own Incompetence In Connection With The Stephen Lawrence Investigation

It was one of the unforeseen misfortunes of public life that Macpherson gave 'the lack of police urgency and poor police motivation' as one of the independent bodies of evidence for police racism, in addition to those dealt with in the previous four chapters. For after its strictures on police efficiency had been written, the Macpherson report itself added a major item to the catalogue of mistakes made in connection with the Stephen Lawrence investigation.

Many of the people who had given police information had had their identities protected throughout the inquiry's proceedings. Some were regarded as facing a 'high risk' of intimidation, injury or worse.

Yet their identities were included in the appendices to the Macpherson report when it was first issued. One thousand copies had been circulated before the mistake was seen. That is why the appendices are now marked 'Revised'. The report in the *Daily Telegraph* said that disclosure of the identities of the source of police information had surprised officers at Scotland Yard and 'appalled' those in Kent.

Errol Kelly, a married carpenter with five children, had no connection with the Lawrence case. His house, however, was used in the police inquiry. This was one of the addresses wrongly revealed by Macpherson. The family was told it was in danger and had to be rehoused at a secret location. A consultant psychiatrist testified that the experience appeared to have triggered a mental illness in Kelly. It was alleged that, in his deteriorated mental condition, his anger with the police and Macpherson resulted, three months after the report was published, in his attacking police officers and motorists outside his home with a samurai sword.[1]

Most people with a detailed enough knowledge of the inquiry's evidence to spot the error did not see the report until after publication. No one in the legal team of the counsel for the inquiry saw the report with its potentially fatal mistakes. Nor did the Kent Police Service, nor the Police Complaints Authority, nor Metropolitan police officers.

Sir William Macpherson wrote a letter of apology to the Home Secretary saying that it was 'entirely the inquiry's responsibility', but that there was 'no single source for blame in these circumstances'.[2]

Lack of urgency and poor motivation in the Stephen Lawrence murder investigation could have been due to a whole range of factors like inexperience, shortage of staff or other resources, depressed morale (including depressed morale due to unfounded accusations of racism), laziness, and a host of other matters that could properly be grouped under the heading of 'lack of proficiency' in general, or 'lack of proficiency' in this particular case.

It could have been due to another range of factors grouped under the heading 'undesirable and correctable, but non-racist, reactions to the conduct of others'. Or it could have been due to the plain bribery of certain officers by Clifford Norris to protect his suspected son. So much anti-police sentiment from so many political and other quarters having attached itself to the Lawrence case, police corruption was for long as strong a candidate (and for some anti-police supporters of the Lawrence's probably as attractive a candidate) as was racism as the explanation for lack of urgency and motivation.

In the case of *Quereshi v London Borough of Newham* the Court of Appeal held that failure on the part of an employer to take steps to counter racial discrimination *could* be evidence from which unlawful prejudice could be inferred. But L.J. Leggatt added: 'Incompetence does not, *without more*, become discrimination merely because the person affected by it is from an ethnic minority'.[3]

What The Lawrences Alleged Against The Police

Michael Mansfield QC set out the family's basic position. The magnitude of the failure of the police investigation in this case, he said, could not be explained by mere incompetence. It could not be explained by lack of direction by senior officers. Nor could it be explained by poor execution or lack of application by junior officers. 'Deeper forces' had to be considered.

The first of these deeper forces was in operation because Stephen Lawrence was black. As a result of his being black, racism 'permeated the investigation'. The second, collusion, was also a racist matter. The murderers were white. Being white, 'they were expecting some form of protection'.[4]

Michael Mansfield began by quoting something that Vernon Johns, a black Baptist minister in *Alabama*, had said *in 1948*. 'It is safe to murder Negroes.' Whether that was intended as evidence, or was simply an apt way to describe the current situation as his clients saw it, is not clear. The climate in which racism 'flourishes', Mansfield said, was created, in part, 'by law enforcement agencies that fail to take speedy and effective and committed action to pursue illegality'.

The actual errors and failures identified by the Kent Police Service, were only 'the symptoms', Cathcart says in summarising Mansfield's address. 'The disease was far worse than "mere incompetence". The investigation was infected by *conscious* racism.'[5]

The 'Evidence' Of Professor Holdaway

Professor Holdaway 'ends his statement to the inquiry with the following *perceptive* assessment', Macpherson says. 'A failure to undertake an adequate investigation; a lack of competent management' was (vaguely) 'compounded by' the police's failure to put 'race relations' at the centre of the murder investigation'.[6]

But this would be convincing as 'evidence' only if Professor Holdaway's evidence, if any, were to be produced by Macpherson. It is not enough to appeal merely to what the report calls the 'indictment', the mere assertion, of a self-selected academic, who is then treated by Macpherson on the *analogy* of an 'expert witness'.

Macpherson

Immediately preceding this 'perceptive assessment' Macpherson had put a more obviously police-racist gloss on the matter. It was put in the form of a question. 'Did the officers involved act sluggishly, and in a way which they would not have acted had the victim been white and the attackers black?'[7]

Police incompetence

Police incompetence was not an issue at the Macpherson inquiry; it was taken as given.[8] On the incompetence of the investigation Macpherson adopted, with few variations, the findings of the Kent Police Service. The Metropolitan Police Service did not quarrel with Kent. Macpherson, however goes over all the evidence of incompetence again.

There had been a series of errors. The suspects should have been arrested not later than the first weekend after the murder, instead of allowing 11 days to elapse. The police surveillance of the suspects in the first week descended at times to farce, if anything can be said to be a farce where a murder is concerned. The importance of anonymous information on the suspects was not sufficiently recognised. Potential witnesses were handled unskilfully. There was poor organisation when the arrests were made. Leads were not pursued quickly or systematically enough. The quality of leadership, the keeping of records, the management of the office, were all criticised.[9] Macpherson added next to nothing to Kent.

Detective Superintendent Ian Crampton, the first Senior Investigating Officer

'The question of the early arrest of the suspects', Macpherson says, 'is ... central to the whole inquiry.'[10]

Macpherson acknowledges that it is *not at all certain* that DS Crampton, the first SIO, made a bad decision in not arresting the Acourts, Dobson, Knight and Norris as soon as their names had been put to the police, and their reputations were firmly known—especially that members of the gang had knifed the white youth Stacey Benefield. 'We wholly understand', the Macpherson report says, 'that early arrests might *not* have led to the conviction of any of the suspects.' If the arrests *had* been made earlier, and if no scientific evidence had been forthcoming, and if no satisfactory identification had taken place, then the prosecution would almost certainly not have proceeded in public or private form'.[11]

What can this possibly mean but that, *without the benefit of hindsight*, DS Crampton's decision not to arrest the gang as soon as they were firm suspects was a *reasonable* one?

But having said that, Macpherson, *with* the benefit of hindsight, identifies the failure to arrest the suspects early as being the crux of the failure of the whole police investigation. DS Crampton had committed a 'fundamental error'.[12] It was *the most fundamental fault in the investigation of this murder'*.[13]

DS Crampton had come to the case as Senior Investigating Officer (SIO) only temporarily, as the duty officer who on the night of the murder was on call for major incidents. It was known from the beginning that he would be returning to his own case in two or three days' time. He was due to attend the Central Criminal Court in connection with it on Monday 26 April 1993.

Macpherson doubts that there was a 'decision', at any rate a strategic decision. If there had been, it would have been noted—and not just as a matter of bureaucracy—and passed on as a strategic decision to other officers. The justification for it would also have been noted, and been known to officers consulting the policy log later. In the absence of a 'for and against' log of arresting or delaying arrest, Macpherson says, the decision must be regarded as at best 'ill-considered'—that is to say, it was a mistake, an error of judgement.[14]

Another possible reason not to arrest the suspects as early as the first weekend after the murder, Macpherson considers, was that DS Crampton 'simply allowed the investigation to drift'.[15]

DS Crampton's own reasons, as given to the inquiry, were that he was looking for 'a potential real live witness' to give weight to the valuable but anonymous tip-offs he was receiving. By the time he had the information that gave grounds for arrest, 36 hours had passed, and all *obviously* bloodstained clothing and weapons would have been disposed of. Evidence for forensic examination would remain. His 'negative strategy' was then to obtain evidence in order to arrest, rather than arrest in order to obtain evidence.[16]

At the inquiry he did not attempt to defend the failure to arrest within two or three days of the murder. 'The strategy I adopted was unsuccessful', he said. The failure to obtain enough evidence for conviction told him quite clearly that the strategy of arresting the suspects during the time he was SIO might well have been the better one.[17]

Detective Superintendent Brian Weeden, the second Senior Investigating Officer

DS Weeden perpetuated the wrong decision DS Crampton had made. 'He did not exercise his own critical faculties', with the result that the arrests were delayed until 7 May 1993, eleven days after the murder.[18]

Detective Chief Superintendent William Ilsley

The error made 'in judgement and decision making' was the fundamental error, too, Macpherson says, of DCS Ilsley. He 'allowed himself to go along with the weak and unenterprising decisions of his SIOs'. Both DS Weeden and DCS Ilsley 'carried on the "strategy" laid down by Mr Crampton in connection with the arrests'.[19]

Detective Inspector Bullock

DI Bullock is the one other officer who is picked out for special mention in connection with the fundamentally flawed decision of the earliest days of the police investigation of the murder. 'He was often passive, and not up to the job', and in particular he failed to process properly vital information supplied by a man called James Grant.[20]

Police racism

DS Crampton's error in deciding to obtain more firm evidence before arresting the suspects was for Macpherson, then, not just *a* fault, but *'the most fundamental fault'*. His erroneous strategy was persevered with for several days by his successor, DS Weeden, with the support of their superior, DCS Ilsley.

But the fact of *incompetence* had already been established by the Kent Police Service, and Macpherson was adding nothing by repeating what the report of the Kent Police Service had spelled out in detail.

What Macpherson was claiming to do was to *explain* the incompetence, with *police racism* as the cause. Here is where the police investigation centrally failed. Here is where police racism would have to be shown to be operative. To *show* racism *here*, by Macpherson's own logic, one would have thought, was essential if the report's thesis was to have any weight at all.

DS Crampton's racism

DS Crampton was not one of those who showed their racism by reluctance to treat the murder as a racist crime. It is true that he had made a note in his policy file that there was 'a *possible* racial motive'. But he explained to the inquiry that this entry was made because if it turned out that it was committed for 'other than *purely* racist reasons' he would not have 'committed himself by a different form of entry in the policy file'.

This satisfied Macpherson, 'bearing in mind', the report says, 'Mr Crampton's *repeated* and *firm* assertion that this was *without doubt* a racist murder'.[21]

All that Macpherson does, therefore, is to *exonerate* DS Crampton from even this faint suspicion of racism.

Apart from that entry on the file, that the racial motive was only 'possible', no evidence at all is produced by Macpherson to show that DS Crampton's failures *in the police investigation* were due in any way to racism of any kind.

According to Macpherson, then, DS Crampton's error was the 'most fundamental' of the failed investigation, but according to Macpherson, too, DS Crampton showed no racism in committing his error. By any ordinary standards of logic, therefore, Macpherson, by saying so, had effectively demolished his own basic argument that police racism was the explanation of police incompetence in the Lawrence case.

DS Weeden's racism

The evidence in the Macpherson report for DS Weeden's racism appears only in its discussion of his liaison with the family and Imran Khan. It will be recalled that he 'stereotyped' Imran Khan and 'lost patience' with him.

No evidence at all is produced by Macpherson to show that DS Weeden's failures *in the police investigation* were due to racism.

DCS Ilsley's racism

No evidence at all is produced by Macpherson to show that DCS Ilsley's failures *in the police investigation* were due to racism.

DI Bullock's racism

No evidence at all is produced by Macpherson to show that DI Bullock's failures in the police investigation were due to racism.

This is surely one of the most remarkable aspects of the Macpherson report. We are told that DS Crampton made a basic error of judgement; that DS Weeden did not exercise his critical faculties; that DCS Ilsley went along with the decisions of his subordinates; that DI Bullock was passive and not up to the job.

If all those allegations are true in those cases, they are common enough and adequate explanations for failure.

But 'the lack of police urgency and poor police motivation in some areas of the investigation' is one of the five *specific* areas which, according to Macpherson's own enumeration, provide evidence of police *racism*. If it were more important as a cause of failure than (or even just additional to) bad judgement, passivity, not being up to the job, and so forth, racism would have to be *shown* by Macpherson in the relevant case and context to at least *exist*.

Not a single example of racism is given under the heading of 'lack of police motivation'.

Cathcart had written, as we have already remarked in our Introduction, that as the inquiry reached its conclusion *no* evidence had been produced of even a *single* act of 'deliberate, malicious' racism. As 'even one of several primary *causes of the failure of the Stephen Lawrence investigation*', Cathcart writes, Macpherson had not been able to show 'racism in *any* form'.[22]

From a sympathiser with Macpherson, those are strong words.

'But', Cathcart continues, 'this did not mean that the Met had won the argument, for the chairman still had the power to infer racism'. His occasional remarks in later sessions 'left the impression that he might do just that'.[23] The officers had lost the *argument*, according to Cathcart's view of the matter, because the chairman had the *power* to infer racism *in the absence of evidence*.

'The only explanation or excuse offered to us for the failures and mistakes in this case are that they were the result of incompetence or misjudgement. Such explanation or excuse cannot in our view negate the reasonable inferences and conclusions which we make from the evidence that we have heard.' If there were such evidence, why was it not put in the report?

The report says that the warning given by the Court of Appeal that proof of incompetence was not proof of racism had been 'heeded'. 'But upon all the *facts*', Macpherson continues, 'we assert that the conclusion that *racism* played its part in this case is *fully justified*. Mere incompetence cannot of itself account for the whole catalogue of failures, mistakes, misjudgements, and lack of direction and control which bedevilled the Stephen Lawrence investigation.'[24]

Even though by including the phrase, only 'played its part', Macpherson gives itself a very low threshold to surmount, what its 'facts' on racism were in this connection remain a mystery.

9

The Everyday and the Sociological Use of the Word 'Institutional'

Macpherson's key concept and principal contribution to current opinion on racism in the police and in English society generally is 'institutional' racism. 'There must be an *unequivocal acceptance*', Macpherson says, 'of the problem of *institutional* racism and its nature'—that is to say, an unequivocal acceptance of the Macpherson report.

'Institution' and 'institutional' are words in common use. 'Institution' has a two-fold meaning. The first is 'a large, complex organisation with a long history and of some importance', such as a religious or educational organisation.

The second is 'one of the complex sets of rules that govern the aims of the organisation, and how that business will be carried out by its employees or other participants'. Such rules cover not only conduct, but also what people must believe and feel about various bodies of 'facts' and what moral judgements they must make upon the facts. (For example, 'God' exists. He requires human conduct to conform to ten commandments, at least, in the spirit required by his Son who took human form 2000 years ago. It is a fact that the commandments are divine, and a fact that their words were spoken by God and Jesus Christ. The moral imperative is to obey them. These 'facts' must be acted upon, also, with appropriate feelings of love, 'childlike' faith and trust, and so on.)

Sociologists have tried to standardise the usage of the term when it is used within the discipline. There is broad agreement that 'institution' and 'institutional' should be used, as they are used ordinarily. They are sociological labels for important, complex *organisations* of long standing. They are also sociological labels for any of the large, complex *sets of rules* that make up the structure of the institution as an organisation.

Sociological usage differs somewhat from ordinary usage in two respects. The first is in the preference given to the use of the term to describe the complexes of rules and appropriate beliefs and attitudes rather than as a 'concrete group of human personalities'. 'A Church is

93

an association and communion an institution ... a family is an association and primogeniture an institution.'[1] The second is that sociology emphasises more than does ordinary language that 'institution' (either as an association of people or as a normative complex) refers to what is formal, written, clear, agreed, known, inculcated, values-laden and enforced.

There are many types of situation in which people's actual beliefs about what 'the facts' are, and about what conduct, ethical convictions and emotions should be, deviate from institutional rules and requirements. Sociology uses a variety of other terms to label these different situations.

Some of the best-known sociological studies from the earliest days of the discipline's existence have been concerned with the unofficial 'cultures' that have developed within the institutional framework of organisations.[2] Some of these cultures have made the association work more effectively. Some of them have subverted the work of the association and its formal institutions. Labels like 'the culture' of, say, a factory are sometimes used to describe the actual beliefs, practices and effective controls that operate within the formal framework of the factory's institutions and the institutions of the wider society of which it is a part. Labels like 'sub-culture' are sometimes found to be convenient to describe small groups of people whose practices and beliefs, as help or hindrance, depart from those required institutionally.

Where departure from institutional requirements is merely an *individual* response, the term 'deviant' and 'deviance' has often been used to emphasise the non-institutional nature of the individual's conduct, belief, value, or attitude.

The Macpherson inquiry's method of developing *its* concept of institutional racism is to string together a large number of statements from different sources that *mention* 'institutional' racism. The resemblance between some of the different sources lies only in their use of those two words, 'institutional' and 'racism', together.

The diverse statements Macpherson quotes on institutional racism fall into distinctly different categories. The report reads as though they all contribute to the authority of the concept of 'institutional' that the report finally develops. In fact the Macpherson concept sits uncomfortably with most, and is quite incompatible with some.

The Commission for Racial Equality

The submission of the Commission for Racial Equality (CRE) to Macpherson reads:

Institutional racism has been defined as those established laws, customs and practices which systematically reflect and reproduce racial inequalities in society. If racist consequences accrue to institutional laws, customs and practices, the institution is racist whether or not the individuals maintaining those [institutional laws] have racial intentions.[3]

The CRE's submission emphasises that 'institutional' refers to 'organisational *structures*, *policies*, processes and practices'.[4]

The observation that, within an organisation the rules of which require racist conduct, individual employees or members, whatever their own thoughts and preferences on the matter, will be acting in a racist way when they are acting institutionally is in line with both standard and sociological usage. An individual within such a racist organisation can do—if he is to keep his job, must do—racist things, even if he or she is personally not a racist at all. (This is likely to have been the case with at least some bus drivers, say, before Rosa Parks and the bus boycott broke segregation on the buses in Montgomery.)

If a person remains in such an organisation without duress, he or she bears the guilt, of course, of racist conduct, even if he or she can say, 'I've nothing against you. I'm just doing my job'.

Stokely Carmichael

Even Macpherson's most curious 'authority' on what 'institutional' racism means, uses 'institutional' roughly in its everyday and sociological sense. Macpherson in fact introduces the term 'institutional' racism in the first place by saying that it was by no means a new term or concept. Stokely Carmichael, the report says, defined 'institutional' racism in 1967.

The passage from Carmichael quoted by Macpherson is part empirical assertion about American society, part campaigning rhetoric. It does not *define* institutional racism. It says where 'institutional' (undefined) racism 'originates from' and what it 'relies on'.

But the notion that 'institutional' means practices that are 'active', 'respected', 'declared', 'inescapable', and so on, is strongly expressed. That was Carmichael's experience of racism in the American South in the mid-1960s. Blacks were oppressed by laws, rules, policies, attitudes and values. Those laws, rules and policies were observed and where necessary enforced by the police, churches, universities, schools, private clubs, hotels, public transport companies, shops and so on. The appropriate values and attitudes were inculcated into children and adults of all races through all channels of education and persuasion. 'Institutional racism originates in the operation of *established* and *respected* forces in society', writes Carmichael in the quoted passage. 'It relies on the active and pervasive operation of [racist] attitudes and practices.' Racism is institutional for Carmichael when it permeates society at the 'institutional level'.[5]

The prominence given to Carmichael's opinion of what 'institutional' should mean is curious for three reasons. The first is that, although a gifted and highly educated man (the *Economist* described him as 'super-bright'), he had no special qualifications either for defining terms in common use or for improving sociological definitions. Of course everyone is entitled to do either of these things. But there must be some special reason to take and present what they say as authoritative.

The second is that his fame rests upon his opposition to Martin Luther King when he was alive, and his advocacy of violence when King was killed. A New Yorker of Jamaican origin, Carmichael attended Howard University, where he enthusiastically committed himself to the Martin Luther King form of anti-racism, that is to say, delivery on the 'promissory notes' of the Founding Fathers and non-violent resistance to oppression in solidarity with similarly inclined white people.

But he came to feel that Dr King put too much stress on integration, and on making legal and 'accommodative' demands for equality of opportunity and for social treatment that did not depend upon skin colour, but upon educational and economic success, and on 'character'. Within the constraints of the laws of the land made by democratically elected governments and the constraints imposed by the objective conditions of success, there was much room for cultural self-expression. Martin Luther King mobilised blacks and their white allies in massive peaceful demonstrations to win the equality to which they all were legally entitled.

Carmichael thought that Dr King ought to be organising blacks alone to win power for themselves, and magnifying instead of trying to reduce the importance of colour. In the place of 'Jim Crow' conciliation within the existing social system, there should be violent disruption of it. Instead of co-operation there should be confrontation. Instead of adjustment there should be repudiation. By 1966 Carmichael 'was on the way to becoming as committed to separatism as any Verwoerdian' in South Africa. When James Meredith was shot, the first black American admitted to the University of Mississippi, Carmichael coined the phrase 'black power'. When King himself was assassinated Carmichael called a press conference to fan the flames of riot and arson. 'White America will live to cry since she killed Dr King.' He parted company with the Black Panthers in 1969 when their violent militancy weakened, and they opted to seek support among whites.

White society would never be improved by reform. No black person could make a success of his or her life by obeying its rules. Success be 'established laws, customs and practices' in a public or private organisation. '[Institutional?] racism is rooted in *widely shared* attitudes, values and beliefs.' People in the organisation have to work within the institutional framework if they want to remain in employment or as members, irrespective of what they would personally intend or prefer.

Otherwise the passage is full of perhaps not very important, but puzzling ambiguities and obscurities. For example, Dr Bowling strangely puts the point about the disjuncture between the wishes of the individual and the demands of the institution within which he or she operates, which is universal and unavoidable, as if it were exceptional or even as that there can be institutions in which there is no trace of it (which is *almost* a sociological impossibility). He writes, 'Discrimination *can* [not 'almost always will'] occur irrespective of the intent of the individuals who carry out the activities of the institution [the laws, customs, practices, values, etc. of which are discriminatory]'. Why Dr Bowling wishes to define institutional in terms of 'a range' of public and private bodies, rather than any one or all of them—the usual connotation—is not clear. Nor is it clear either why the discrimination has to be 'severe' for it to count as 'institutional', or what is to count as 'severe'. In its usual dictionary and in the more elaborate sociological meaning of 'institutional' the idea of structure rather than process is prominent. The significance of 'process' being used and underlined by Dr Bowling is therefore obscure. What is the difference between a 'result' and an 'outcome'? What makes the difference so important that 'outcome' is underlined?

But what follows is astonishing. Dr Bowling continues with a 'thus', as if there was some logical deduction from the previous passage and the one that follows. Not only is there no logical or factual link whatsoever, but jumping without transition to policing, he introduces a completely contrary consideration. '*Thus* policing can be discriminatory ... *in the face of* official policies geared to the *removal* of discrimination.'[2]

The new idea in his own discourse that Dr Bowling may be attempting to express is an entirely familiar and banal one. Institutional policies, which are always applied through institutional rules, institutionally inculcated values, institution-wide attitudes and so forth (which is what makes them institutional policies) can be subverted or sabotaged by recalcitrant individuals within the organisation. A powerful intimidatory system can exist parallel to the controls of the official institution.

Alternatively he might be attempting to express the equally familiar and everyday, but entirely different idea that, without anybody

---

could only come when white society was intimidated into concessions by riot or overthrown by rebellion. The 'panegyric' that rang from Marx and Engels 'in honour of violent revolution', the inevitability of which they 'proudly and openly declared', (as Lenin had written), resonated with Carmichael as a ready-made rhetoric of revolt, easily transferred from the proletarian to the black man.[6]

Eventually he left the United States altogether. The black man could only succeed by separation. He emigrated to Guinea. He urged all other black Americans to leave America. 'The land in Africa, not America, is ours. Our primary objective should be Africa.' Carrying a pistol and dressed in the green fatigues of a Guinean soldier, he answered the telephone with, 'Ready for the revolution!'

What makes the prominence accorded by Macpherson to Carmichael as an expert on the definition of 'institutional' racism most curious of all is the fact that Carmichael was deeply and overtly (not 'unintentionally', 'unwittingly' or 'unconsciously') not only anti-Zionist but also anti-Semitic. 'The only good Zionist is a dead Zionist.' He called for an all-out war against Israel. '*We must take a lesson from Hitler.*'[7]

When we see Macpherson castigating the police for incompetence in the heat of a murder investigation, what are we to deduce about the Macpherson report's competence from its prominent and deferential use of Carmichael as an authority to support the Macpherson use of 'institutional' when, even apart from Carmichael's extremely dubious 'anti-racist' credentials, Carmichael's use contradicts it?

The prominence given to Carmichael scarcely shows either Macpherson's sophistication in handling, much less inventing, concepts; or its deep knowledge of the history of race relations and revolutionary violence; or its expertise in sorting data-based, anti-racist Lawrence wheat from the chaff of a heterogeneous assortment of campaigning groups and individuals, some well-meaning, who coalesced only because the Lawrence affair provided them with the opportunity to attack 'English society' and especially to attack the police.

Lord Scarman

Scarman: 'Institutional' racism emphatically does not exist anywhere in Great Britain.

Another definition which corresponds to normal usage is that of Lord Scarman; yet Macpherson seems to appeal to Lord Scarman's 'authority' in defence of the Macpherson usage of 'institutional'.

In his 'seminal' report on the Brixton riots of 1981, Macpherson writes, Lord Scarman rejected the allegation that the MPS was an 'institutionally' racist force. 'The *direction* and *policies* of the Metropolitan Police are not racist. I totally and unequivocally reject the attack made upon the ... impartiality of the senior direction of the force.'[8]

Lord Scarman also responded to the suggestion that 'Britain is an "institutionally" racist society'. Lord Scarman said that if 'institutional' is taken to mean 'knowingly' and 'as a matter of policy', then he rejected the allegation. In his final judgement on the Brixton riots Lord Scarman said emphatically, '"*institutional*" racism *does not exist* in Great Britain'.[9]

Scarman's criticisms of the MPS lay elsewhere—in 'errors of judgement'.[10]

Scarman: Non-institutional racism does exist in the MPS and everywhere in Great Britain.

People can end up by being discriminated against by the unforeseen and unwanted *effects* of policies that are not in themselves intended to be discriminatory (or are plainly and specifically *intended* to be *non*-discriminatory), and that are applied by people who did not wish to discriminate. That Lord Scarman embraced this possibility was not surprising. That is a particular example of a common phenomenon to which common sense and administrative experience alert people from the Cabinet Office to the lowliest social club committee.

Since 1976 the Race Relations Act had widely prohibited conduct that in its effects was discriminatory, even when no one concerned intended to discriminate. (Any law can prohibit or prescribe 'effects', without being able to prevent them or bring them about.) Lord Scarman had not said, 'if the suggestion being made is that unwitting, unconscious and unintentional racism should be called institutional racism, then that suggestion deserves serious consideration'. Scarman said that if the suggestion being made was that practices might be adopted by public bodies that are 'unwittingly discriminatory against black people', then such an allegation deserves serious consideration and, where proven, swift remedy.[11] (The police and the judiciary had been excluded from the 'unintended' racism provisions of the 1976 Act.)

10

'Institutional' As Institutional Failure

The failure of an association or other social entity to achieve what its policies, rules and inculcated attitudes set out to achieve, or to avoid what they are designed to avoid, is a thoroughly common occurrence. Of course such failure can be called 'institutional'. But results that stem from the institutions of an association that is striving to avoid those results are 'institutional' in quite a different way from the same results if they are achieved in the fulfilment of an association's policies. Racism in an apartheid state is quite different from racism in a state whose laws forbid racial discrimination and insult. Yet some of the authorities Macpherson quotes with approval write as though they are 'institutional' in the same sense, or even as if *institutional failure* was the *only* meaning of 'institutional'.

Dr Benjamin Bowling

Macpherson is respectful to an unexpected degree to some of the people who made contributions to the inquiry. It is not always obvious why. The inquiry was grateful, says Macpherson, for the contribution made by Dr Benjamin Bowling. Dr Bowling's whole paper is of such extraordinary merit, for Macpherson, that it has to read in full, a 'summaries of such work can be unhelpful'. Sir William and his three advisers actually express the hope that Dr Bowling would *forgive* them for quoting only one important passage. Clearly, for Macpherson, i must have been the most important one. Whatever the quoted writer might think, or however their ideas appear 'in context', it is only ho the writers' ideas are quoted by Macpherson that is relevant here. D Bowling begins conventionally enough:

> Institutional racism is the *process* by which people from ethnic minorities a systematically discriminated against by a range of public and private bodies. the result or *outcome* of established laws, customs and practices is radica discriminatory, then institutional racism can be said to have occurred. Althou racism is rooted in widely shared attitudes, values and beliefs, discriminati can occur irrespective of the intent of the individuals who carry out the activit of the institution.[1]

Many of the elements of the ordinary meaning of 'institutional' a retained here by Dr Bowling. To be labelled 'institutional' there mu

deliberately sabotaging anything, and everybody doing their conscientious best, benignly intended institutional policies, rules, attitudes, values and practices often have unforeseen and undesired—even disastrous—effects. This is so much a staple of sociology that, in one of the best-known of sociological essays, Robert K. Merton took that view that the study of the unforeseen consequences of what he called 'purposive' social action *is* 'sociology'.[3] There can be few clearer examples of the unintended consequences of purposive social action than the Macpherson inquiry itself. (Of course it did not require a sociologist to reveal to an ignorant world that 'the best-laid schemes o' mice an' men/ Gang aft agley'.)

Dr Bowling says that policing can be discriminatory 'without this being ... recognised'. What he means by this, however, is again quite unclear. Does Dr Bowling mean 'without the fact that it is discriminatory being recognised by anyone'? Or does he mean 'without the fact that it is discriminatory being recognised by the policy- and rule-makers and the policy- and rule-enforcers'? Or does he mean 'without the fact that it is discriminatory being recognised by the people who are doing the discriminating'?

No doubt any of these things *can* be the case. They all exist. And it is true, of course, that as Macpherson says 'history shows that "covert" insidious racism is more difficult to detect' than overt non-insidious racism. (It is a tautology.) It is also true, of course, that as Macpherson says 'institutions ... *can* operate in a racist way without at once recognising their racism'.[4]

But the question Macpherson is addressing is not the interesting and important academic one of what range of institutional structures, of personal conduct within institutions, and of unforeseen consequences is *possible*. That can be the subject of endless armchair and common-room discussion and speculation. Macpherson's question is an *empirical* one, which requires *evidence* in the *specific case* if it is to be answered.

The 1990 Trust

The 1990 Trust in its submission wrote: 'Racism can be systemic and therefore institutional without being apparent in broad policy terms'. What that means is not clear. 'Systemic' can only mean here 'of or relating to a system as a whole', and the 'system' can only be 'the group and its institutions'. The 'therefore' expresses nothing more than another tautology. An institution's 'broad policy' is, presumably, the expression in some form of its fundamental aims and methods, from which are derived the rationale for its rules, roles, values and hierarchical controls.

The statement appears to mean, therefore, that *racism* can be the regular consequence of an institution's *non-racist* or anti-racist, institutionalised, policies, rules and stated and inculcated values. The racist consequences stem from the non- or anti-racist institution. Therefore the racism is 'institutional' racism. If that is what the 1990 Trust is saying, then its contribution falls under this heading of 'institutional' not as institutional aim or method, but as institutional failure.

The best-known case of anti-racist policies having racist results was the Reconstruction imposed on the Confederacy by the victorious Union after the American Civil War. Within the framework of political, legal and economic equality, the South developed racist institutions in its own area. Slavery could not be restored, but the reaction of southern whites was to suppress the new-won rights of the southern Negro (as he was then respectfully called) and maintain for two generations, in spite of all the guarantees of the American constitution, a colour-caste system, to some extent through the peremptory terror of lynch-law.

But the 1990 Trust, in discussing how racism can be 'made apparent' pays little attention to its own definition of 'institutional' police racism. Racism within the police, the 1990 Trust says, can be detected in how '*existing policy* is *ignored*' and in how 'operational'—presumably non-racist, institutional—police decisions are carried out in a racist manner or with racist consequences.[5]

Perhaps the Trust intended simply to mention 'institutional' police racism (as was by then *de rigueur* in such discussions), and then pass on to what on its own definition is non-institutional police racism. Or perhaps it did intend to include, in the category of 'institutional' racism, the racism that it says can be 'made apparent' in the ways it describes. Whatever may be the case, it is a puzzle why its remarks, then, should be accorded such prominence in Macpherson's discussion of what *'institutional'* means.

11

'Institutional'
as Counter-Institutional Subculture

The 1990 Trust touched on the phenomenon of subcultures appearing within an organisation that are devoted to subverting the organisation's aims. The reasons for such subversion will appear to one person as ethically good and to another as ethically bad. Some of the other contributors quoted with approval by Macpherson place these anti-institutional sub-cultures at the centre of their definition, or at least of their treatment, of 'institutional'.

The Metropolitan Police Service (MPS) Black Police Association

Macpherson does not say in so many words that he endorses the statements submitted by the MPS Black Police Association; but in the context his approval is obvious. Their quality and utility are certainly higher than that of much that Macpherson quotes from what the report refers to as 'academics and activists'.

The submissions of the MPS Black Police Association use the same jargon as the anti-racist academics and activists. They do not say that 'some police officers are sometimes unaware that black people will take offence at this or that word, or this or that kind of behaviour towards them'. They say 'unconscious' racism. Of course they use the term 'institutional' racism.

But they concentrate on the anti-institutional racist subculture or subcultures in the police service. 'Institutional racism permeates the Metropolitan Police Service. This issue above all others is central to their attitudes, values and beliefs [the attitudes, values and beliefs of officers of the MPS], which lead officers to act, albeit unintentionally and for the most part unwittingly, to treat others differently solely because of their ethnicity or culture.'[1]

Although it is peculiar to use the word institutional to describe something that is subversive of the institutions to which it refers, the MPS Black Police Association is *clearer* about what *it* means by 'institutional' racism than are others quoted by Macpherson. It means for the Association something its members actually experience every day. It is something on which data can be collected. And it does contain some elements of the conventional use of the term 'institutional'.

The MPS Black Police Association sees the formal MPS structure as institutionally non-racist. It sees individual officers as mainly non-racist. But within the formal institutional structure there is the sub-structure of definite, known, sanctioned ways of behaving and talking, and definite, known values that have to be subscribed to (or at least not openly challenged). The MPS Black Police Association did not claim that the perceptions of fact and the judgements of value which constitute this subculture within the formal institutional structures were malicious. But it did claim that their net *effects* were detrimental to 'black individuals on the street'. Officers of goodwill were therefore 'unconscious as to the nature of what they are doing'—unaware of the effects of their actions.

A spokesman for the Association said 'our' culture. 'Interestingly I say "we" because there is no marked difference between black and white in the force essentially. We are all consumed by this occupational culture ... which we say is all-powerful in shaping our views and perceptions.'

The same emphasis on the tension between the demands of the institution, and the subcultures with different aims and objectives that constantly arise in opposition to them, was expressed by Sir John Woodcock in 1992 when he was HM Inspector of Constabulary. The *culture* of the police he said 'actually makes it totally improbable that *all* police officers will behave *as the system lays down* that they should'.[2]

All that seems good sociology, anthropology and social psychology to us, and we should not be surprised if it were largely borne out by empirical research.

The Metropolitan Police Service Commissioner

Sir Paul Condon wrote to the inquiry about 'institutional' racism. The head of all very large organisations—or of an organisation of any size that has to produce results and not just words—is primarily concerned with keeping the conduct of the members of the organisation in line with its objectives and modes of realising them. There is always and everywhere a tendency for the employees and members of an organisation to go their own way if they have a chance. That is why institutions exist: to organise people in a way that maximises the possibilities of regular, predictable and effective co-operation.

Sir Paul therefore begins by recognising that one of the dangers for any non-racist organisation is that of drifting into racism. There will almost always be individual dissidents from benign policies. 'I recognise', he wrote, ' that individual officers can be and are overtly racist.' Some officers worked too much in the light of their stereotypes of other people, not enough on their experience of how individuals actually behaved. The result in practice was differentially detrimental outcomes for black citizens. There were, that is, 'bad apples' in the MPS.

But it was 'much more' than a matter of bad apples. There was also an 'institutional' problem. If too many members of an organisation are allowed to drift too far into racism, then their views of what the facts of race are, and what ethically should be done in the light of those facts will begin to appear in unofficial and disapproved subcultural groups in the organisation. Then it can develop into a general, still unofficial, racist culture within what are increasingly the 'dead-letter' institutional rules. Finally the institutional rules, values and attitudes themselves can change.

Any association is responsible for the conduct of people acting under its instructions or with its authority. Racism can therefore grow without the intention or wish of the institution, as a result of institutional 'neglect'. If it allows through neglect racism to continue to grow, then racism itself could become institutionalised in the body's rules, procedures and discipline. 'I acknowledge', wrote Sir Paul, 'the danger of institutionalisation of racism.'[3]

He had acknowledged the *danger* of institutionalisation, but had not said outright that racism was *now* institutionalised in the MPS. How could he, so long as he was using the term as it had been universally used, prior to the novel and opposite meaning that Macpherson was to give it? It would have been difficult to find a line or even a word in the institutional rules and disciplinary procedures of his service that could be called 'racist'. If such a line or word were to be pointed out, it would be eliminated with despatch and enthusiastic agreement.

But that was not good enough for Macpherson. 'Sir Paul will go thus far', the report says, 'but he will not accept that there is *institutional* racism within his force.'[4]

12

'Institutional' as that which is Unidentifiable from Any Evidence

'The B vocabulary', Orwell wrote in *Nineteen Eighty-Four*, 'consisted of words which had been deliberately constructed for political purposes: words, that is to say, which were intended to impose a desirable mental attitude upon the person using them.' The aim was to create a person who was 'naturally orthodox' (in Newspeak a 'goodthinker'). 'The Party told you to reject the evidence of your senses. It was their final, most essential command.' The goodthinker will in all circumstances know, without having to find out for himself, and without taking thought, what is the true belief about what the facts are, and the desirable emotion in response to them.[1]

Lord Scarman

In spite of the fact that he uses the phrase 'if "institutional" is taken to mean ...', as if there were some endless array of equally acceptable usages, in his report on the Brixton riots Lord Scarman makes it absolutely clear that he is using the word in its conventional sense. But it is obviously a great advantage if the prestige of Lord Scarman can be attached to any quasi-legal or pseudo-legal argument about a concept.

'Lord Scarman further said', says Macpherson, '"Racialism and discrimination against black people—often hidden, sometimes unconscious—remains a major source of social tension and conflict".'[2] (This was not a specific reference to the police.) Although Macpherson selects this remark from Lord Scarman's report as being particularly apposite to its own discussion of 'institutional' racism, the remark mixes many things. What does it mean?

Does it mean 'hidden' from people of goodwill by their own ignorance —they are unaware of the disadvantages brought by their attempts to bring advantages to other people? (That is the perennial peril of all private and state 'welfare', not just anti-racist, institutions.) Does it mean 'hidden', from people of goodwill, by people of ill will who themselves are acting in a racist manner? Is 'unconscious' here no more than a synonym for 'unaware'? Does racism that is 'unconscious' in that case mean that the perpetrator would easily correct his conduct if he or she were made aware of its reception or consequences? Or does racism that is 'unconscious' mean that, under the guise of the ego's goodwill, the id is wreaking revenge on people who are threats to one's prestige or image of superior sexual potency, and that the 'unconscious' will find ways of turning intended benefit into actual harm until the anti-racist of this type has undergone a successful course with a psychoanalyst? Or does it mean all these things?

'Thus', says Macpherson, 'Lord Scarman accepted the existence of what he termed "unwitting" or "unconscious" racism. To these adjectives can be added "unintentional".'[3]

Macpherson regrets that Scarman continued to use the word 'institutional' in its ordinary sense, for 'if the phrase "institutional racism" had been used to describe not only explicit manifestations at direction and policy level, but also unwitting discrimination at the organisational level, then the reality of indirect racism at its more subtle, hidden and potentially more pervasive nature would have been addressed [in 1981]'.

Is it Macpherson's suggestion or insinuation that Scarman proved the existence of all the elements of what 'institutional' racism 'really' is, and only fell into error by not calling 'subtle', 'pervasive', 'unwitting', 'unintentional', 'hidden' and 'unconscious' racism 'institutional'?

The President of the Association of Chief Police Officers (ACPO)

Chief Constable John Newing, President of ACPO, wrote to the inquiry about the racism that is *'inherent'* in the whole of British society. This society-wide 'inherent' racism 'shapes our attitudes and behaviour'. 'Those attitudes and behaviour' are then either 'reinforced' or 're-shaped' by the 'culture of the organisation the person works for'.

The notable thing about this definition is that it uses only two identifiers. As a special kind of racism it is 'inherent'; and it is inherent 'in the wider society'.

All kinds of racism are *present* in the wider society. They can be shown to be present by undertaking empirical studies of what people have decided should be the rules of their organisations; how strictly they implement those rules; what people say; what people do. It can be shown where racism exists, in the forms that it exists, to the degree it exists. The degree to which racism is *present*, and changes in its intensity and distribution over time, can be shown, and can only be shown, by studies of rules of organisations and of the speech and conduct of people. In the absence of evidence from these sources, the prospects of obtaining evidence on any large scale on thoughts that are not externalised in rules and personal conduct are negligible.

What sort of investigation could be undertaken to demonstrate that racism is not just present as shown by the evidence, but 'inherent'?

'Inherence' is the core of the President of ACPO's definition of 'institutional racism'. Macpherson quotes it with approval. The inquiry was 'encouraged' by it.[4]

Dr Robin Oakley

In her statement to the Macpherson inquiry Mrs Lawrence said:

> Police have a preconceived notion of what black people are like, and their behaviour demonstrates this yet again. According to my understanding the only regular dealings police have with black families is when they are criminals. So coming across a black family who have no criminal background is new to them—an alien concept.[5]

Dr Robin Oakley observes in his submission that 'police work, unlike most other professional activities has the capacity to bring officers into contact with a skewed cross-section of society with well-recognised potential for producing negative stereotypes of particular groups.'

Dr Oakley uses the contradictory term 'skewed cross-section'. He expresses himself in a confusing way. He almost certainly does not mean what he says, that it is the 'skewed cross-section of the population' that has the potential for producing negative stereotypes of other groups. He must mean police work itself has that potential.[6] Dr Oakley does not go so far as Mrs Lawrence. Mrs Lawrence's view was that the very idea of a non-criminal black family is 'alien' to the police, and that the first time that the officers concerned had ever come across a law-abiding black family was when they met hers.

'Predominantly hidden' racism

Macpherson gives a strongly approving account of Dr Robin Oakley's two submissions to the inquiry. Again, surprising deference beyond the requirements of politeness is expressed: 'it is perhaps impudent to quote short extracts from his work'.[7] With Dr Oakley we move far from conventional usage of the word 'institutional', and move towards a new way of using it. Oakley's new meaning is the one that Macpherson accepts, and Macpherson's concept of 'institutional' racism comes to play a dominant role in the public's perception and evaluation of police racism in the Lawrence affair.

Dr Oakley describes a form of racism that is *undetected*. It is:

> usually *covert* rather than overt, *unintended* so far as motivation is concerned, acted out *unconsciously* by individuals, and an expression of collective rather than purely individual *sentiment*.[8]

He says that it is '*predominantly*' hidden. It is thus not only undetected, but by this account by ordinary means undetectable.

If the racism does not express itself overtly, what does the covert racism consist of, and how can its existence be demonstrated?

Dr Oakley's is an empirical statement, that *usually* police racism is *unconscious*. What studies, using what means, has Dr Oakley undertaken that enable him to know what the police officers do not consciously know themselves?

What is 'collective racist sentiment' that is not 'individual racist sentiment'? If the racist sentiment is not expressed 'purely' by individuals, what expresses the rest of the racist 'sentiment'? Where is this non-individual 'sentiment' to be found? Most importantly, how did Dr Oakley find so certainly what is covert, unconscious, and collective without being expressed by individuals, not only in the police service but also, as he says, pervasively 'throughout the culture and institutions of the whole of British society'?

Dr Oakley's main concern is with the defects of the Scarman report. According to Dr Oakley, in spite of Lord Scarman's use of the words 'hidden', 'unconscious' and 'unwitting', the concept of racist conduct that unfortunately—in Dr Oakley's view—became established following the Scarman report *was* one of *overt* discrimination, hostility by *individuals* and *personal* prejudices. On that diagnosis, the cure for police racism would be to weed out prejudiced individuals at the selection stage so far as possible, and apply disciplinary sanctions against anyone who displayed prejudice as a police officer. It followed from—for Dr Oakley—Scarman's unacceptable views that all the police need to, and properly could, do was to ensure that everything racist was removed from its own policies, procedures and training courses on the one hand, and on the other that officers should be recruited and dismissed on the basis of their overt conduct. What is for Oakley Scarman's faulty analysis 'appears also to have informed the conclusion of the Police Complaints Authority' that racism had not affected the Lawrence murder investigation. The Kent Police Service in its long and well-resourced investigations into the MPS's handling of the Lawrence case found a myriad of things to criticise severely, but failed to find racist police conduct.

This failure to find racism was due to the fact, then, that they were looking in an archaic police way for what is ordinarily called 'evidence' that identifiable *individuals* had been doing *overt* racist things. According to Dr Oakley, and the Macpherson report that agrees with him, they should have been looking for 'collective sentiments' that individuals were not expressing, and for racism that the 'racists' were not conscious of.[9] It *is* 'pervasive'. It is just that it cannot be shown to exist by ordinary standards of evidence.

The 'much greater' challenge than racism that can be seen, heard and felt, is for Dr Oakley and Macpherson the racism that is 'subtle', 'concealed', 'predominantly hidden', and yet has the power of 'an in-built persuasiveness'.

Who can see what is invisible? Only the adepts of the anti-racist illuminati.

In her statement to the Macpherson inquiry Mrs Lawrence makes it clear that *she* was not aware that she was the victim of racism *until it was pointed out to her after all these years by one of the anti-racist groups*.

Nor was she aware that, before he was murdered, Stephen must also have had been the unwitting victim of racism. So far as any *awareness* of racism on her part was concerned, before he was attacked Stephen had only one single 'brush with racism', as Mrs Lawrence described it, and that was when he was a young child in primary school. One of the boys who used to be his friend had called him racial names. Stephen was one of the few black children in the class, 'so the *majority of his friends were white*'. When his former friend called him names, Stephen '*had the support of his white friends* against this boy and they used to get into fights'. 'When I went to the school', Mrs Lawrence told the inquiry, 'I told the Head that if a child is being racist to him, then Stephen was justified in sticking up for himself. *That was the end of it.*'

'With hindsight you need groups like the ARA to point out issues to you because *someone like myself was not aware* that this sort of thing was happening on a daily basis.'[10]

This 'concealed' and 'hidden' racism—hidden even from the victim himself or herself, as in the case of Mrs Lawrence until she was enlightened—is 'institutional' racism. This new concept of 'institutional' racism, Dr Oakley says, must be given a 'clear *analytic* meaning'. The addition of the word 'institutional', he says, identifies the *source* of the differential treatment. This source 'lies *in some sense* within the organisation'.

In case that was not clear enough for the slow-on-the-uptake, analytical enough for pedants, or even informative enough for the run-of-the-mill reader, Dr Oakley adds that 'the production of differential treatment is "institutionalised" in the *way the organisation operates*'.[11] Dr Oakley tells us that the 'much discussed concept of racism referred to as institutional racism' means 'not solely' (but by implication then at least partly) the 'deliberate actions of a small number of bigoted individuals'.

Two questions immediately arise in relation to that part of Dr Oakley's definition of 'institutional' racism:

1. How can the 'deliberate actions of a small number of bigoted individuals' be called 'institutional', unless they are acting according to the rules and policies of the institution, in which case

their numbers presumably would not be small, and the racism would be unambiguously 'institutional' in the ordinary sense of the word?

2. Why does Dr Oakley's concept as it stands require a *small* number?

In addition, Dr Oakley's concept specifically of police institutional racism means 'a more systematic tendency that could unconsciously influence police performance generally'.[12] Again a number of questions arise.

1. 'More systematic' than what?

2. A 'tendency' to do what?

3. What is 'unconscious influence'?

4. Must it be performance 'generally', rather than performance only in relation to colour, ethnicity and culture?

It would be difficult to construct a vaguer 'concept' than Dr Oakley's concept of institutional racism. But one thing is clear about it. It is that it has taken leave entirely of the normal sense of 'institutional'. All that remains of 'institutional' is that this 'subtle', 'covert', 'unconscious', 'unwitting' racism, takes place in institutions.

Dr Oakley does not restrict his contribution to clarifying a concept. He provides all the empirical expert evidence that Macpherson could need on whether or not police racism interfered with bringing the Lawrence investigation to a successful conclusion. Dr Oakley brushes past the racism not only of the Metropolitan Police, but of all police services, as a datum too obvious to be commented upon, by remarking that such institutional racism is '*in fact*' in no way specific to the police service. It is '*pervasive throughout the culture and institutions of the whole of British society*'.[13]

Macpherson

Macpherson makes two statements about what it itself calls its 'long trawl through the work of academics and activists'.[14] The first statement is that 'the concept' of institutional racism is 'generally accepted'. The second is that the long trawl 'produces varied words and phrases in pursuit of the definition', that is to say, plainly, that Macpherson found many academics and activists using the two words together, 'institutional' and 'racism', but no general agreement on what 'institutional' racism means. Macpherson deals with the CRE definition of institutional racism, that of Scarman, that of Carmichael, and of all others who used the term in the ordinary way without any criticism and apparently with approval. But it transpires that all the report was doing was mustering their authority for its use of nothing more than the phrase. Then, without explicitly saying that its meaning is to be completely different from the CRE's, Scarman's, Carmichael's and that of the others who use 'institution' conventionally, it chooses to follow only those 'academics and activists' like Dr Oakley who use the term unconventionally.

'We accept', the report says, 'that there are dangers in allowing the phrase to be used to express overall criticism of the police without addressing its meaning.' What the report then provides is its own concept of 'institutional' racism as a 'standpoint' that can be 'understood by those that are criticised'.[15]

Racism, for Macpherson, 'consists of conduct or words or practices which disadvantage or advantage people because of their colour'. Macpherson adds 'ethnic origin' to 'colour' as a criterion. An anomaly of Macpherson's use of the term 'racism' is that it covers also conduct or words or practices that disadvantage or advantage people because of their *culture*. This spread a fine-meshed and treacherous net very wide indeed.[16]

'Institutional' racism, for Macpherson, is not racism at its clearest and most public—the racism prescribed by the laws of the state and by the explicit policies and written enforced rules of public and private associations, underpinned by approved and sanctioned values and attitudes (e.g. apartheid). It is racism at its most secret and obscure. It is the racism that cannot be pinned down.

Indirect racism

Occasionally there is a hint that Macphersonian institutional racism retains the normal connotation at one remove. This is the case where the laws, rules, attitudes and hierarchical control of a country or an association are not racist, but the non-racist country or association nevertheless in its operations does disadvantage people of a given colour or ethnic origin.

As a by-product of efficiency

One kind of indirect discrimination refers to institutional rules that, though apparently impartial and necessary, bring disadvantages to a racial or cultural group. Some of these general rules that result in discrimination are necessary for reasons of staff safety, or for other reasons of institutional efficiency. For example, if police officers are required to wear a certain kind of helmet, Sikhs who must wear turbans cannot comply with that rule, and therefore cannot join the police service. If a minimum height is stipulated, then a lower proportion of people from a racial group with a low average height cannot enter in proportion to their numbers. Whether any particular rule ought to be suspended in order to accommodate the disadvantaged group is a matter to be decided in each particular case. But the rule is in itself a sensible and 'necessary' one.

Stop and search would fall into this category. (We are not talking here, of course, of stop and search powers being abused by racist police officers.) The rules say that the police may and should stop and search on reasonable suspicion. 'Reasonable suspicion' falls more frequently on people in the streets than people in their homes. Black youths spend more time on the streets than white youths. They are therefore disproportionately stopped and searched under this impartial institutional rule. Similarly, the institutional rule that requires police officers to act on information received about suspicious activities. If information is received less frequently on the suspicious conduct of white youths than on the suspicious behaviour of black youths, then an impartial rule would again disadvantage innocent people because of their colour.

Unpredictable indirect discrimination where all efforts have been made to eliminate discrimination

Institutional laws, rules, controls, values and attitudes might be designed generously to compensate previously disadvantaged groups. They might grant privileged access to employment, membership, or office. But even a country or organisation practising positive discrimination is institutionally racist in the new sense if it fails in fact to redress, and of course if it exacerbates, the disadvantages suffered because of colour or ethnic origin. (On the Macpherson definition disadvantages suffered because of 'culture' also.)

On this definition, therefore, if the most radical and rigorous *antiracist* policies, rules and attitudes were *successfully* introduced into the structure and processes of the Metropolitan Police Service, but *for whatever bad reason* of public backlash or what Veblen called 'the conscientious withdrawal of efficiency' by the workforce, actually resulted in worse policing and more crime being suffered by people because of their colour, ethnic origin or culture, 'institutional' racism would have worsened. This is the classic case of the unforeseen and undesired consequences of purposive social action, discussed above.

Perhaps Macpherson has generally shied away for this reason from conceptualising 'institutional' in this way, for it is an accurate description of the system that produced the Macpherson report itself.

Invisible racism

At the press conference held on the day following the murder of Stephen, Neville Lawrence had so little experience of 'race relations' as an issue, or was so little preoccupied with it, that when he was asked whether he blamed 'the BNP' he replied, 'What's that?'[17]

His attitude and experience of the police before the murder of his son is also indicated by his speech at a National Black Police Association meeting in 1999. He said that the police had to win back the reputation they had when he came to Britain in the 1960s—presumably, in the context, their good, non-racist, reputation with black working men like himself.[18]

In her statement at the Macpherson inquiry Mrs Lawrence makes it clear that Stephen reached the age of 18 without having any experience of police racism. 'Stephen's attitude to the police', she told the inquiry, 'was *always*: "Well, if I'm not doing anything wrong how could they do that to me?"' Stephen, she said, did not mistrust the police. He had never been in any sort of trouble. He had never even spoken to the police.[19]

Overwhelmingly, Macpherson uses 'institutional' to describe, not what is most obvious and concrete about social life, but what is most elusive.

The 'more subtle concept of racism', Macpherson says, is 'referred to as institutional racism'[20]—the kind of police racism, for example, that could evade the notice of a highly intelligent and gregarious black boy who had mixed with black and white children and adults for 18 years.

Macpherson thus almost completely reverses the usual meaning of institutional. When racism cannot be seen in conduct or words ('coloured' being the worst word that the inquiry could discover, unless 'Negro' is worse yet), and when racism is clearly prohibited in all the policies, rules and permitted attitudes of the institution, then what is *left* is what Macpherson calls 'institutional'. It is the racism for which there is no evidence in the ordinary sense, that can only be 'inferred', that we simply *know* exists. It is the racism that cannot be seen, that cannot be proven. This was precisely the view that Doreen Lawrence expressed to the inquiry, that *unprovable* racism *is* 'institutional' racism. 'There is overt racism where people are blatantly racist in your face and then the other covert racism, *and how do you prove it*? Racism is *institutionalised*.'[21]

For Macpherson (and through the enormous influence of the report, for educated English opinion in general) this 'corrosive disease' of 'institutional' racism can be defined as follows:

> The collective failure of an organisation to provide an appropriate and professional service to people because of their colour, culture, or ethnic origin. It can be seen or detected in processes, attitudes and behaviour which amount to

discrimination through unwitting prejudice, ignorance, thoughtlessness, and racist stereotyping which disadvantage minority ethnic people. It persists because of the failure of the organisation openly and adequately to recognise and address its existence and causes by policy, example and leadership.[22]

'Thus in this Inquiry we have looked to see whether racism *of this type* lay behind the steps taken, or not taken, or pursued inadequately.'[23] Racism that is unwitting, ignorant, thoughtless, hidden, unintentional and so forth is by definition either very difficult to detect or actually undetectable. Having adopted this as its—and everyone's post-Macpherson—definition, therefore, Macpherson has put the question of racist motive, intention, and in the ordinary sense racist conduct more or less outside the boundaries of empirical verification or rebuttal. The report side-steps altogether the problem of showing that 'racist' conduct has taken place. Macpherson simply announces that in its inquiry and from now on, if any category of colour, ethnic origin *or culture*, which is also a minority, shows a statistical excess (of undefined proportions) in police statistics, then that excess is proof that the police service is 'institutionally racist'.

If there is a statistical deficiency in the percentage of officers from such categories who are recruited, remain, or are promoted to higher positions, then that is proof of 'institutional' police racism.

There is no need to consider to what extent young people from any of the minority colour, ethnic and cultural categories are proportionately less inclined to join the police service. (This is in spite of the fact that between 'cultural' categories, *by definition*, there are likely to be cultural differences in how highly service with the police is evaluated as a career.)

There is no need to examine whether any rule, regulation, training programme, approved value or permitted attitude of any police service *is* racist when measured against any criterion whatsoever.

If there is a statistical surplus of suspects stopped, or searched, or apprehended from any category defined by colour, ethnic origin or culture—how large a surplus it has to be we are not told—then the police service is 'institutionally' racist. There is no need to examine whether any officer did say or did do anything in particular at all, or whether the opinions of any individual officer was rabidly racist or fervently anti-racist. Passing beyond the police, if a statistical surplus from any such minority category is convicted, the courts are then proven *by that fact alone* to be guilty of 'institutional' racism.

Since the Macpherson report was issued, Professor Ellis Cashmore, of Staffordshire University, has interviewed police officers in Derbyshire, Norfolk and the West Midlands. The black officers he interviewed, he reports. have no doubt that there is a 'persistence of racism among *individual* white police officers'. But, in the opinion of many black officers, Macpherson's emphasis on 'institutional racism' has deflected attention from this fact.[24]

Macpherson recommends that the definition of a racist incident should continue to be '*any* incident which is perceived to be racist by the victim or *any* other person'.[25] Any incident (not any 'crime') that involves interaction with any person from the minority of 'colour, ethnic origin or culture', is racist if anyone at all, whether from the minority or from the majority, says he or she thinks it is. For all practical purposes this expands the occasions for racial offence being perpetrated and taken to infinity, and it reduces the empirical evidence needed for establishing racial offence for all practical purposes to zero.

Macpherson's recommendations say that any racist incident that is a crime, and any racist incident that has *nothing to do* with a crime, must be 'investigated with *equal commitment*' by the police.[26] No person of good will would recommend anything but that both types of incident must be treated seriously and diligently. But no society, and no organisation within it, can operate except on the basis of distinguishing more important from less important incidents, and giving *due* 'commitment' to one rather than another according to its position on a scale of finely graded priorities.

The report also recommends that consideration should be given to changing the law so that, where there is a prosecutable offence which involves 'racist language', then prosecution should be allowed for the use of such language '*other than in a public place*'.[27] That is to say, people ought to be prosecuted for remarks made in private, including in their own homes. The origin of this recommendation is, presumably, the laudable anti-racist frustration that the video recordings of conversations in the flat of one of the suspects would not be accepted in any court of law against the foul-mouthed and racist gang. As Macpherson said, quoting someone else's phrase with approval, the video did not add 'one iota' to the evidence. 'There was', Macpherson says, 'virtually no probative value in these recordings as to the 1993 murder.'[28]

Macpherson does say briefly that the appearance of the Acourts, Norris, Dobson, Knight and others at the inquiry highlighted the fact that 'society allows such people to become or to be as they are'. But Macpherson mentions only one thing that was wrong about their thuggish, ignorant lives. Their example, Macpherson says, shows the 'need for education and example at the youngest age, and an overall attitude of "zero tolerance" of racism'.[29] (This proposal has, of course, our approval, as has 'zero tolerance' in other areas of criminal and sub-criminal anti-social life.[30])

A sense of proportion here would have put these youths into the context of their threat to English society. English society had produced them; English society was failing to contain the effects of the their morals and activities, and those of people like them. Macpherson's failure to put the suspects into this context, the context of their all-round characteristics and all-round impact on all their fellow-citizens, meant that the bugging of a private home, justified in the case of *Gary Dobson's flat* to secure evidence about *murder*, is extended by Macpherson's recommendation to *any home*, to secure evidence about *words*.

None of this account of what Macpherson says is hyperbolic. Emerging from the muddled 'evidence', Macpherson's final definition of the two words separately and together, 'institutional' racism, and at any rate the main thrust of the policies he derives from the definition, are things that Cathcart *could* properly describe as 'unequivocal'. But 'unequivocal' does not mean 'correct' or 'justified' or 'practically useful' or even 'harmlessly eccentric'. A concept and its social policy implications can just as well be unequivocally ruinous.

13

Macpherson's Anthropology

Our Anthropological Comments

People have different beliefs about what is true of the world and eternity. They have different values. They have different ways of behaving associated with these beliefs and values.

How majority and minority cultures can relate to one another

In associating or coping with others either unlike or like itself, any particular group adopts its own strategy of domination, or submission, or accommodation, or withdrawal. A group's or individual's strategy for coping with others is, of course, itself a central element in its or his world-view.

At one extreme, a distinctive cultural majority, *if there is one*, may seek to compel or cajole any minority of colour, ethnic origin or culture sharing the same territory to abandon completely its own way of looking at the world and handling life.

Many societies with a distinctive majority culture have set the assimilation of minorities as their ideal goal.

In many societies minorities have regarded themselves as being fortunate in thus being invited to be part of the majority culture. Thus there used to be an annual ceremony at Soldier Field, Chicago, in the course of which different sets of people dressed in their national costumes and chatted in their national languages—Poles, Austrians, Lithuanians, and so forth—and paraded into an enormous 'melting pot'. They all emerged speaking English and dressed as 'Americans', the men in their Sunday suits, all with an Eversharp pencil in their top pocket.[1] In 1960, when 'segregation' was what Southern whites were fighting to maintain and 'integration' what nearly all black activists were demanding, Dan Wakefield wrote of the aspirations of the black middle class and black students, that:

> they may have big cars, but they can't drive them to big vacation resorts. They may have fine homes, but they have to be built within the confines of the Negro ghetto. They may have good clothes, but they can't wear them to the best restaurants and theatres. The young Negro students, for better or worse, want to partake in the real middle class values and rewards of American society. They

want the *same* pursuit of happiness as the whites, and the want to be able to pursue them in the *same* way.[2]

In other societies there has been bitter and centuries-long opposition to assimilation.

At the other extreme, a minority, even a powerless and persecuted minority, might relate to the majority only on its own terms and try to make the majority adjust to its values and beliefs about the 'facts' of this world and the next.

In the case of some minorities this strategy is well worked out. Jehovah's Witnesses, for example, patiently try to persuade their neighbours that they too can survive Armageddon into Jehovah's new life on an earth purged of sin and hardship.

In the case of other minorities the refusal to conform to the majority culture is based on a vague and constantly nagging complaint that conformity is a snare and an illusion. Efforts on their part to conform will never really be rewarded. The majority is not treating them fairly. They are being 'victimised' and nothing can improve for them until the victimisation stops.

The replacement of cultural beliefs by individual beliefs

In modern societies 'cultures' (including the distinctive national culture of the indigenous majority on which 'patriotism' is based) tend to weaken.

Securing the adherence of individuals to distinctive groups proves hard to maintain. The rules of political parties, business firms, churches, sports associations, working men's clubs and so on need only be obeyed for so long as one is a member. The social solidarity, unity of outlook, loyalty, collective pride, and mutual trust of people who are related as kinsfolk; or who worship in the same church; or who live in the same neighbourhood; or who work in the same factory or office; or who are members of the same trade union; or who come from the same West Indian island or English town; or who have a shared history of a tragedy or success, and so forth, give way to individualism.

This is because the costs of social solidarity are high, and in the circumstances of modern urban life they can be avoided. The family tends to disappear as a long-term focus of long-term fidelity, and sex, procreation and who will raise the children (if any), for how long, each becomes a separate matter of individual adult choice and negotiation. The neighbourhood tends to lose its community character. 'Loyalty' to any particular political party or trade union tends to become anachronistic.

The costs of individualism then have to be paid by someone. But they do not always have to be paid only by the people who benefit from the freedom to exercise their own individual choices. (This is clearly the case where sex and procreation are concerned. The benefits of freedom from life-long marriage are reaped by adults, the costs of unmarried parenthood and divorce are borne also by children.)

In the past 30 or 40 years in particular a recognisable 'English' majority culture has become increasingly difficult to identify, as the population has fragmented into a variety of ways of sexual, religious, political and leisure life.

There is enormous scope within the law for the expression and practice of 'cultural' beliefs and requirements, whether minority or majority 'ethnic'.

The population of this country in 2000, therefore, is a mosaic of 'cultures'. Individuals drift in and out of associations and cultural commitments increasingly at will.

The law of the land

The exception is the state. Anyone present on United Kingdom soil is subject to the law of the land, and has no choice about it. The principal sense in which there is a majority culture is in the acceptance by the majority of the current law of the land as the framework within which they have to act, and to which they have to accommodate their current cultural choices.

The essence of the law of the land is that its injunctions and prohibitions have to be obeyed by everyone under threat of punishment. In principle, neither the requirements of the law, nor the punishment if they are not met, can be avoided.

We are a multi-cultural society *in so far as the content of each different culture is lawful*. The law is what the sociologist Talcott Parsons called a *universalistic* element in our society. It applies to everyone, and it applies to everyone in the same way.

Mrs Lawrence, in her statement, demanded such 'universalistic', colour-blind treatment from the police. Their job, she said is 'to uphold law and order for everyone'. 'I am asking for someone who is impartial and will treat people as individuals and equals.'[3]

Colour-consciousness

Taking account of colour, being colour-conscious, in one's conduct towards other people *in the public domain* is taken by some people, probably by most, as being the essence of racism.

More often than not colour-consciousness is associated with claims to genetic superiority that are severely detrimental to those to whom genetic inferiority is attributed.[4]

Slavery remained legal in the American South until as late as 1865.[5] Colour-consciousness has had its other numerous victims. In re-establishing white dominance after the emancipation of the slaves, for example, the murder of blacks through lynch-law was widely practised, with the silence, where it was not with the connivance, of the police, the churches and the 'respectable' people of the community. The NAACP calculated that in the 30 years from 1889 to 1918 there were 3,324 lynchings in the USA, with most lynchings taking place in the 1890s. In the towns of the northern USA murders, sometimes mass murders in anti-black race riots, took the place of the lynchings in the countryside in the South.[6]

Macpherson's Implied Anthropology

Doreen Lawrence ended her statement to the inquiry by praising Stephen because he 'did not distinguish between black and white'. Neville Lawrence throughout his ordeal retained his old-fashioned view that prejudice, whether for or against people of a particular colour, had no place in the work of a police officer. 'When he puts his uniform on', he told the inquiry, 'he should forget all his prejudices. If he cannot do that, then he should not be doing the job.'[7] Coming early in the report, these statements, both of which deplore colour-conscious-ness, are picked out by Macpherson in bold type and italics. Most people, probably, agree with the Lawrences on that point.

Later, however, Macpherson argues that colour-blindness is itself the problem. Police officers should not be colour-conscious to the detriment of black people. But they *should* be colour-conscious for the benefit of black people. They should not be 'colour-blind'. Macpherson quotes various authorities to support this unexpected view.

Here we are concerned only with Neville Lawrence's point, not Mrs Lawrence's. Mrs Lawrence is talking about people in private life and in voluntary associations. Neville Lawrence is directly addressing the much narrower but crucial issue of equality *before the law*.

The authority of Lord Scarman

'Lord Scarman said', Macpherson writes, 'that there can be " ... failure to adjust policies and methods to the needs of policing in a multi-racial society".' Macpherson appears to take that as giving authority to its own proposition that 'such failures can occur simply because police officers may mistakenly believe that it is legitimate to be "colour-blind" in ... the management and investigation of racist crimes and in the relationship generally with people from minority ethnic communities. ... A colour-blind approach fails to take into account the nature and needs of the person or the people involved'.[8]

The authority of Mr Dan Crompton

Mr Dan Crompton, Her Majesty's Inspector of Constabulary—again, a mere assertion by an 'authority'—more obviously does support Macpherson's view. As he 'helpfully' told the inquiry, 'it is no longer enough to believe all that is necessary is to treat everyone the same. ... It might be said it is about treatment according to need'.[9]

The authority of Professor Simon Holdaway

Among the publications seen by the inquiry, Macpherson lists four books by Professor Simon Holdaway. Macpherson appeals to the 'authority' of Professor Holdaway's assertions as evidence that the investigation of the murder of Stephen Lawrence was unsuccessful, at least in part, because it was sabotaged, not by police officers' racism, but by their 'colour-blindness'.[10]

No evidence is quoted from Professor Holdaway's books. On the subject of the police's failure to treat the murder as a purely racist crime, Macpherson quotes only Professor Holdaway's 'perceptive assessment' of the issue. Yet the 'perceptive assessment' is nothing but an eccentrically worded single assertion that something about 'racism' in the police led to the failure of the investigation.

It reads, in the relevant part:

a lack of a particular approach to the investigation of a racial attack [was] compounded precisely because the officers in charge did not place race at the centre of their understanding of the Lawrence murder and its investigation ... Race relations were consistently underplayed or ignored.

That is to say, in Professor Holdaway's formulation, that the failure of the police to undertake an adequate investigation in the Lawrence case was due to the following:

1. The lack of an approach that put race at the centre of a murder that was racist at its centre;

2. This was compounded by the lack of an approach that put race at the centre of a murder that was racist at its centre;

3. Race was not put at the centre of a murder that was racist at its centre.

It is difficult to discern what 'evidence' of any kind is contained in that statement. It is impossible to see what is 'perceptive' about it. 'Say it three times and it is true' is acceptable as a children's game. It comes as shock to see it praised in a public inquiry.[11]

Macpherson

Macpherson follows the approving reference to Professor Holdaway's conclusion, that colour-blindness was the cause of the investigation's failure, by mixing its own conclusive assertions with its own 'open-minded' queries to which the conclusive assertions give the answer. It *was* a 'purely' racist crime; it had been 'palpably identified' as such. Had there been 'an adequate and thoughtful understanding' of the special action to be taken when a crime was 'purely' racist? 'Did the officers involved behave at each stage as "colour-blind"?'

The colour-blind approach is 'flawed'.[12] By being 'colour-blind' the police in the Lawrence case were 'denying the relevance and particular reactions and needs of the victims and their families'.[13] Detective Constable Linda Holden and Detective Sergeant John Bevan, for example, were found guilty of racism by Macpherson ('unwitting' racism) because they had failed to treat the Lawrences 'within *their own* culture and as a *black* grieving family'.[14]

Here, therefore, treating people differently *in the application of the laws of the land* because of their colour, ethnic origin or culture is not prohibited, but demanded. In order to secure *equality of feelings of satisfaction* with the ways they are treated by the police, then they must be accorded *inequality* of *treatment* in the ways they are treated by the police.

Historically, the struggle for equality started with the demand for equality of legal and political rights. However often it is said, it is not true that in this country today there is one law for the rich and one for the poor. It was once true that there was one law for one group and another law for another group, rich and poor; town and country; men and women; clergyman and layman; Jew, Catholic or non-conformist and Church of England. With very few remote exceptions and residues (e.g. the Act of Settlement) it is true no longer. Not for centuries have there been any laws that have given any countenance to differences in the skin colour of British citizens. (There have been laws that have been more restrictive of black and Asian people entering Britain and becoming British citizens. That is a grievance. We are not belittling its importance by saying that it is a different one.) There is the continuing struggle to see that the equal laws are *applied* equally to all citizens.

The fight was won for equal legal and political rights and duties. Then that for state provisions to ensure equality of opportunity was fought. Free, universal and compulsory state education for the young, gradually extending up the age range, was established. The élite grammar schools in the state sector were largely replaced by comprehensive schools. University education was vastly expanded. Equality of opportunity was also sought in state provisions to ensure that in all circumstances all citizens were guaranteed the minimum of food, clothing, shelter, medical care, and access to facilities for physical and mental improvement such as fine art in public galleries, playing fields, swimming pools, and so forth, without which other opportunities could be taken up only with extreme difficulty. (In Sunderland the libraries of the university, with their banks of computers giving access to the world wide web, are open to all. The only restriction is on borrowing books.)

State provisions for equality of opportunity being well-advanced, the battle-ground shifted to state provision for equality of outcomes—those groups that have not succeeded in obtaining equality through the mechanisms of equality of opportunity are granted quotas in the ranks of the successful.

But there is a *reductio ad absurdum* of any well-meaning cause. Has the point been reached with the demand *for state provisions* to ensure equality of *subjective feelings of satisfaction*?

All victims and their families

It is difficult to see how the abandonment of colour-blindness can be described as anything but a recommendation that the police *should* stereotype victims and victims' families. What else can responding to victims and their families in accordance with their perceived 'culture', colour or ethnicity be called but 'stereotyping'?

'The black community' can be a reference to a set of people who share no more than a single characteristic, the way their skin is pigmented. Spokesmen and spokeswomen, elected, employed, or self-appointed, who object to people being treated unfavourably by others solely because of their colour can be said to be speaking for 'the black community' in this extremely loose sense. They can be confident that they are speaking for everybody who is black.

But 'community' in ordinary language and in technical sociology, anthropology and social psychology is used in precisely the opposite sense to 'any set of people who share a single observable outward characteristic'. It is used of a set of people who are held together because they share the same values over a wide range of human activities.

Macpherson overturns the old idea that black people should not be treated differently from white people in the public domain. The report demands that they should be treated differently because of their distinctive culture. Macpherson contains no evidence that such a unitary culture exists. Except in what seems to be the suggestion that Duwayne Brooks' behaviour was cultural, and he should have therefore been dealt with more skilfully by anthropologically well-informed police constables, there is no information on the different content of that culture to which the police should respond differently.

In a recent study of children of mixed parentage Tizard and Phoenix concluded that there was no such phenomenon as 'a unitary black culture'.[15]

Just as Marxists created the myth of the proletariat as a unified body 'for itself', or had liked to believe that working-class solidarity must, already did, or inevitably would override all other loyalties and attachments, so *a* unitary black culture, *the* 'black community', is the ideological creation of those who want to create such uniformity and solidarity, or who wishfully think that underlying apparent black cultural and black anomic diversity such potent solidarity already 'really' exists.

All suspects

The pre-Macphersonian idea is obviously sound, also, in relation to suspects. It is quite wrong in terms of justice, and utterly wasteful in terms of effective policing, to regard everybody from *any* broad category of the population as a 'suspect'. This is as true for any broad category within the majority population as it is for the broad category of each minority population taken as a whole.

When it is done in a thoroughly colour-blind fashion it is right and efficient to profile groups within the majority population, and within each minority population, that are known to produce unusually large proportions of what Macpherson calls 'potential criminals or trouble-makers'.

In demanding *the abandonment* of colour-blindness Macpherson is explicitly demanding also that mere membership of a colour, culture or ethnic category should disqualify the police from engaging in *any* profiling in relation to that minority category.[16] That is indeed, once again, throwing out the baby with the bathwater.

The Obscurities Of The Macpherson Doctrine That The Police Must Not Be Colour-Blind

Colour-consciousness as a legal police obligation?

Is the doctrine applicable only to the police officer's *range of discretion* within the unchanged national laws?

Few people, probably, would object to the notion that police officers should react to even the ill-conduct of surviving victims and victims' families with sensitive regard and exemplary restraint to all their cultural and personal traits, in so far as police officers can be trained to recognise and respond appropriately to them—and given the time to behave in this way.

Few people, probably, would object to the notion that the principle of sensitive regard to the peculiarities of the situation should apply to *everyone*, regardless of his or her colour, culture or ethnic status, or minority or majority status. Most people, probably, would, on the contrary, regard it as inappropriate that the principle should be presented as one to be applied to minorities *per se*, rather than one that applied to minorities *by virtue of the fact that it applies to all without exception*.

Or do these principles apply, on the contrary, not just to a police officer's use of his or her discretion, but also to changes in the national laws, which would make special policing provision for minorities of colour, ethnic origin and culture? This is what 'The Rotterdam Charter', favourably quoted by Macpherson, demands: 'The police must accept the need to adapt ... their *legal* responsibilities to the needs of a continually changing population'. This is what a 'multi-ethnic' society 'demands'.[17]

Colour-consciousness in relation to suspects?

If suspects have been arrested according to colour-blind principles, do these principles of how people from minority groups should be treated apply to them, as well as victims and their families?

'Suspects' is a category that is necessarily rich in people who object to the police interfering with them.

Also by definition, the police officer does not know whether, within the category of 'suspect', the particular individual falls into the sub-category of innocent citizen or guilty criminal. Necessarily, therefore, when dealing with a suspect, the police officer has to take firm control of a situation that would otherwise be exploited if the suspect is a criminal.[18]

To recommend that police officers should deal with anyone who is especially unco-operative, excitable, or anti-police with more than normal restraint and tolerance because that is their 'culture' is simply to invite others to develop or to claim to be part of the same 'culture'.

There is a passage in John Buchan's *The Thirty-Nine Steps*, first published in 1915, in which one of a group of suspects is made to say, 'We want to assist the law, like all Englishmen'.[19] The perennial popularity of the book, and of Alfred Hitchcock's 1935 film of it, suggests that this pro-police attitude struck a chord of approval among English people at the time and subsequently.

There are two models. One model is that of an impartial police service, acting in accordance with current English law, and a public opinion that favours pro-police attitudes above anti-police attitudes. The other model is that of a police service that favours people who show anti-police attitudes (who come from an anti-police 'culture') above people who show pro-police attitudes, and a public opinion that is neutral between anti-police and pro-police cultures, in the name of multi-culturalism.

What is the source of information on 'the culture' of a suspect, a victim, or a victim's family?

Macpherson writes about the police service relating in a particular way to each 'minority' defined by colour, ethnic origin and culture. The report uses such terms as *the* black *community*.

If there is such *a* black community, Macpherson does not indicate where the information is to be found on what its characteristic responses are to questions of English law or particular English laws, to the police, or to 'law and order' itself.

Is each individual police constable expected to be his or her own instantaneous expert anthropologist?

Where is the line to be drawn between what applies to everybody, and what applies to someone from a particular 'culture'?

Nor does Macpherson indicate where the line—a very important line— has to be drawn between police officers impartially applying the law to all citizens, (their primary, 'universalistic', role) and their paying attention to the peculiarities of the individual case (the secondary, subsidiary, concessionary, 'particularistic' role of police officers).

Unwitting racism can arise from colour-blindness

What relation Macpherson's doctrine of the illegitimacy of 'colour-blindness' has to 'racism' is not clear. Macpherson does not say directly that to be colour-*blind* is to be *racist*.

With typical obscurity the report says that 'unwitting' racism 'can arise' from 'unfamiliarity with the behaviour or cultural traditions of people or families from minority ethnic communities'.

Obviously all varieties and degrees of racism, including the most virulent and open racism, *can* 'arise from' ignorance. It is not clear, therefore, whether or not the inclusion of the word 'unwitting' is meant to imply that conduct where there is 'unfamiliarity' is itself 'racist' conduct.[20]

This conjectural statement at the very least associates 'colour-blindness' with racism. It contributes nothing at all to factual evidence about police conduct in the Lawrence affair.

14

The Political Uses of Disruptive and Separatist Anti-Racism

A striking thing about the Lawrence affair is the manner in which it rapidly fell into line with a set of assumptions of fact and of value, and a set of particular policy implications associated with these assumptions, that by the late 1980s had become anti-racist orthodoxy. This orthodoxy was the creation of a long history of political, journalistic, religious and academic endeavour of the same kind as Hayek described in *The Intellectuals and Socialism,*[1] and its tenets found wide support within the social-affairs intelligentsia.

Traditional Marxism

The attraction exerted by anti-police rhetoric from whatever source is well illustrated by the prominence and praise that the report grants to a largely irrelevant passage from Sir John Woodcock's old lecture, in which Sir John, as Her Majesty's Inspector of Police, in a sense the country's most senior police officer, presents a carbon-copy of Marx's theory that the liberties of the citizen are just so many 'police traps'. Whether rights are permitted to be exercised or are prohibited, Marx wrote, 'this *always* happens *solely* in the interests of ... the safety of the bourgeoisie'.[2]

To use Sir John's words, '*Never* really were the police the police of the whole people, but [*always*] a mechanism set up to protect the affluent from what the Victorians described as the dangerous classes'.[3] Marx's words, identical in meaning except for the inclusion of 'the dangerous classes', are that the state is 'nothing but a mechanism for the oppression of one class by another'.[4] The 'dangerous class' is also a term Marx uses, and it is probably for that reason it is still known today as a 'Victorian' term.

But Marx himself has no time for members of the 'dangerous class', the *lumpenproletariat*, as contrasted with the proletariat. He probably thought it was a good idea, poor though he was, that he should be protected from them by the London bobby. In *The Communist Manifesto* he calls members of the dangerous class 'the social scum'.[5] In *The Eighteenth Brumaire of Louis Bonaparte* Marx calls them again 'scum', but adds the word 'offal', and lists with evident disgust some of them: 'jailbirds', 'vagabonds', 'procurers', 'brothel keepers', 'swindlers', 'tricksters', and the whole 'disintegrated mass' of 'bohemians' from all social classes who sponge on the 'labouring nation'.[6] Elsewhere he includes the homeless.[7] If any of them tried to join in the revolution, Marx wrote, decent people ought to string them up straight away on the nearest lamp post.

To ordinary non-affluent people—the 'labouring nation'—who suffer from the crimes and insecurity imposed on them by their neighbours, the idea pronounced by HM Inspector of Police, that the police service is needed by nobody but the affluent, is incredible. Yet this is included in the Macpherson report as particularly 'apt in the context of this Inquiry'.[8] *Vous n'êtes que des blagueurs.* You are nothing but windbags.[9]

The 'Marxism' Of The Frankfurt School And The Student Politics Of The 'Sixty-Eighters'

Herbert Marcuse

The best known and most influential source of the anti-police, pro-minority world-view so prevalent among the social-affairs intelligentsia since the late 1960s, the deification of the dangerous class, is to be found in the work of Herbert Marcuse. The intellectual and philosophical basis of this world-view has gradually faded from knowledge, leaving only the all-important residues of belief and attitude. It is a contemporary error of radical chic to believe that Marcuse's views on the dangerous classes are Marx's.[10]

Marcuse argued that, in spite of its pride in its 'freedom' and its 'tolerance', Western society was in reality repressive ('repressive tolerance' is one of Marcuse's phrases). The complacency of the masses had been purchased with an abundance of goods and services that money could buy. What money could not buy was falling into decay and disrepute. As the dupes of their false consciousness, the masses were intellectually and spiritually willing captives to the system. The proletariat had been 'pacified'. Within our successfully administered but 'intolerable institutions', within our rich but grossly unjust and humanly destructive society, the revolutionary potential can only come from those who do not enjoy its dubious but narcotic benefits. Society must for its own good be radicalised through the refusal to heed pleas for agreement and conciliation; through the repudiation of 'the appearance of wisdom'; through resistance, subversion and vociferous dissent.

He believed that the barbarian within advanced society must not be tamed, but assisted, for the true barbarism may well be the 'continued empire of civilisation itself'. Whoever repudiates, escapes from, or defies society and its tool, the state, is properly to be regarded, not as someone to be brought under control, but as society's saviour. Prominent among Marcuse's potentially revolutionary 'outcasts and outsiders' are 'the exploited and persecuted of other races and colours' and 'the victims of law and order'. They are part of that 'elemental force which violates the rules of the game and, in doing so, reveals that it is a rigged game'.[11]

These ideas had already been introduced in the 1920s in the neo-Marxist works of writers like György Lukács. The proletariat, the 'ordinary' working class, had failed to fulfil its historic revolutionary mission in Western Europe and the United States. 'False conscious-ness' prevailed everywhere save in the ranks of the enlightened vanguard. Revolutionaries needed to control, therefore, 'the means of mental production' in the media of entertainment, information, education and the arts, before they would be able to secure control of the means of material production. (The subtitle of *One Dimensional Man* is 'a study in the *ideology* of advanced industrial society'.)[12] The common thread is that mere appearances are deceptive. Only those beings of superior virtue who are trained in the mysteries of correct interpretation can discern what is 'really' there.

And what is really there is *bad*. No one but the permanent critic of society, two of the leading intellectuals of neo-Marxist and anarchist student movements of the 1960s wrote, can count as a bone fide intellectual or artist. If the intellectual or artist willingly emerges from his or her natural element, which is denunciation, he or she becomes 'merely means at the disposal of the existing order'. When criticism becomes affirmation, its truth evaporates. 'The findings on fact' often deceptively contradict what those who are virtuous and enlightened know to be 'really' true. It is therefore necessary to break free from the facts, reject the tyranny of 'the instrumentalisation of science' and struggle against 'the present triumph of the factual mentality'.[13]

The task of the intellectual and artist, that is, is to correct everyone else's false consciousness.

The new term to describe the task of all revolutionaries was 'decons-truction'. After a false start in the 1970s when the traditional attempt had been made to deconstruct the economy, immense success was won in deconstructing the monogamous family and the fine mesh of legal and informal norms that had sustained it. The religious guardians of culture and its educational transmitters, on the promise that it would be well nourished and there was nothing to fear for its safety, delivered the traditional family bound and gagged to those whose sole ambition was to destroy it.[14]

Karl Popper's opposition

The notable opponent of the philosophy, sociology and politics of Marcuse and the Frankfurt School was Karl Popper. Popper saw in these revolutionary ideas of the disruptive, anarchistic and, according to its own lights, 'humane' left, all the traits of a nascent totalitarianism. Marcuse and other neo-Marxist writers became popular among the students in the 1960s. (Much-used words in German and French for these students, 30 years on, translate as 'the sixty-eighters'.) Popper had already by then dealt with the mind-set and philosophy of the enemies of an open society.[15] The reception enjoyed by the anti-science stance of the Frankfurt School brought Popper to the fore in defence of scientific method in the study of social affairs.

For Popper the 'irrefutability' of any alleged findings (like Macpherson's 'irrefutable' findings on 'racism') is not a sign of their evidential strength, but of their evidential worthlessness. The non-scientific mode of thought turns anything that can been seen or inferred into proof of the case that is being made or the theory that is being propounded.

Killing, enslaving, excluding, mistreating, insulting, despising or shunning a black person because he or she is black is obviously racism on any definition of the term. But for Macpherson, so is being nice to a black person, objecting to the bad behaviour of a black person, being indifferent to a black person, keeping one's distance from a black person, or not knowing oneself to be a racist. But being patronising, disliking, keeping one's distance, lacking insight into one's own personality and other undesirable ways of relating to black people are also found abundantly in social situations not involving colour, ethnicity or culture at all.

Macpherson nearly always lacks what is essential to true evidence, that is, the declared and systematic means that would enable it to say, and the reader to see, that a particular finding is evidence *of what is alleged*, and could not equally be evidence of something else. The report lays no rules upon itself about how it proposes to distinguish between, on the one hand, those examples of 'undesirable conduct' that would have occurred in a white-white social situation and which therefore would not have anything to do with racism, and, on the other hand, those which would have only occurred in a black-white social situation. Macpherson, that is, pays no attention, in Popperian terms, to the crucial scientific principle of the empirical *falsifiability* of its statements. The essential difference between scientific and other versions of reality is that science allows observable data to *disprove* its own statements.[16] For most of the anti-racists who advised or endorse the Macpherson inquiry, on the contrary, there is no action, gesture, or 'unconscious' thought but that can be, and is, turned with enthusiasm into further 'proof' for their theory of pervasive racism.[17] They are not worried about that. As the heirs of critical neo-Marxists of the 1960s, they are anti-Popperians in attitude, even where they are not anti-Popperians in their settled ideology.

In spite of Popper's efforts, that is, the ideas of the revolutionary students of the 1960s had spread far and wide through the ranks of influential social-affairs intellectuals by the 1990s. In his lecture Her Majesty's Inspector of Police, no less, as we have seen, was daringly displaying his 'Marxist' credentials, post-1968 style. The origin and details have been gradually forgotten. What remains is the unexamined doctrine of the rejection of scientific method in the study of social phenomena; the exceptional insight, sophistication and virtue of those intellectuals who adopt the victims' standpoint to expose the hidden truth; and the political fraud of deceptive freedom, repressive institutions and bogus democracy.[18]

Trotskyism

In the 1970s and 1980s the more old-fashioned Marxism of Leon Trotsky enjoyed an Indian summer in this country. (It is old fashioned in its faith in the virtue and revolutionary ardour of the 'multi-millioned masses' of the industrial proletariat rather than minorities.[19] They cannot always be seen, but all 'the moles of revolution' are down there digging.[20]) Trotskyism is distinct in the special emphasis it places on two aspects of Marxism.

First, Trotsky strongly recommended to his followers that where they were not themselves numerous, they adopt the technique of 'entrism'. That is to say, Trotskyists should infiltrate themselves in sufficiently large numbers into the ordinarily ill-attended rank-and-file meetings of trade unions and left-inclined political parties (in this country, especially the Labour party) and elect one another to office in the organisation.

It is also incumbent upon the Trotskyist, however, to make revolutionary use of any sizeable body of discontented people. 'He who does not seek and does not find the road to the masses is not a fighter but a dead weight to the party.'[21]

This was already a well-established Communist principle. The genuine outrage of Communists of goodwill often coincided in the 1920s and 1930s with the Comintern's propaganda interest in discrediting the USA. Probably the best-known example is the case of the Scottsboro boys. Nine youths between the ages of 13 and 20 were condemned to death in 1931 for assault on two white girls. (One of the nine was reprieved.) The Communists ousted the NAACP in the control of the world-wide protest movement that developed.

The black activist Walter White says in his memoirs that no one knew what to be more astounded at—the way in which the Democratic government let the injustice pass, or the impudent way in which the Communists 'cashed in' on the issue.[22]

Trotsky himself thought mainly in terms of workers, women and 'youth'. He dealt with race relations only briefly in his discussion of countries that are 'backward by their very essence'.[23] But, especially with the aid of the Marcusian ideas that were part of the intellectual atmosphere of the post-1968 period, Trotskyists could easily extend this to the struggles of ethnic minorities and their allies against disadvantageous discrimination, and attempt to control and keep aflame any racist issue.

The second distinctive characteristic of Trotskyism as a form of Marxism is its doctrine of 'the transitional programme'. This is the doctrine that discontent must never be allowed to die down until, under Trotsky's 'spotless banner', the conquest of power by the proletariat abolishes every reason for discontent.

If grievances are acknowledged and concessions are made to remove them, then new demands must be made to rekindle discontent, so that 'daily agitation' can continue at the old level. Each new demand has to be one that 'the masses' believe that the established system should meet. But the Trotskyist needs to know that the demand is one that the system *cannot possibly meet* without destroying itself.

As Marx said, 'The *demands* of the *workers* must everywhere be governed by the *concessions* of the *democrats*'.[24] As Trotsky, following Marx, said, 'The Fourth International advances a system of transitional demands, the *essence* of which is contained in the fact that they will be directed against the *very bases* of the bourgeois régime'.[25] A prime target, of course, is the effectiveness of the bourgeois state's police force. The state is no more than 'bodies of armed men'. If anyone is already armed against the state and its 'armed thugs of counterrevolution', then far from decommissioning their arms at the state's behest, the arming of the proletariat as a whole must be demanded as 'an imperative element to its struggle for liberation'.[26]

The Indian summer ended when the most successful of the Trotskyist factions, the Militant Tendency, lost control of Liverpool city council and its known adherents were expelled from the Labour party, and when the 1984-85 miners' strike, with its Trotskyist demands that *no* pit should *ever* be closed on *economic* grounds, ended in defeat and the disappearance to an insignificant rump of the once mighty National Union of Miners. The leader of the strike, Arthur Scargill, was left to form his own Socialist Labour Party. Imran Khan stood as the candidate for the Socialist Labour Party in an east London constituency in the general election of 1997.[27]

But race relations became more important to ex-Communists and ex-Trotskyists when communism and all openly communist parties in the

West collapsed. Following the disintegration of the USSR, adherents of this philosophy of social justice, believers in the efficacy of these means for obtaining it, and practitioners with these skills, were homeless. They moved en masse in the 1990s into good causes that still had a good name, including 'anti-racism'.

The Wide Spectrum Of Anti-racist Views

'Institutional racism' is the first fruit of their coalition across the wide spectrum of anti-racism—that is to say, all but a small minority of people in this country. Created by people of slack, self-righteous good-will who still carried, or had been gradually influenced by, the mélange of doctrines from the 1960s, 'institutional racism' could have been made to specification as an instrument for the deconstruction of police effectiveness. The almost universally favourable reception of this specialised concept—because general anti-racist sentiment is properly so deep and widespread—must have exceeded, in particular, all the hopes of those displaced by the decay and then disintegration of (to use a term from Macpherson) 'overt' Marxism as their intellectual and moral home.

The use of what Lenin called 'termites and useful idiots', has been for over a century, of course, the standard practice of the destabilising left. But rarely has the tactic been so obvious or so successful as in the case of 'institutional racism'. Feeble leaders of major churches, professional bodies and other organisations, charged with conserving what is valuable in our cultural heritage, collapsed at the sight of this dishonest fabrication in a chorus of mutually applauded *mea culpa*s.

Their intellectual slackness and moral confusion are caught exactly in Byron's old lines: The magnet of their course is gone/Or only points in vain/The shore to which their shivered sail/Shall never shift again.[28]

15

Stereotypes and Prejudice

There are two sides to any stereotype. There is the stereotype from the point of view of the person observing the carrier of the stereotype. There is the stereotype from the point of view of the person evincing the signals of the stereotype.

Any given stereotype, at one extreme, can be largely the creation of the observer. At the other extreme it can be largely the creation of the carrier. In real life there is are mixtures of the two, ranged along a continuum between these two poles.

The Observer-created Stereotype

Stereotypes of all human beings

One of the most important of stereotypes is that of 'the human being'. What behaviour can be expected of people, just as people? Much political controversy originates in divergent conceptions of 'human nature'.

At one extreme there is the altruistic-anarchist view, that people are fundamentally co-operative, creative, self-sacrificing and peaceable. If they behave badly, it is because they have been corrupted by their exercise of power or their subjection to the power of others. Remove all control, and human nature itself will create a harmonious, productive and happy society for all. Human beings are fundamentally rational, and rational thought and rational persuasion lead to individual freedom and communal solidarity.[1]

At the other extreme there is the stereotype of the human being as someone who is weak and selfish, and whose natural tendency is towards aggression, vice, corruption, and self-degradation. If there are not in existence intense systems for inculcating values and for maintaining the complicated patterns of permitted social interaction, there will be (in Hobbes' well-known words) 'no arts; no letters; no society; and what is worst of all, continual fear, and danger of violent death; and the life of man solitary, nasty, poor, brutal, and short'.[2]

These most general of stereotypes have been the basis of the worst tyrannies of the left, which operate towards the one extreme, of rational human beings as 'really' good; and of the right, which operate

135

towards the other extreme, of irrational human beings, when they depend only on themselves, as bound to fall into evil and violent ways.[3] Strangely, this type of stereotyping is rarely attacked as stereotyping at all.

Stereotypes of broad categories

Innate physical characteristics

It is strange that this type of stereotyping is ignored, because the broader the category that is stereotyped, the less useful the stereotype is. Thus, to know only that a person is a man rather than a woman is to have very little useful information on what to expect of him. The fact that he is not a woman says nothing about his kindness, his efficiency, his intelligence, his reliability, his education, his driving skills, or his suitability for a particular private appointment or public office.

The same applies to the colour of a person's skin.

Such stereotypes are of no utility, or in the case of sex of next to no utility.

Cultural origin and choice of value-system

People sharing the same culture respond to others in a particular way. That is what 'culture' means. 'Stereotyping' someone who is French means having the expectation that he or she will react in 'French' ways. English people are not offended if one says 'Good day!' to them. But it is likely that a French person would find '*Bonjour!*' abrupt, and would expect to hear '*Bonjour, monsieur!*', or '*Bonjour, madame!*'.

The stereotype that is useful alerts the user to the *chances* that certain conduct and certain responses will occur.

Stereotyping is useless or worse when one or both of two things happen.

One is that the calculation of the chances proves to be outdated, or wrong for some other reason: the idea that English people normally have bacon and eggs for breakfast, for example, or that pizza or curry and chips are regarded as foreign dishes instead of being seen as part of the staple diet of children on working-class estates.

The other is far more important. The stereotype is useless or harmful when the conduct and responses of the individual concerned do not correspond to one or other features of the stereotype. The stereotype is useful for initial orientation only. It is useless or harmful when it is held onto *when it is in conflict with experience*.

People in any easily identified group or category share in the reflected glory, or bear the stigmata of the reputation of their group or category. The collective reputation is acquired through the good or bad conduct, the successes or failures of, usually, a small minority of its members.

People who become or remain Catholics, or Protestants or Muslims or Hindus can provisionally be taken to have oriented themselves to the world and eternity in certain ways that affect their conduct and responses. The readers of the *Guardian* are a very mixed bunch, as are the readers of the *Daily Telegraph*. It would be discarding useful information for interaction, however, to assume that there will not be an average difference in the response of readers of the *Guardian* and the readers of the *Daily Telegraph* over a wide range of political and social concerns. If one 'stereotypes' a young man on the basis that he reads the *Socialist Worker*, and assumes that he has a certain level of intolerance towards and dislike for people who believe or express views that are not his, that is much more useful than stereotyping a reader of the *Sunderland Echo*.

The good and bad name of the group or category

'A good name' and 'a bad name' are synonyms for 'a favourable stereotype' and 'an unfavourable stereotype'. If your parents and brothers and sisters have a 'good name' or a 'bad name', then people will take that into account in their initial, duly favourable or duly cautious, dealings with you. If your neighbourhood has a bad name for debt default, people will wisely take that into account in making you a loan.

You yourself can do nothing about the fact that your parents have a reputation as model citizens. Knowing nothing about you people *initially* give you credit for a good upbringing.

You yourself can do nothing, at a given point in time, about the fact that, at that given point in time, your neighbourhood has acquired a bad name, and *initially* the neighbourhood's reputation rubs off on you.

The 'bad name' of the family, neighbourhood, school, country, or ethnic group might be undeserved in the case of the particular individual. But nearly all group or category 'bad names' are based on experience. That is why the good people in any group or category object so strongly to the people who do give that group or category a bad name. It affects them too. And that is why the group itself often takes measures to control the conduct of its own internal worst enemies.

Internationally, the term for a violently racist youth, and his uniform, is now the English word 'skinhead'. All English people suffer from the bad reputation that skinheads have given the English, just as all English people once benefited from the good reputation of English 'fair play', 'gentlemanliness', and so forth, which used to be the English words typically untranslated in foreign usage.

The ban on what is now called 'grassing up' members of your group or category was originally highly functional. It was a realistic recognition of the fact that the power of internal public opinion is more effective than authoritative control from the outside. One of the main reasons for the collapse of community control in neighbourhoods that were once respectable working class in culture is that the original reason for 'not grassing up' anybody has been forgotten. The rule that once was the foundation of community control is now a rule that benefits, and greatly benefits, only the badly behaved.

The Stereotyping Invited By The Carrier Of The Stereotype

If people dress themselves as 'English football fans' abroad, then people abroad (and their police services) have to respond to them in the first instance in terms of the bad name their predecessors gave them. Ten years ago, especially, sensible people calculated in the first instance that the chances of appallingly bad behaviour from an 'English football fan' were high, as compared with the chances of any kind of bad behaviour from, say, a middle-aged, middle-class husband and wife with their children, dressed by Marks and Spencer, getting off the ferry with the family car at Calais for their foreign holiday.[4]

From his observations as a GP and prison doctor in Birmingham, Theodore Dalrymple gives a vivid account of the adoption in the past few years of the stereotypical traits of English underclass boys by an emerging underclass of English Indians within the highly successful category of English Indians generally.

> Although their complexions are by no means adapted to it, tattooing is fast on the increase among them. Other adornments—a ring through the eyebrow or the nose, for example—are membership badges of the clan. Gold in the front teeth, either replacing an incisor or framing it with a rim of gold, is virtually diagnostic of heroin addiction and criminality. Such decorative dentistry is imitative of the black underclass and is intended as a signal of both success and dangerousness.
> [Such] young Indians have adopted, too, the graceless manners of the class to which they aspire to belong. They now walk with the same vulpine lope as their white compatriots, not merely as a means of locomotion, but as a means of communicating threat. ...
> When a member of the developing Indian underclass consults me, he slouches in the chair at so obtuse an angle to the floor that I would not have thought it possible, let alone comfortable, for a man to retain the position. But it isn't comfort he's after; he is making a statement of disrespect in the face of what he supposes to be authority.[5]

Some people play games with stereotypes at other people's expense, and protect or enjoy themselves by deliberately sending the wrong signals that they are formidable, dangerous, charming or reliable. Part of the enjoyment can be that of deliberately inviting prejudice and then denouncing others for being prejudiced when they receive the signals and act upon them.

When the signals are taken at their face value, that is not proof that people who have stereotyped them were to blame in reacting as they did. They had been deliberately misled.

The Indispensability Of Responding To The Signals Of Self-Chosen Stereotypes

The advantage of 'accusations' that police officers stereotype people is that it is obviously true. It is obviously true because everybody stereotypes people. Social life would not be possible without the economy of stereotypes. Clothing, speech and gesture are all ways in which people signal to others, prior to interaction, that certain attitudes and reactions can be expected of them.

At the local derby match, Newcastle football thugs dress and adorn themselves in one way. They are signalling, 'We are people who are willing to attack you under slight provocation if you come from Sunderland'. (And vice versa.) When they go to the same match, St John Ambulance Brigade men and women dress and adorn themselves to indicate clearly and immediately that they can be looked to with safety for assistance in case of injury. Anyone who ignored those signals would be a complete fool. But in real life no one is such a fool. It is only in abstract academic discussion or sophisticated articles in broadsheet journals that the proposition can be entertained that 'one must not stereotype people'.

In an emergency, most black or white people will wisely stereotype a man or woman that comes along with a fluorescent yellow coat, a black hat with a black and white checked band, and 'police' written on his or her chest. The stereotyped response, with few exceptions, will be different from and more favourable to the stereotypical signals carried by almost anybody else. When PC Geddis got out of the car in civilian clothes, he had only to say 'I am an off-duty policeman' to transform his reception, for most people, in his favour.

Duwayne Brooks was perfectly entitled to wear a cap carrying the slogan, 'Stay black!', and trousers with machine-gun bullet holes sewn into them, as he was on the night of the murder. He was not entitled to insist, and no one was entitled to insist on his behalf, that no one should read any message into this choice of clothing. He is entitled to adopt a personal style of 'hating the police' and of shouting and swearing in a crisis. He is not entitled to expect that the consequences will be no different from those experienced by a person who eschews the use of foul language in addressing strangers in public, and who genuinely or tactically defers to the authority vested in public officials.

In any interaction where there are consequences for the individual, responding to the self-chosen stereotype presented by the other person is indispensable. To ask for anybody to deal with everybody in all circumstances on the basis of what the other person is 'really' like is to ask the impossible.

Nobody can run his or her professional or personal life as if he or she were an encyclopædic enthographer (and as if the ethnography of every group were known).

Nobody can run his or her professional or personal life as if he or she were as sensitive to the nuances of personality as a consultant psychiatrist.

The individual has no option but to use the rough-and-ready knowledge accumulated by others over time and over a range of occasions beyond the range of any single individual.

Stereotyping is not prejudice (judgement *in advance of* experience) but judgement on the experience of the *chance* that a person from this group or category is *more likely* to behave in one way rather than another.

In the light of his research Professor Cashmore concludes that the stop and search figures are not driven by blind prejudice. 'Many officers have been driven by a performance culture where arrest figures are crucial.' To use the acceptable concepts 'targeting' or 'profiling' in place of the unacceptable concept of stereotyping, stopping and searching black youths with baseball caps and jewellery does, in fact, produce, in a disproportionate number of cases compared with many other possible categories, *evidence of crimes*. It produces, therefore, high arrest figures that are professionally valuable to the officers concerned.[6]

Erroneous Stereotypes

As is already clear from the above discussion, stereotypes can be, of course, wrong. That is a matter that has to be settled by the facts of each case. Here we are simply making the general point. We are not talking about the accuracy of any particular stereotype.

Making Demands That Cannot Possibly Be Met

The demand that members of given professional groups should be made to act without responding to the self-chosen stereotypes of others, as distinct from the demand that they should not be prejudiced in the above sense of persevering in holding the stereotype when it has been shown not to apply to the particular case, is a demand that they make themselves ineffective in anything they do—a not unwelcome result for anti-police advocates. Faced by being judged by standards that are impossible to reach, the response cannot be other than either inaction or deception.

Prejudice is evil when an opinion about how another person will behave remains unaltered *in spite of the evidence that in the particular case the group or category stereotype does not apply.*

Mrs Lawrence provides a striking example of stereotyping in her statement to the Macpherson inquiry.

> If I could, I would change every single police officer in the country and get a black person in charge of investigations. I would like to get someone who is truly black and not token black ... *No* black person can *ever* trust the police.[7]

Let us say that some black person holding that view meets a reasonable and decent police officer in the future, and *whatever* that police officer did was interpreted as proving that he or she is a 'racist' police officer—kindness or rudeness, consideration or indifference. Then she would have gone beyond using her personal (though obviously wildly overgeneralised stereotype) to being prejudiced, in this sense of being impervious to the conduct of the individual.

As we have said, we are not making any reference here to the accuracy of any particular stereotype. Nor are we discussing how far in any particular case a useful and accurate stereotype has degenerated into prejudice and bigotry.

We are making four *general* points. The first is that stereotyping is humanly unavoidable. The second is that any given stereotype can be justified or unjustified. It can be too 'strong' or (rarely) too 'weak'; but whether it is too strong or too weak *depends on the facts* relating to the group or category in question. The third is that prejudice is the refusal to treat an individual case on its merits. In that case, whatever the conduct it is interpreted in such a way as to keep the stereotype intact. The fourth is that these are three separate issues, and each is to be separately dealt with adequately on its own.

16

Conclusion

The Welcome For Macpherson

The Macpherson message on institutional racism was *received* as being *unequivocal*. The crucial passages in Macpherson where the absence of evidence is admitted, and the innocence of both the Metropolitan Police Service and individual officers is insisted upon, were all lost in the report's welter of assertion, 'evidence', 'inference' and 'expert' testimony. This is shown by the fact 'unequivocal' is the word Cathcart uses to describe Macpherson's findings.[1] Lord Falconer, a Cabinet Office minister, said that the Macpherson report 'had *proved* that our society and particularly the police are *riddled with racism*'.[2] It is also shown by the fact that by January 2000 so sceptical a newspaper on the subject as the *Daily Telegraph* was able to remark, in passing, that the Macpherson report *had* claimed that racism was 'rife' in the police.[3] Current affairs programmes such as BBC 2's 'Newsnight' would routinely cite Macpherson as having established beyond discussion that the MPS and the police generally were racist. Before it was only the blacks who knew it, 'suddenly it was everybody'.[4]

Cathcart celebrates the Lawrences and the Macpherson report as having transformed the debate about racism in England. Ideas such as 'unconscious or institutional racism' had been 'thrust into the mainstream while notions that were easier to live with, such as the bad apple theory, have lost much of their authority'.

He also expresses his satisfaction that as the result of the efforts of the Lawrences and Macpherson 'it is now less widely accepted that people should be treated equally and more widely accepted that people should be treated according to their needs'.[5]

The Fanatical Mind-set

From the point of view of the militant anti-racist, only racists (or their unwitting but nevertheless all-too dangerous allies) can be interested in *any* facts or arguments about racism. What needs to be known is known. Racism is pervasive. No good-thinking person can therefore be interested in the irrelevant and confusing minutiæ of how good an argument is that points this out.

People have massacred other people solely because of racism. Rigid caste systems of labour, prestige, power and material rewards have been maintained on the basis of racism. People are insulted because of racism. Guilty of none of these things, some people nevertheless secretly and silently despise others they perceive as belonging to an inferior race. Some people are conscious of no racism in their own outlook. They act in a 'colour-blind' fashion, and judge purely on conduct and character. This can 'give rise' to racism.

But to point out these differences is racist. For racism is an absolute evil. There are no significant gradations of 'more' or 'less'. This is a characteristic trait of fanaticism, whether religious or secular. Robespierre, speaking fanatically of 'freedom' before the Constituent Assembly in August 1791, said that there are no two ways of being free. Either you are *entirely* free or you are *entirely* a slave. What is more, you are either *wholly* for the cause as defined by the fanatic, or you are *wholly* against it. 'If you do not do *all* for liberty, you have done *not a thing*.' To oppose the person in the forefront of the self-evidently true and good demand is to commit lese-majesty. To oppose the demand itself is to commit lese-humanity.[6]

So far as the militant anti-racist is concerned, whatever the intentions of people who nit-pick among the arguments, or who say slavery was a long time ago, or that racism is comparatively mild in its effects in this country, they are all *pro-racist*. The *effects* of what they do is racist. As the old Communists used to say, they may or may not be formally right but they are objectively wrong. They blunt the edge of anti-racist ardour. All the *relevant* facts and all the *reasonable* arguments about race have already been settled and are already known to all good-thinking people. All that remains is to inculcate the correct conclusions into this and future generations.

Sorel argued the same case in his *Reflections on Violence*, where he set out the conditions for a successful working-class revolution. When you already know what is right and necessary, you do not need more or better facts. You need, to use the term in Sorel's sense, a *myth*, any version of 'the facts' that is *motivationally effective* in the struggle of the righteous for elementary justice. 'It is the myth in its entirety that is alone important.'[7]

The Betrayal By The Intellectuals[8]

The Macpherson report escaped and escapes serious challenge from the people whose job it is to think about what can roughly be called the 'intellectual integrity' of such things, and write or speak about them —the social-affairs intelligentsia in the universities, serious printed and electronic journalism, the churches, and elsewhere.

This freedom from criticism can hardly be because of the factual soundness of Macperhson's propositions or the scientific utility of its definitions.

Some people do not criticise the Macpherson report because they agree with its sentiments. It is easy to be in complacent agreement with ideas that are so finely in tune with the spirit of the times. Embracing them brings no trouble.

But paucity of critics may be also due to the silence of those who *do* perceive that the Macpherson report is empirically and intellectually shoddy, but who also say nothing. Such silent dissenters are concerned, on the arguments stated (or rather the mind-set described) at the beginning of this chapter, that *any* criticism from them about facts or tactics, or even any comment they make, will lead to their being condemned for condoning racist oppression.[9]

John Pierson, writing about this phenomenon in social work, one of the bastions of anti-racist thinking and practice of the Macpherson type, writes that this doctrine has atrophied into a few slogans. 'Society and its institutions are oppressive.' 'Power holders are there to be excoriated.' 'Those who are not with us are against us.' Anyone who attempts to question *in any way* the tenets of anti-racism proves by that very fact that he or she is a racist, and for that reason is not worthy of a hearing.[10]

In 1991 the Central Council for Education and Training in Social Work (CCETSW—'Settsoo') published its guidelines on the content and implementation of the new Diploma in Social Work.[11] This document[12] set out in detail the new orthodoxy, and *the measures that would be implemented to ensure full compliance with it*. This would not be only compliance with correct conduct, it would be compliance with correct thought.

The first tenet of the new doctrine, from which everything else flowed, was 'the *self-evident* truths' contained in the statement that '*racism is endemic in the values, attitudes and structures of British society*'.[13]

No dissent from this proclamation would be tolerated. Colleges and courses that did not accept it would lose their licence to train social workers. Evidence of doubt was evidence of unsuitability to teach or practise social work.

The Training Manual fleshed out the requirements of the *Rules*. It stated that 'steps need to be taken to promote permeation of all aspects of the curriculum by an anti-racist analysis'. All 'racist materials' had to be withdrawn from the syllabus. What 'racist materials' were, was to be decided by CCETSW.[14] The manual explicitly dismissed all liberal ideas about freedom, tolerance and individualism. It rejected the traditional academic belief that you have to win people over by rational persuasion, not emotional arguments, and that you must not interfere with other people's freedom of speech.[15] In the *Rules*, 'freedom of speech' does not include the freedom to express any opinions or adduce any facts or use any words that are or can be construed as 'racist' or favourable to 'racism'.

The manual states that 'anti-racist *practice* requires the adoption of explicit *values*'. The first of the 'values' is that individual problems have roots in 'political structures' and '*not* in individual or cultural pathology'. A second 'value' is that racial oppression and discrimination are everywhere to be *found* in British society, even where they *seem* to be *invisible*.[16] (These are both badly-expressed statements about *facts*. The 'values' are that one should have a blind belief that they are true.)

The Spectrum Of Anti-racism

We can consider, say, Booker T. Washington's work and views as representing one end of the scale on black response to oppression. Booker T. Washington believed in the power of black self- and mutual improvement, especially through education and down-to-earth training. As these steadily succeeded, they would open all doors to all blacks, and lead to equality of opportunity, neither assisted nor hampered by the colour of any person's skin.[17] The first priority, for Washington, was to counteract the debilitating effects of slavery. 'Friction will pass away in proportion as the black man ... can produce something that the white man wants and respects.'[18]

W.E.B. du Bois, Washington's younger contemporary, whose views used to be thought to be opposed to his, differed with him only in setting the black's sights higher. He had to fight the temptation of the line from the Blues, 'Been down so long that "down" don't bother me'. For du Bois the harmonisation of American race relations could only occur between two self-respecting, cultured and educated races.[19]

These sentiments were, in fact, an inspiration to English working men. Approval of them was one of the reasons that the English working class at the cost of considerable hardship (especially in the Lancashire cotton trades) supported the North against the South in the Civil War. The leader of the Northumberland miners in the decades straddling the nineteenth and twentieth centuries, Thomas Burt, pays tribute to the American slave, Frederick Douglass, for the influence for good (as Burt saw it) that he had on his life, and that of many other workers like him. Burt's own autobiography is entitled, not pitman *to* privy councillor, but pitman *and* privy councillor.[20]

We can consider, say, Malcolm X's work as representing a view, on the question of segregation versus integration, nearer the other end of the scale. The white race is incorrigibly prejudiced and exploitative. Blacks who are in a minority in white societies are permanent victims. They are, to use Booker T. Washington's striking phrase that summed up all he hated, 'disburdened of responsibility'.[21] They can expect no reasonable concessions or any justice. They cannot succeed in white society. They have to obtain what they can 'by any means necessary'.[22] This is the same message, that is, that has already created in the past 40 years the anomic neighbourhoods of the white underclass.

Since the 1960s influential black opinion has shifted sharply away from the pole of policies represented by Booker T. Washington, to the pole represented by Malcolm X.

Which strategy seems to the general public to be that of a given group? It is that which they hear about in the most effective messages from those who claim to speak for a category or group. Unfavourable stereotypes can be created not just by hostile propaganda of a group's opponents, but by the advocacy of its supporters.

'Stephen has never been in trouble. We brought our children up to respect the law. As far as I know Stephen had never even spoken to a policeman', Neville Lawrence said in his statement to the inquiry. 'Stephen had friends of all races. We brought Stephen up in the belief that you did not see colour as a problem. I do not see colour as a problem.' Stephen attended Trinity Church in Woolwich from an early age. He was christened there. He was also blessed at a Seventh Day Adventist Church. He went with the family to church every Sunday. He was in the cubs and later the scouts. He was involved in numerous activities. He frequently took part in charitable events.

Stephen was able and conscientious at school, and was supported strongly by his parents. Neville Lawrence records in his statement to the inquiry: 'I remember we went to see the Head of his House before he went to school and there were so many good reports about him. We used to go to all his open evenings to make sure that he did not fall behind. His favourite subject was art. One of the things we discovered was that he wanted to be an architect so he was very good at drawing.'

Stephen obtained a work-experience placement with a well-known black architect, Arthur Timothy. Arthur Timothy asked Stephen to return to work for him once he had finished his training.

Stephen was also a good sportsman, integrated and popular in his clubs. Here, too, he had the support of his parents.

I used to take him to a group near Schofields Park. He joined a club and used to go twice a week. We used to go and take him to meetings all over the country. When the London Marathon started, there was a mini-marathon which Stephen took part in and did very well. I think he came 16th out of several hundred.

'Stephen has never said anything to me about having problems concerning race so as far as I know he didn't have any.'[23]

Neville Lawrence's mother was a Seventh Day Adventist. Neville Lawrence himself attended a Catholic school, 'so from an early stage religion has been part of my life'. Neville was the archetypal self-improving working man, uncomplaining and resilient, even as the victim of racial discrimination.

He married Doreen in 1972, and throughout his family life he was a model husband and father of the respectable working class. When he could not get a job with one employer, he trained himself to be useful to another. When he could not find an employer, he supported his family by being self-employed. He was an upholsterer by trade, went to work for the borough council in a factory. He regarded the job as temporary and below his potential, so he took the three-year evening course for his City and Guilds in tool-making. He passed. All the white students got places in factories, he says, but he did not. 'I had wasted three years studying.' He took the knock and went into furniture making. Then he worked in a suede and leather factory.

> When the work got scarce we started looking for work in the newspaper. There were lots of jobs giving work out to people who sewed at home so I used to go and pick up the work from the factory and sew it at Aspinal Road, where I lived before I got married. I then got to know Doreen's mother who was also a machinist but she only did dresses and things. While I was looking for a job for myself I used to look for work for her as well and I used to collect her work and take it to her.

Just after they were married the employment situation changed. At that time the work was scarce so he started to do painting and decorating. He worked with two plasterers, and decided that he should learn to plaster. He and about 15 others put up £1,000 each and joined (sic) a company.

At the time of the murder he had been looking after his family and doing plastering and decorating for 20 years.[24]

He was exactly the kind of man whose adjustment to domestic and working life was one that the intellectual consensus sneered at for so long in the old respectable white working class. He became a hero only when he was forced by his son's horrible death into being a victim.

Doreen Lawrence, too, was a self-improving pupil, a model employee, and a devoted wife and mother. She obtained her CSEs at school and worked with NatWest as a bank clerk for three or four years. She left work to look after Stephen when he was born. She took part-time work when Stephen was 18 months old. She was studying for her BA in Humanities at the time of Stephen's murder. As a BA graduate she was studying for her MSC in therapeutic counselling at the time of the Macpherson inquiry.

The Lawrences' previous life was structured on the integrationist and self-help/mutual aid model of Frederick Douglass and Booker T.

Washington. Although they were black, the signals that Neville Lawrence and his son sent out by their clothes, lifestyle and demeanour meant that they never had anything to do with the police in their ordinary lives, nor the police with them.

Yet through their experience of their son's murder they, of all people, became the most influential couple in English history in strengthening those who reject what they contemptuously dismiss as 'Uncle Tomism' among either whites or blacks, and choose the Malcolm X and Stokely Carmichael model of victimhood, confrontation and separation.

Radical whites, especially when well placed and sophisticated, no less than radical blacks, detest and mock their family devotion, their lifestyle and their demeanour; they mock and detest this family-centred lifestyle in the respectable white working class no less than in the respectable black working class. Yet the murder of Stephen Lawrence, at the hands of youths whose way of life is one of the main products of the deconstruction of the past 40 years, has been the occasion for another substantial victory for the deconstructionists. That is the supreme irony of the fateful meeting of the stricken Lawrences, an unworldly High Court judge, a feckless social-affairs intelligentsia, and what is currently fashionable in political militancy.

Notes

Preface

1 *Report by the Police Complaints Authority on the Investigation of a Complaint against the Metropolitan Police Service by Mr N. and Mrs D. Lawrence*, (The Kent Report), Cm 3822, London: The Stationery Office, December 1997, p.3.

2 Macpherson, W., *The Stephen Lawrence Inquiry*, Cm 4262-I, London: The Stationery Office, February 1999, p. 322.

3 Macpherson, *The Stephen Lawrence Inquiry,* Cm 4262-I, p. 246.

4 Cathcart, B., *The Case of Stephen Lawrence*, London: Penguin Viking, 1999, p. 208.

5 Macpherson, *The Stephen Lawrence Inquiry*, Cm 4262-I, pp. 240 and 242.

6 Macpherson, *The Stephen Lawrence Inquiry*, Cm 4262-I, pp. 237-38.

7 Cathcart, *The Case of Stephen Lawrence*, 1999, p. 271.

8 *Report by the Police Complaints Authority on the Investigation of a Complaint against the Metropolitan Police Service by Mr N. and Mrs D. Lawrence*, (The Kent Report), pp. 3-4.

9 *Report by the Police Complaints Authority on the Investigation of a Complaint against the Metropolitan Police Service by Mr N. and Mrs D. Lawrence*, (The Kent Report), pp. 5-6 , p. 10 and p. 12.

10 *Report by the Police Complaints Authority on the Investigation of a Complaint against the Metropolitan Police Service by Mr N. and Mrs D. Lawrence*, (The Kent Report), p. 13. (Emphasis added.)

11 Macpherson, W., 'Brief history of the inquiry', *The Stephen Lawrence Inquiry: appendices*, Cm 4262-II (Revised), London: The Stationery Office, February 1999. [No page numbers supplied.]

12 Macpherson, *The Stephen Lawrence Inquiry*, Cm 4262-I, p. 20.

13 Macpherson, *The Stephen Lawrence Inquiry*, Cm 4262-I, p. 28.

14 Macpherson, 'Brief history of the inquiry', *The Stephen Lawrence Inquiry: appendices*, Cm 4262-II (Revised). [No page numbers supplied.]

15 Macpherson, 'Brief history of the inquiry', *The Stephen Lawrence Inquiry: appendices*, Cm 4262-II (Revised). [No page numbers supplied.]

16 Macpherson, *The Stephen Lawrence Inquiry*, Cm 4262-I, p. 33.

Introduction

1 'Statement of Doreen Lawrence, 8 March 1998', Macpherson, W., *The Stephen Lawrence Inquiry: appendices*, Cm 4262-II (Revised), London: The Stationery Office, February 1999. [No page numbers supplied.]

2 Cathcart, B., *The Case of Stephen Lawrence*, London: Penguin Viking, 1999 p. 316.

3 Macpherson, W., *The Stephen Lawrence Inquiry: appendices*, Cm 4262-II (Revised), London: The Stationery Office, February 1999. Appendix 14 and Appendix 15. Cathcart, B., *The Case of Stephen Lawrence*, London: Penguin Viking, 1999, pp. 315-17.

4 Macpherson, W., *The Stephen Lawrence Inquiry*, Cm 4262-I, London: The Stationery Office, February 1999, p. 185.

5 Macpherson, *The Stephen Lawrence Inquiry*, Cm 4262-I, p. 54. (Emphasis added.)

6 Macpherson, *The Stephen Lawrence Inquiry*, Cm 4262-I, p. 52 and p. 53.

7 Macpherson, *The Stephen Lawrence Inquiry*, Cm 4262-I, p. 51.

8 Macpherson, *The Stephen Lawrence Inquiry*, Cm 4262-I, p. 52.

9 Cathcart, B., *The Case of Stephen Lawrence*, London: Penguin Viking, 1999, pp. 412-13. (Emphasis added.) Macpherson, *The Stephen Lawrence Inquiry*, Cm 4262-I, p. 24. (Emphasis added.)

10 Cathcart, *The Case of Stephen Lawrence*, 1999, pp. 412-13. Macpherson, *The Stephen Lawrence Inquiry*, Cm 4262-I, p. 24.

11 Macpherson, *The Stephen Lawrence Inquiry*, Cm 4262-I, p. 20. (Emphasis added.) The 'inappropriate expressions' Macpherson is referring to here are 'coloured' and 'Negro' instead of 'black'. Macpherson inappropriately writes 'negro'. The evidence presented at the inquiry on the use of such an inappropriate expression mainly concerned one officer. Inspector Steven Groves persisted in thinking that 'coloured' was only a term of description, not of abuse. See our section on 'The crowd and Inspector Groves' (pp. 23).

12 Cathcart, *The Case of Stephen Lawrence*, 1999, pp. 412-13. (Emphasis added.) Macpherson, *The Stephen Lawrence Inquiry*, Cm 4262-I, p. 24.

13 Cathcart, *The Case of Stephen Lawrence*, p. 357.

14 Quoted Macpherson, *The Stephen Lawrence Inquiry*, Cm 4262-I, p. 20.

Chapter 1: The Main Issues

1 Cobbett, W., *The 'Autobiography' of William Cobbett: the progress of a plough boy to a seat in parliament*, Reitzel, W. (ed.), London: Faber and Faber, 1933.

2 Hate Crimes Statistics Act, 23 April 1990.

3 These Louisiana provisions, making it unlawful for any person in the commission of an underlying crime to select the victim because of his or her 'actual or perceived' 'race, age, gender, religion, colour, creed, disability, sexual orientation, national origin, or ancestry', became effective on 15 July 1997. §107.2 Hate crimes, *West's Louisiana Statutes Annotated: revised statutes*, St. Paul, Minn: West, 1999. Volume 9A.

4 Macpherson, W., *The Stephen Lawrence Inquiry: appendices*, Cm 4262-II (Revised), London: The Stationery Office, February 1999. Appendix 5. Day 2 of Part I of the inquiry, 24 March 1998. (Emphasis added.)

5 Macpherson, W., *The Stephen Lawrence Inquiry*, Cm 4262-I, London: The Stationery Office, February 1999, p. 6.

6 Macpherson, *The Stephen Lawrence Inquiry*, Cm 4262-I, p. 41.

7 Macpherson, *The Stephen Lawrence Inquiry*, Cm 4262-I, p. 42.

8 Macpherson, *The Stephen Lawrence Inquiry*, Cm 4262-I, pp. 299-300.

9 'Mr E. Lawson QC appearing on behalf of the inquiry', Macpherson, *The Stephen Lawrence Inquiry: appendices*, Cm 4262-II (Revised), p. 50. (Emphasis added.)

10 Macpherson, *The Stephen Lawrence Inquiry*, Cm 4262-I, p. 27.

11 In, for example, Durkheim, E., *The Division of Labour in Society* (1893), Glencoe, Ill: The Free Press, 1947, p. 368. Durkheim, E., 'Anomic suicide', *Suicide* (1897), London: Routledge and Kegan Paul, 1952.

12 The lines of verse are from Wordsworth's 'Mutability'.

13 Clough, S., 'Family tenacity traps musician's killers', and 'Musician's racial killer sentenced to life in jail', *Daily Telegraph*, 22 and 23 December 1999.

14 Weber, M., 'Politics as a vocation', Gerth, H.H., and Mills, C. Wright, (eds.), *From Max Weber: essays in sociology*, London: Routledge and Kegan Paul, 1948, pp. 115-16. (Emphasis added.) 'Politik' has a wider connotation than 'politics' in English. Depending on the context, it can be taken to mean either that or 'policy'. Some of Weber's discussion is about politics and politicians, but here it is legitimate to widen the reference of his remarks to all social activists.

Chapter 2: The Methods of Inquiry used by Macpherson

1 An English theologian (was it William Paley?) who was highly respected in his day and for long after death, and by no means a crank, once wrote that the existence of angels is more certain, though less obvious, than the existence of the meal on the plate before him. The existence of angels, for him, was vouched for explicitly by God; the existence of his dinner was not.

2   *Royal Commission on Tribunals of Inquiry*, London: HMSO, 1966.

3   Sir Richard Scott, Chancery Bar Association, 2 May 1995.

4   Macpherson, W., *The Stephen Lawrence Inquiry*, Cm 4262-I, London: The Stationery Office, February 1999, p. 41.

5   'It is right that we should say at once that no collusion or corruption is proved to have infected the investigation of Stephen Lawrence's murder. It would be wrong and unfair to conclude otherwise.' Macpherson, *The Stephen Lawrence Inquiry*, Cm 4262-I, p. 45.

6   Macpherson, *The Stephen Lawrence Inquiry*, Cm 4262-I, p. 29. (Emphasis added.)

7   For example, Assistant Commissioner Ian Johnston is described as making an 'abject' apology for the failures of the MPS in connection with the murder of Stephen Lawrence. Macpherson, *The Stephen Lawrence Inquiry*, Cm 4262-I, p. 218.

8   Uncorroborated testimony of one's own evil deeds was the basis of the belief in witchcraft. The most distinguished thinkers of their time had been convinced that there were witches, simply on the grounds that without coercion women did claim that they had anointed themselves with the fat of murdered babies, had flown on goats or broomsticks, had copulated with the devil at witches' Sabbaths, and eaten boiled children. The French philosopher Jean Bodin was one of those who took the fact of uncoerced confession as being proof of the truth. Yet he was one of the most 'liberal' men of his epoch. He was the French founder of anti-slavery thought. He was an early anthropologist. As a member of the Estates-General of Blois in 1576 he damaged his career by opposing the resumption of the war against the Huguenots. ['Jean Bodin' and 'Slavery', *Encyclopædia Britannica*.] In this country the last notable example of the confession-trial was the proceedings connected with the 'Popish Plot' of 1678. An Anglican priest, Titus Oates, accused the Jesuits of plotting to murder Charles II. A wave of terror swept London, and a pseudo-judicial process was used to obtain confessions of being guilty of being a Catholic and of implication in the plot. Thirty-five people were executed. Oates was hailed as the saviour of his country. But as the frenzy subsided, inconsistencies were discovered in his story. He was convicted of perjury, flogged, and imprisoned.

9   Cathcart, B., *The Case of Stephen Lawrence*, London: Penguin Viking, 1999, p. 359. (Emphasis added.)

10 Cathcart, *The Case of Stephen Lawrence*, 1999, p. 357.

11 Macpherson, *The Stephen Lawrence Inquiry*, Cm 4262-I, p. 8.

12 Macpherson, *The Stephen Lawrence Inquiry*, Cm 4262-I, p. 7.

13 Koestler, A., *Darkness at Noon*, London: Cape, 1940, p. 223 and p. 227.

14 Macpherson, *The Stephen Lawrence Inquiry*, Cm 4262-I, pp. 51-52.

15 Macpherson, *The Stephen Lawrence Inquiry*, Cm 4262-I, p. 51.

16 Cathcart, *The Case of Stephen Lawrence*, pp. 349-50. (Emphasis added.)

17 Talmon, J.L., *The Origins of Totalitarian Democracy* (1952), London: Mercury, 1961, pp. 127 and 129.

18 Macpherson, *The Stephen Lawrence Inquiry*, Cm 4262-I, p. 6.

19 Macpherson does not disclose why he thinks the Kent Police Service inquiry, because it 'concentrated on discipline', was not an inquiry that dealt with 'what happened and why'. On the face of it every inquiry that concentrates on establishing the facts of the case concentrates also on the special area of its investigation.

20 Macpherson, *The Stephen Lawrence Inquiry*, Cm 4262-I, p. 7.

21 Cathcart, *The Case of Stephen Lawrence*, 1999, p. 315.

22 Macpherson, *The Stephen Lawrence Inquiry*, Cm 4262-I, p. 8.

23 'Lawrences sue police for £500,000', *Daily Telegraph*, 29 January 2000. Included in the claim was the cost of burying Stephen in Jamaica to forestall desecration in England, the costs of visits to the grave, and compensation to Mrs Lawrence for loss of earnings due to psychiatric damage brought on by the investigation and the effects it had on her university studies. It was reported that 16 of the writs were withdrawn three weeks later. The Lawrences were offered around £180,000 by the Metropolitan Police, but they rejected the offer. Steele, J., 'Met calls for Lawrence damages to be rejected', *Daily Telegraph*, 19 February 2000.

24 Macpherson, *The Stephen Lawrence Inquiry*, Cm 4262-I, p. 31.

25 Macpherson, *The Stephen Lawrence Inquiry*, Cm 4262-I, p. 8.

Chapter 3: The Crowd in Hannibal House

1 For an account of this nature and extent of this change, see Dennis, N, 'Sociology and the spirit of sixty-eight', *British Journal of Sociology*, Vol. 40, No. 3, September 1989.

2 The language of *Race Traitor* is that 'whiteness is the principal scourge of mankind'; the key 'to solving the social problems of our age is the abolition of the white race'. Horowitz, D., *Hating Whitey and Other Progressive Causes*, Dallas: Spence, 1999. Horowitz was a student radical at Berkeley in the 1960s. He supported the Black Panthers until they killed one of his friends. He was a member of the exploratory committee that attempted to draft Colin Powell as presidential candidate in 1996. His daughter-in-law is black.

3 See, for example, Weber, M., 'Politics as a vocation', *From Max Weber: essays in sociology*, Gerth, H.H. and Mills, C. Wright, (eds.), London: Routledge and Kegan Paul, 1948, pp. 77-78.

4 Hobbes, T., *Leviathan* (1651), London: Penguin, 1985, p. 106.

5   Le Bon, G., *The Crowd* (1930), London: Transaction Publications, 1995.

6   The short form of the Kent report was presented to Parliament and is reproduced in full as an appendix to the Macpherson report. Macpherson, W., 'Report by the Police Complaints Authority on the investigation of a complaint against the Metropolitan Police Service by Mr N. and Mrs D. Lawrence', *The Stephen Lawrence Inquiry: appendices*, Cm 4262-II (Revised), London: The Stationery Office, February 1999.

7   Cathcart, B., *The Case of Stephen Lawrence*, London: Penguin Viking, 1999, p. 293.

8   Cathcart, *The Case of Stephen Lawrence*, 1999, p. 319.

9   Cathcart, *The Case of Stephen Lawrence*, 1999, pp. 339-41. (Emphasis added.)

10 Cathcart, *The Case of Stephen Lawrence*, 1999, pp. 388-90.

11 Macpherson, W., *The Stephen Lawrence Inquiry*, Cm 4262-I, London: The Stationery Office, February 1999, p. 20.

12 Richmond, A.H., *The Colour Problem: a study of race relations*, Harmondsworth: Penguin, 1955. The dedication page quotes the UN Declaration of Human Rights. 'All human beings are born free and equal in dignity and rights... They should act towards one another in a spirit of brotherhood.'

13 Macpherson, *The Stephen Lawrence Inquiry*, Cm 4262-I, p. 28.

14 Mandela, N., *Long Walk to Freedom*, London: Little, Brown, 1994, p. 234.

15 Macpherson, *The Stephen Lawrence Inquiry*, Cm 4262-I, pp. 83-84.

16 Macpherson, *The Stephen Lawrence Inquiry*, Cm 4262-I, p. 322.

17 Cathcart, *The Case of Stephen Lawrence*, 1999, pp. 323-24 and p. 355. (Emphasis added.)

18 Cathcart, *The Case of Stephen Lawrence*, 1999, p. 328.

19 Macpherson, *The Stephen Lawrence Inquiry*, Cm 4262-I, pp. 31-33.

20 Cathcart, *The Case of Stephen Lawrence*, 1999, p. 328 and pp. 359-60.

21 Home Office, *Criminal Statistics England and Wales*, London: HMSO, 1930, p. xiv; FitzGerald, M., 'What do searches contribute to tackling crime?', *Final Report on Stop and Search*, 16 December 1999, p. 8, see: 'http://www.met.police.uk/police/mps/mps/mis/stop9.htm'; and Harlow, J., 'Rolex gang foxed by rich woman's Swatch', *Sunday Times*, 26 December 1999.

22 FitzGerald, 'What do searches contribute to tackling crime?', 1999, p. 5, see: 'http://www.met.police.uk/police/mps/mps/mis/stop9.htm'.

23 FitzGerald,'What do searches contribute to tackling crime?' 1999, Appendix 1, p. 2.

24 FitzGerald, 'What do searches contribute to tackling crime?', 1999, p. 11.

25 FitzGerald, M., 'Executive summary', *Final Report on Stop and Search*, 16 December 1999, p. 4, see: 'http://www.met.police.uk/ police/mps/mps/mis/stop9.htm'.

26 Harlow, J., 'Rolex gang foxed by rich woman's Swatch', *Sunday Times*, 26 December 1999.

27 London: Home Office, 2000.

28 Singh, G., 'Open up', *Fabian Review*, Vol. 112, No. 2, summer 2000.

29 *Daily Telegraph*, 19 January 2000.

30 *Daily Telegraph*, 19 January 2000.

31 Just such an interview was conducted when Marian FitzGerald and the representatives of special interest groups were interviewed on the BBC's 'Today' radio programme, 18 January 2000.

Chapter 4: Mr and Mrs Lawrence's Treatment at the Hospital

1 Steele, J., '"Supergrasses" who testified against detectives are jailed', *Daily Telegraph*, 5 February 2000.

2 Macpherson, W., *The Stephen Lawrence Inquiry*, Cm 4262-I, London: The Stationery Office, February 1999, p. 20.

3 Macpherson, W.,*The Stephen Lawrence Inquiry: appendices*, Cm 4262-II (Revised), London: The Stationery Office, February 1999, Appendix 17.

4 Christopher, W., *Report of the Independent Commission on the Los Angeles Police Department*, Los Angeles: City of Los Angeles, 1991.

5 Macpherson, *The Stephen Lawrence Inquiry*, Cm 4262-I, p. 30.

6 FitzGerald, M., 'Executive summary', *Final Report on Stop and Search*, 16 December 1999, p. 5. (Emphasis added.) See: 'http://www.met.police.uk/police/mps/mps/mis/stop9.htm'.

7 Macpherson, *The Stephen Lawrence Inquiry*, Cm 4262-I, pp. 29-30.

8 Orwell, G., 'How the poor die' (1946), *Collected Essays*, London: Mercury Books, 1961, p. 351.

9 Macpherson, *The Stephen Lawrence Inquiry*, Cm 4262-I, pp. 78-81. (Emphasis added.)

10 Macpherson, *The Stephen Lawrence Inquiry*, Cm 4262-I, p. 81. (Emphasis added.)

11 Macpherson, *The Stephen Lawrence Inquiry*, Cm 4262-I, p. 81.

Chapter 5: The Initial Treatment of Duwayne Brooks as Evidence of Police Racism

1 'Statement of Doreen Lawrence, 8 March 1998', Macpherson, W., *The Stephen Lawrence Inquiry: appendices*, Cm 4262-II (Revised), London: The Stationery Office, February 1999. [No page numbers supplied.]

2 Macpherson, W., *The Stephen Lawrence Inquiry*, Cm 4262-I, London: The Stationery Office, February 1999, p. 63.

3 Macpherson, *The Stephen Lawrence Inquiry*, Cm 4262-I, p. 53.

4 Cathcart, B., *The Case of Stephen Lawrence*, London: Penguin Viking, 1999, pp. 14-16.

5 The statement is dated 6 April 1998. It was read at the inquiry on 15 May 1998 in the absence of Duwayne Brooks, who had been excused cross-examination on medical grounds. Our punctuation is not always that which appears in the statement, which is under-punctuated. We have inserted what seems to us standard punctuation (as distinct from our italics). The added punctuation marks simply express Mr Brooks's meaning more clearly to the reader, without altering it. The original punctuation and possible differences in nuance incorrectly introduced by us can be consulted and assessed by referring to the appendix to the Macpherson report which reproduces the statement. Macpherson, 'Statements to the inquiry of Mr Brooks', *The Stephen Lawrence Inquiry: appendices*, Cm 4262-II, [no page numbers given in the appendices]. (Emphasis added.)

6 Macpherson, *The Stephen Lawrence Inquiry*, Cm 4262-I, p.162.

7 'Statements to the Inquiry of Mr Brooks', Macpherson, *The Stephen Lawrence Inquiry: appendices*, Cm 4262-II, [no page numbers given in the appendices]. (Emphasis added.)

8 Macpherson, *The Stephen Lawrence Inquiry*, Cm 4262-I, p. 15.

9 Cathcart, *The Case of Stephen Lawrence*, 1999, p. 155.

10 Macpherson, *The Stephen Lawrence Inquiry*, Cm 4262-I, p. 16.

11 Macpherson, *The Stephen Lawrence Inquiry*, Cm 4262-I, p. 56.

12 Macpherson, *The Stephen Lawrence Inquiry*, Cm 4262-I, p. 56.

13 'His conduct at the scene was described ...' not 'At the scene his conduct was described ...'

14 Macpherson, *The Stephen Lawrence Inquiry*, Cm 4262-I, p. 19.

15 Macpherson, *The Stephen Lawrence Inquiry*, Cm 4262-I, p. 16.

16 Macpherson, *The Stephen Lawrence Inquiry*, Cm 4262-I, pp. 15-16.

17 Macpherson, *The Stephen Lawrence Inquiry*, Cm 4262-I, pp. 15-16. (Emphasis added.)

18 Macpherson, *The Stephen Lawrence Inquiry*, Cm 4262-I, pp. 15-16. (Emphasis added.)

19 Macpherson, *The Stephen Lawrence Inquiry*, Cm 4262-I, p. 306. The first identification parade took place on 7 May 1993. It involved Jamie Acourt. Duwayne Brooks failed to identify him. The second parade on 13 May 1993 involved Neil Acourt, David Norris and Gary Dobson. Duwayne Brooks picked out Neil Acourt. The third parade was held on 3 June 1993. It involved Luke Knight. Duwayne Brooks picked him out. (Pp. 154-56.) Immediately after the Luke Knight identification Duwayne Brooks travelled in a car with DS Crowley. Duwayne Brooks did not deny the main substance of the conversation. He had picked out Neil Acourt because he had been prompted on his appearance by a friend. He had picked out Luke Knight because he had the physical appearance and clothing of the person in the ID parade whom the police were keeping in custody (p. 162). Macpherson says, 'We believe DS Crowley's evidence is substantially correct' (p. 164). At the Central Criminal Court Mr Justice Curtis took into account only what Duwayne Brooks agreed he had said to DS Crowley (p. 164).

20 Macpherson, *The Stephen Lawrence Inquiry*, Cm 4262-I, p. 292.

21 Macpherson, *The Stephen Lawrence Inquiry*, Cm 4262-I, p. 292.

22 Macpherson, *The Stephen Lawrence Inquiry*, Cm 4262-I, p. 295.

23 Macpherson, *The Stephen Lawrence Inquiry*, Cm 4262-I, pp. 295-96. (Emphasis added.)

24 Macpherson, *The Stephen Lawrence Inquiry*, Cm 4262-I, p. 295. (Emphasis added.)

25 Macpherson, *The Stephen Lawrence Inquiry*, Cm 4262-I, pp. 15-16.

26 Macpherson, *The Stephen Lawrence Inquiry*, Cm 4262-I, p. 61. Emphasis added.)

27 Macpherson, *The Stephen Lawrence Inquiry*, Cm 4262-I, p. 61.

28 Macpherson, *The Stephen Lawrence Inquiry*, Cm 4262-I, p. 56.

29 Macpherson, *The Stephen Lawrence Inquiry*, Cm 4262-I, p. 56.

30 'Statements to the inquiry of Mr Brooks', Macpherson, *The Stephen Lawrence Inquiry: appendices*, Cm 4262-II, [no page numbers given in the appendices].

31 'Statement of Doreen Lawrence, 8 March 1998', Macpherson, *The Stephen Lawrence Inquiry: appendices*, Cm 4262-II, [no page numbers supplied.] (Emphasis added.)

32 Macpherson, *The Stephen Lawrence Inquiry*, Cm 4262-I, p. 16.

33 FitzGerald, M., 'Stops, searches and dissatisfaction', *Final Report on Stop and Search*, 16 December 1999, p. 4, see: 'http://www.met.police.uk/police/mps/mps/mis/stop9.htm'.

34 Macpherson, *The Stephen Lawrence Inquiry*, Cm 4262-I, p. 16. (Emphasis added.)

35 Cathcart, *The Case of Stephen Lawrence*, pp. 136-37, and p. 189.

36 'Statement of Duwayne Brooks as provided to the inquiry': dated 6 April 1998, read at the inquiry 15 May 1998. Macpherson, 'Statements to the inquiry of Mr Brooks', *The Stephen Lawrence Inquiry: appendices*, Cm 4262-II, [no page numbers given in the appendices].

37 Macpherson, *The Stephen Lawrence Inquiry*, Cm 4262-I, p. 19. (Emphasis added.)

38 Macpherson, *The Stephen Lawrence Inquiry*, Cm 4262-I, p. 19. (Emphasis added.)

39 Macpherson, *The Stephen Lawrence Inquiry*, Cm 4262-I, p. 30.

Chapter 6: The treatment of Mr and Mrs Lawrence in Family Liaison as Evidence of Police Racism

1 'Mr. E. Lawson QC appearing on behalf of the inquiry', Macpherson, W., *The Stephen Lawrence Inquiry: appendices*, Cm 4262-II (Revised), London: The Stationery Office, February 1999, p. 59.

2 Cathcart, B., *The Case of Stephen Lawrence*, London: Penguin Viking, 1999, pp. 109-10.

3 Cathcart, *The Case of Stephen Lawrence*, 1999, p. 111.

4 Macpherson, W., *The Stephen Lawrence Inquiry*, Cm 4262-I, London: The Stationery Office, February 1999, p. 301.

5 Macpherson, *The Stephen Lawrence Inquiry*, Cm 4262-I, p. 303.

6 Macpherson, *The Stephen Lawrence Inquiry*, Cm 4262-I, p. 183. (Emphasis added.)

7 Macpherson, *The Stephen Lawrence Inquiry*, Cm 4262-I, p. 182. (Emphasis added.)

8 Macpherson, *The Stephen Lawrence Inquiry*, Cm 4262-I, p.185.

9 Cathcart, *The Case of Stephen Lawrence*, 1999, p. 328.

10 Cathcart, *The Case of Stephen Lawrence*, 1999, p. 328.

11 'Statement of Doreen Lawrence, 8 March 1998', Macpherson, *The Stephen Lawrence Inquiry: appendices*, Cm 4262-II. [No page numbers supplied.]

12 'Mr. E. Lawson QC appearing on behalf of the inquiry', Macpherson, *The Stephen Lawrence Inquiry: appendices*, Cm 4262-II, pp. 60-61.

13 Cathcart, *The Case of Stephen Lawrence*, 1999, p. 329.

14 Cathcart, *The Case of Stephen Lawrence*, 1999, pp. 329-30.

15 Kafka, F., *The Trial* (1925), Harmondsworth: Penguin, 1953.

16 Macpherson, *The Stephen Lawrence Inquiry*, Cm 4262-I, p. 295.

17 Macpherson, *The Stephen Lawrence Inquiry*, Cm 4262-I, p. 295. (Emphasis added.)

18 Macpherson, *The Stephen Lawrence Inquiry*, Cm 4262-I, p. 182 and p. 184.

19 Macpherson, *The Stephen Lawrence Inquiry*, Cm 4262-I, p. 185.

20 Macpherson, *The Stephen Lawrence Inquiry*, Cm 4262-I, p.183. (Emphasis added.)

21 Macpherson, *The Stephen Lawrence Inquiry*, Cm 4262-I, p. 302. (Emphasis added.)

22 Macpherson, *The Stephen Lawrence Inquiry*, Cm 4262-I, p. 340.

23 'Statement of Doreen Lawrence, 8 March 1998', Macpherson, *The Stephen Lawrence Inquiry: appendices*, Cm 4262-II (Revised). [No page numbers supplied.]

24 Cathcart, *The Case of Stephen Lawrence*, 1999, pp. 125-26.

25 Macpherson, *The Stephen Lawrence Inquiry*, Cm 4262-I, pp 295-96.

26 'Statement of Doreen Lawrence, 8 March 1998', Macpherson, *The Stephen Lawrence Inquiry: appendices*, Cm 4262-II (Revised). [No page numbers supplied.]

27 Mrs Lawrence had suggested to DCS Ilsley that the cells of the suspects should be bugged. DCS Ilsley had replied, 'We don't do things this way. No way!' 'I could remember that he was very angry because he assumed that I had been told to ask the question.' Macpherson, *The Stephen Lawrence Inquiry*, Cm 4262-I, p. 11 and again on p. 12. Mrs Lawrence had worked at a school first as a lunchtime supervisor, and then as a special needs helper. The teachers at the school had encouraged her to take an Access course (she had no A-levels) to qualify for university, and one of them had obtained a prospectus for her and advised her on which courses to attend. 'Statement of Doreen Lawrence, 8 March 1998', Macpherson, *The Stephen Lawrence Inquiry: appendices*, Cm 4262-II (Revised). [No page numbers supplied.]

28 The Rt. Hon. The Lord Scarman, OBE, *Report to the Rt. Hon. William Whitelaw CH, MC, MP, Secretary of State for the Home Department, on the Brixton Disorders of 10-12 April 1981*, Cmnd 8427, London: HMSO, November 1981, p. 62.

29 Cathcart, *The Case of Stephen Lawrence*, 1999, pp. 355-56.

30 Macpherson, *The Stephen Lawrence Inquiry*, Cm 4262-I, p. 116.

31 Macpherson, *The Stephen Lawrence Inquiry*, Cm 4262-I, pp. 116-17.

32 Macpherson, *The Stephen Lawrence Inquiry*, Cm 4262-I, p. 116.

33 Macpherson, *The Stephen Lawrence Inquiry*, Cm 4262-I, p. 117.

34 Macpherson, *The Stephen Lawrence Inquiry*, Cm 4262-I, p. 117. (Emphasis added.)

35 Macpherson, *The Stephen Lawrence Inquiry*, Cm 4262-I, p. 117. (Emphasis added.)

36 'Mr. E. Lawson QC appearing on behalf of the inquiry', Macpherson, *The Stephen Lawrence Inquiry: appendices*, Cm 4262-II (Revised), p. 61.

37 Cathcart, *The Case of Stephen Lawrence*, 1999, pp.107-08.

38 'Statement of Doreen Lawrence, 8 March 1998', Macpherson, *The Stephen Lawrence Inquiry: appendices*, Cm 4262-II (Revised). [No page numbers supplied.]

39 Macpherson, *The Stephen Lawrence Inquiry*, Cm 4262-I, p. 301.

40 Macpherson, *The Stephen Lawrence Inquiry*, Cm 4262-I, p. 303.

41 Cathcart, *The Case of Stephen Lawrence*, 1999, pp.113-14.

42 Macpherson, *The Stephen Lawrence Inquiry*, Cm 4262-I, p. 302.

43 Macpherson, *The Stephen Lawrence Inquiry*, Cm 4262-I, p. 303.

44 Macpherson, *The Stephen Lawrence Inquiry*, Cm 4262-I, p. 305. (Emphasis added.)

45 Macpherson, *The Stephen Lawrence Inquiry*, Cm 4262-I, p. 305. (Emphasis added.)

46 Macpherson, *The Stephen Lawrence Inquiry*, Cm 4262-I, p. 306. (Emphasis added.)

47 Cathcart, *The Case of Stephen Lawrence*, 1999, pp.105-07.

48 *May 1991*: the murder of Orvill Blair. 'There was some doubt whether this was in fact a racist crime, but it was so regarded by the community.' He was killed by a man called Snell, who was the victim of Blair's burglary. *February 1991*: the murder of Rolan Adams, a black 15 year old, by an unknown white youth. *July 1992*: the murder by stabbing of Rohit Duggal, a 16-year-old Asian. It was suggested that there was some connection between Thompson, the murderer, and the suspects in the Stephen Lawrence murder. 'Mr. E. Lawson QC appearing on behalf of the inquiry', Macpherson, *The Stephen Lawrence Inquiry: appendices*, Cm 4262-II, pp. 57-58. Macpherson, *The Stephen Lawrence Inquiry*, Cm 4262-I, p. 38.

49 'Statement of Doreen Lawrence, 8 March 1998', Macpherson, *The Stephen Lawrence Inquiry: appendices*, Cm 4262-II (Revised). [No page numbers supplied.]

50 Cathcart, *The Case of Stephen Lawrence*, 1999, p. 123.

51 Macpherson, *The Stephen Lawrence Inquiry*, Cm 4262-I, p.181.

52 Cathcart, *The Case of Stephen Lawrence*, 1999, pp.107-09.

53 Cathcart, *The Case of Stephen Lawrence*, 1999, p.109.

54 Macpherson, *The Stephen Lawrence Inquiry*, Cm 4262-I, p. 181.

55 'Statement of Doreen Lawrence, 8 March 1998', Macpherson, *The Stephen Lawrence Inquiry: appendices*, Cm 4262-II (Revised). [No page numbers supplied.]

56 Joseph Shepherd witnessed the murder. He knew the Lawrences, and it was he who had gone straight to the Lawrence's home to let them know what had happened. 'Weeden' is Detective Superintendent Brian Weeden, second Senior Investigation Officer in the first of the two MPS investigations into the murder. Statement of Doreen Lawrence, 8 March 1998', read on 11 June 1998. Macpherson, *The Stephen Lawrence Inquiry: appendices*, Cm 4262-II (Revised. [No page numbers supplied.] (Emphasis added.)

57 'Statement of Doreen Lawrence, 8 March 1998', Macpherson, *The Stephen Lawrence Inquiry: appendices*, Cm 4262-II (Revised). [No page numbers supplied.]

58 'Statement of Doreen Lawrence, 8 March 1998', read on 11 June 1998. Macpherson, *The Stephen Lawrence Inquiry: appendices*, Cm 4262-II (Revised). [No page numbers supplied.]

59 'Statement of Doreen Lawrence, 8 March 1998', Macpherson, *The Stephen Lawrence Inquiry: appendices*, Cm 4262-II (Revised). [No page numbers supplied.]

60 'Statement of Doreen Lawrence, 8 March 1998', Macpherson, *The Stephen Lawrence Inquiry: appendices*, Cm 4262-II (Revised). [No page numbers supplied.]

61 'Statement of Doreen Lawrence, 8 March 1998', Macpherson, *The Stephen Lawrence Inquiry: appendices*, Cm 4262-II (Revised). [No page numbers supplied.]

62 Cathcart, *The Case of Stephen Lawrence*, 1999, p. 225.

63 'Statement of Doreen Lawrence, 8 March 1998', Macpherson, *The Stephen Lawrence Inquiry: appendices*, Cm 4262-II (Revised). [No page numbers supplied.]

64 Macpherson, *The Stephen Lawrence Inquiry*, Cm 4262-I, p. 185.

65 Macpherson, *The Stephen Lawrence Inquiry*, Cm 4262-I, p. 118. (Emphasis added.)

66 Macpherson, *The Stephen Lawrence Inquiry*, Cm 4262-I, p. 185.

67 Macpherson, *The Stephen Lawrence Inquiry*, Cm 4262-I, p. 23 and p. 28.

68 'Statement of Doreen Lawrence, 8 March 1998', Macpherson, *The Stephen Lawrence Inquiry: appendices*, Cm 4262-II (Revised). [No page numbers supplied.]

Chapter 7: The Failure of Many Officers to Recognise Stephen Lawrence's Murder as a *Purely* Racially Motivated Crime as Evidence of Police Racism

1   Macpherson, W., *The Stephen Lawrence Inquiry*, Cm 4262-I, London: The Stationery Office, February 1999, pp. 29-30.

2   Macpherson, *The Stephen Lawrence Inquiry*, Cm 4262-I, p. 322. (Emphasis added.)

3   Cathcart, B., *The Case of Stephen Lawrence*, London: Penguin Viking, 1999, pp. 212-13.

4   Cathcart, *The Case of Stephen Lawrence*, 1999, p. 234. (Emphasis added.)

5   'Transcript of compilation video IC/3', Macpherson, *The Stephen Lawrence Inquiry: appendices*, Cm 4262-II (Revised), Sequence 49.

6   'Transcript of compilation video IC/3', Macpherson, *The Stephen Lawrence Inquiry: appendices*, Cm 4262-II (Revised), Sequence 50.

7   Cathcart, *The Case of Stephen Lawrence*, 1999, p. 27.

8   On the crime figures from the middle of the nineteenth century until the 1990s see Dennis, N., *Rising Crime and the Dismembered Family*, London: IEA Health and Welfare Unit, 1993, pp. 1-3.

9   'Attacked for being disabled', *Shields Gazette*, 1 February 2000.

10 Clough, S., 'Boys who killed just for fun are sentenced', *Daily Telegraph*, 5 November 1999.

11 These points are the subject of Dennis, N., *The Invention of Permanent Poverty*, London: IEA Health and Welfare Unit, 1997.

12 Orwell discusses mainly Hornung's *Raffles, A Thief in the Night* and *Mr Justice Raffles*, and ('now for a header into the cesspool') James Hadley Chase's *No Orchids for Miss Blandish* and *He Won't Need it Now*.

13 Orwell, G, 'Raffles and Miss Blandish', in Orwell, G., *Collected Essays*, London: Mercury, 1961, p. 255, p. 258 and p. 263. What would Orwell have made of the content of any day's programmes on the BBC 56 years later? What would he have made of the video games that are replacing this too-bland fare in the lives of children, games that make millionaires of young men who design the software that enables the lonely player to feel even more directly that *he* is stealing cars, *he* is killing anybody who gets in the way, and *he* carrying out missions for inner-city criminal gangs?

14 Macpherson, *The Stephen Lawrence Inquiry*, Cm 4262-I, p.157. (Emphasis added.)

15 'Mr E. Lawson QC appearing on behalf of the inquiry', Macpherson, *The Stephen Lawrence Inquiry: appendices*, Cm 4262-II (Revised), pp. 56-57.(Emphasis added.)

16 'Mr E. Lawson QC appearing on behalf of the inquiry', Macpherson, *The Stephen Lawrence Inquiry: appendices*, Cm 4262-II (Revised), p. 47.

17 'Mr E. Lawson QC appearing on behalf of the inquiry', Macpherson, *The Stephen Lawrence Inquiry: appendices*, Cm 4262-II (Revised), p. 47.

18 Macpherson, *The Stephen Lawrence Inquiry*, Cm 4262-I, p. 187. (Emphasis added.)

19 Macpherson, *The Stephen Lawrence Inquiry*, Cm 4262-I, p. 187. (Emphasis added.)

20 Cathcart, *The Case of Stephen Lawrence*, 1999, pp. 347-48.

21 Cathcart, *The Case of Stephen Lawrence*, 1999, p. 350.

22 Cathcart, *The Case of Stephen Lawrence*, 1999, p. 350.

23 Cathcart, *The Case of Stephen Lawrence*, 1999, p. 351. (Emphasis added.)

24 Cathcart, *The Case of Stephen Lawrence*, 1999, pp. 351-52. (Emphasis added.) What is the difference between racial and racist? If there is none, why the change?

25 Cathcart, *The Case of Stephen Lawrence*, 1999, p. 352.

26 Cathcart, *The Case of Stephen Lawrence*, 1999, p. 352.

27 Cathcart, *The Case of Stephen Lawrence*, 1999, p. 412.

28 Macpherson, *The Stephen Lawrence Inquiry*, Cm 4262-I, p. 181. (Emphasis added.)

29 Cathcart, *The Case of Stephen Lawrence*, 1999, p. 234. (Emphasis added.)

30 'Transcript of compilation video IC/3', Macpherson, *The Stephen Lawrence Inquiry: appendices*, Cm 4262-II (Revised), Sequence 7. The versions given in Carthcart and Macpherson differ. The only significant difference is that in the Macpherson transcript Luke Knight, not Neil Acourt, joins in to say, 'At least they're white'.

31 Macpherson, *The Stephen Lawrence Inquiry*, Cm 4262-I, pp. 147-48. Possibly the use of the word 'reflects' saves Macpherson from the accusation of being quite clear for once.

32 Macpherson, *The Stephen Lawrence Inquiry*, Cm 4262-I, pp. 147-48. (Emphasis added.) The ambiguity is introduced here by including the word 'perception'. I can be blamed for allowing myself to be perceived as holding certain opinions, without 'indeed' holding those opinions.

33 Macpherson, *The Stephen Lawrence Inquiry*, Cm 4262-I, p. 181.

34 Cathcart, *The Case of Stephen Lawrence*, 1999, p. 412.

35 Macpherson, *The Stephen Lawrence Inquiry*, Cm 4262-I, p. 183.

36 Cathcart, *The Case of Stephen Lawrence*, 1999, p. 312.

Chapter 8: The Lack of Police Urgency and Poor Police Motivation in Some Areas of the Investigation as Evidence of Police Racism

1   Clough, S., 'Witness blunder created a madman', *Daily Telegraph*, 14 March 2000.

2   Steele, J., 'Report's mistakes puts ten informants at risk', *Daily Telegraph*, 27 February 1999.

3   Macpherson, W., *The Stephen Lawrence Inquiry*, Cm 4262-I, London: The Stationery Office, February 1999, p. 267.

4   Cathcart, B., *The Case of Stephen Lawrence*, London: Penguin Viking, 1999, p. 317. (Emphasis added.)

5   Cathcart, *The Case of Stephen Lawrence*, 1999, p. 318. (Emphasis added.)

6   Macpherson, *The Stephen Lawrence Inquiry*, Cm 4262-I, p. 28. (Emphasis added.)

7   Macpherson, *The Stephen Lawrence Inquiry*, Cm 4262-I, p. 28.

8   It was and is, of course, an issue for the individual officers and their families. The officers' weaknesses were publicly reviled and their careers blighted or ended. Who would want any particular job he did exposed to similar detailed scrutiny and high standards of bureaucratic rectitude? 'Working to rule' is, after all, a method of nearly going on strike. Who does not know that, in matters of what the facts were, and what good judgement would have decided, hindsight delivers superiority on the cheap?

9   *Report by the Police Complaints Authority on the Investigation of a Complaint against the Metropolitan Police Authority by Mr N. and Mrs D. Lawrence*, Cm 3822, London: The Stationery Office, December 1997. This, the Kent Police Service report, appears as appendix 2 in the appendices to the Macpherson report.

10 Macpherson, *The Stephen Lawrence Inquiry*, Cm 4262-I, p. 89.

11 Macpherson, *The Stephen Lawrence Inquiry*, Cm 4262-I, p. 95.

12 Macpherson, *The Stephen Lawrence Inquiry*, Cm 4262-I, p. 89.

13 Macpherson, *The Stephen Lawrence Inquiry*, Cm 4262-I, p. 95. (Emphasis added.)

14 Macpherson, *The Stephen Lawrence Inquiry*, Cm 4262-I, p. 94.

15 Macpherson, *The Stephen Lawrence Inquiry*, Cm 4262-I, p. 96.

16 Macpherson, *The Stephen Lawrence Inquiry*, Cm 4262-I, p. 95.

17 Macpherson, *The Stephen Lawrence Inquiry*, Cm 4262-I, p. 89.

18 Macpherson, *The Stephen Lawrence Inquiry*, Cm 4262-I, p. 318.

19 Macpherson, *The Stephen Lawrence Inquiry*, Cm 4262-I, p. 89 and p. 318.

20 Macpherson, *The Stephen Lawrence Inquiry*, Cm 4262-I, p. 318.

21 Macpherson, *The Stephen Lawrence Inquiry*, Cm 4262-I, p. 90.

22 Cathcart, *The Case of Stephen Lawrence*, 1999, p. 357. (Emphasis added.)

23 Cathcart, *The Case of Stephen Lawrence*, 1999, p. 357.

24 Macpherson, *The Stephen Lawrence Inquiry*, Cm 4262-I, p. 29. (Emphasis added.)

Chapter 9: The Everyday and the Sociological Use of the Word 'Institutional'

1 MacIver, R.M., *Society: a textbook of sociology*, New York: Rinehart, p. 15.

2 For example, the study at the Western Electric factory at Hawthorne, Illinois. Roethlisberger, F.S., and Dickson, W.J., *Management and the Worker*, Cambridge, Mass: Harvard University Press, 1939. Mayo, E., *The Social Problems of an Industrial Civilization*, Cambridge, Mass: Harvard University Press, 1945.

3 Macpherson, W., *The Stephen Lawrence Inquiry*, Cm 4262-I, London: The Stationery Office, February 1999, p. 26. (Emphasis added.)

4 Macpherson, *The Stephen Lawrence Inquiry*, Cm 4262-I, p. 26. (Emphasis added.)

5 Carmichael, S. and Hamilton, C.V., *Black Power: the politics of liberation in America*, Harmondsworth: Penguin, 1967, pp. 20-21. (Emphasis added.)

6 Lenin, V.I., 'The State and Revolution' (1917), in *Collected Works II*, Moscow, Foreign Languages Publishing House, 1945, pp. 154-55.

7 'Obituary: Stokely Carmichael (later Kwame Ture)', the *Economist*, 21 November 1998.

8 The Rt. Hon. The Lord Scarman, OBE, *Report to the Rt. Hon. William Whitelaw CH, MC, MP, Secretary of State for the Home Department, on the Brixton Disorders of 10-12 April 1981*, Cmnd 8427, London: HMSO, November 1981, p. 11, p. 62, and p. 64.

9 *The Brixton Disorders 10-12 April 1981*, Cmnd 8427, 1981, p. 135. (Emphasis added.)

10 *The Brixton Disorders 10-12 April 1981*, Cmnd 8427, 1981, p. 11, p. 62, and p. 64. (Emphasis added.)

11 *The Brixton Disorders 10-12 April 1981*, Cmnd 8427, 1981, p. 11.

Chapter 10: 'Institutional' As Institutional Failure

1   Macpherson, W., *The Stephen Lawrence Inquiry*, Cm 4262-I, London: The Stationery Office, February 1999, p. 27. (Emphasis in the original.)

2   Macpherson, *The Stephen Lawrence Inquiry*, Cm 4262-I, p. 27. (Emphasis added.)

3   Merton, R.K., 'The unintended consequences of purposive social action', *American Sociological Review*, Vol. 1, No. 1, 1936. He himself was more interested in those unintended consequences that turned out to be of service to society.

4   Macpherson, *The Stephen Lawrence Inquiry*, Cm 4262-I, p. 24. (Emphasis added.) Bowling, B., *Violent Racism: victimization, policing and social context*, London: Oxford University Press, 1998.

5   Macpherson, *The Stephen Lawrence Inquiry*, Cm 4262-I, p. 25. (Emphasis added.)

Chapter 11: 'Institutional' as Counter-Institutional Subculture

1   Macpherson, W., *The Stephen Lawrence Inquiry*, Cm 4262-I, London: The Stationery Office, February 1999, p. 24. It will be seen later that Macpherson strongly recommends that black and white people should be treated differently by police officers. Black people should be treated differently from but not worse than white people.

2   Macpherson, *The Stephen Lawrence Inquiry*, Cm 4262-I, p. 35. (Emphasis added.)

3   Macpherson, *The Stephen Lawrence Inquiry*, Cm 4262-I, p. 24.

4   Macpherson, *The Stephen Lawrence Inquiry*, Cm 4262-I, p. 24. (Emphasis added.)

Chapter 12: 'Institutional' As That Which Is Unidentifiable From Any Evidence

1   Orwell, G., *Nineteen Eighty-Four* (1949), London: Twentieth Century Classics, 1974, Appendix p. 84, and p. 216.

2   The Rt. Hon. The Lord Scarman, OBE, *Report to the Rt. Hon. William Whitelaw CH, MC, MP, Secretary of State for the Home Department, on the Brixton Disorders of 10-12 April 1981*, Cmnd 8427, London: HMSO, November 1981, p. 110.

3   Macpherson, W., *The Stephen Lawrence Inquiry*, Cm 4262-I, London: The Stationery Office, February 1999, p. 22.

4   Macpherson, *The Stephen Lawrence Inquiry*, Cm 4262-I, pp. 32-33.

5   'Statement of Doreen Lawrence, 8 March 1998', Macpherson, W., *The Stephen Lawrence Inquiry: appendices*, Cm 4262-II (Revised), London: The Stationery Office, February 1999. Appendix 5. Day 2 of Part I of the inquiry, 24 March 1998. [No page numbers supplied.]

6 Oakley, R., 'Institutional Racism and Police Service Delivery', Submission to the Macpherson Inquiry, 1998.

7 Macpherson, *The Stephen Lawrence Inquiry*, Cm 4262-I, p. 26. Dr Oakley's *Tackling Racist and Xenophobic Attitudes in Europe: case studies*, Council of Europe, 1997, is listed among 'publications seen by the inquiry'.

8 Oakley, 'Institutional Racism and Police Service Delivery', Submission to the Macpherson Inquiry, 1998. (Emphasis added.)

9 Macpherson, *The Stephen Lawrence Inquiry*, Cm 4262-I, p. 22. (Emphasis added.)

10 'Statement of Doreen Lawrence, 8 March 1998', Macpherson, *The Stephen Lawrence Inquiry: appendices*, Cm 4262-II (Revised). [No page numbers supplied.] (Emphasis added.)

11 Macpherson, *The Stephen Lawrence Inquiry*, Cm 4262-I, p. 27. (Emphasis added.)

12 Macpherson, *The Stephen Lawrence Inquiry*, Cm 4262-I, p. 20.

13 Macpherson, *The Stephen Lawrence Inquiry*, Cm 4262-I, p. 26. (Emphasis added.)

14 Macpherson, *The Stephen Lawrence Inquiry*, Cm 4262-I, p. 24.

15 Macpherson, *The Stephen Lawrence Inquiry*, Cm 4262-I, p. 20.

16 Macpherson, *The Stephen Lawrence Inquiry*, Cm 4262-I, p. 20.

17 Cathcart, B., *The Case of Stephen Lawrence*, London: Penguin Viking, 1999, pp. 107-08.

18 Steele, J., 'Police "put a block on promotion for blacks and Asians"', *Daily Telegraph*, 30 November 1999. In the year 1998-99 the number of black police associations rose from five to 22.

19 'Statement of Doreen Lawrence, 8 March 1998', Macpherson, *The Stephen Lawrence Inquiry: appendices*, Cm 4262-II (Revised). [No page numbers supplied.] (Emphasis added.)

20 Macpherson, *The Stephen Lawrence Inquiry*, Cm 4262-I, p. 20. (Emphasis added.)

21 'Statement of Doreen Lawrence, 8 March 1998', Macpherson, *The Stephen Lawrence Inquiry: appendices*, Cm 4262-II (Revised). [No page numbers supplied.] (Emphasis added.)

22 Macpherson, *The Stephen Lawrence Inquiry*, Cm 4262-I, p. 28.

23 Macpherson, *The Stephen Lawrence Inquiry*, Cm 4262-I, p. 28.

24 'Racism tolerated "because it comes from my mates"', *Daily Telegraph*, 30 November 1999.

25 'Recommendations. Definition of racist incident 12', Macpherson, *The Stephen Lawrence Inquiry*, Cm 4262-I, p. 328. (Emphasis added.)

26 'We recommend ... that the term "racist incident" must be understood to include crimes and non-crimes. Both must be reported, recorded and investigated with equal commitment.' 'Recommendations. Definition of racist incident 13', Macpherson, *The Stephen Lawrence Inquiry*, Cm 4262-I, p. 329. (Emphasis added.)

27 The recommendation is that the law should 'allow prosecution' of offences involving racist language where the use of such language 'can be proven to have taken place'. This strikes the layman as a strange formulation. 'Proof' is normally established as the result of being prosecuted. 'Proof' is not normally required before someone can be prosecuted. But a High Court judge wrote the recommendation, so it must be all right. Presumably there are two prosecutions, one for using racist language. If that is proven, then a prosecution for 'an offence involving racist language' can take place. In any case, the recommendation is that someone can be prosecuted for using racist language in his or her own home, or in any other public or private place. 'Recommendations. Prosecution of racist crimes 39', Macpherson, *The Stephen Lawrence Inquiry*, Cm 4262-I, p. 331. (Emphasis added.)

28 Macpherson, *The Stephen Lawrence Inquiry*, Cm 4262-I, p. 40.

29 Macpherson, *The Stephen Lawrence Inquiry*, Cm 4262-I, p. 41.

30 Dennis, N. and Mallon, R., 'Confident policing in Hartlepool' and 'Crime and culture in Hartlepool', in Dennis, N. (ed.), *Zero Tolerance: Policing a Free Society*, London: IEA Health and Welfare Unit, 1997.

Chapter 13: Macpherson's Anthropology

1 As in the case of all social phenomena, perverted extremes can emerge. In the twentieth century technical developments made it possible for the first time for 'totalitarianism' to be put into practice. The Nazis called it their policy of *Gleichschaltung* —'bringing everyone into line'. The Soviet communists called it the production of 'the new man'. People who were neither persuaded by education or propaganda, nor intimidated by terror into falling into line or becoming new men were simply imprisoned or killed.

2 Wakefield, D., *Revolt in the South*, London: Evergreen, p. 123.Wakefield was a white journalist with *The Nation* reporting on his trips to the South in 1955-60. He was highly sympathetic to the new spirit of protest and action represented by the younger blacks around Martin Luther King and the Southern Christian Leadership Conference. (Emphasis added.)

3 'Statement of Doreen Lawrence, 8 March 1998', Macpherson, W., *The Stephen Lawrence Inquiry: appendices*, Cm 4262-II (Revised), London: The Stationery Office, February 1999. [No page numbers supplied.]

4 Colour-consciousness can benefit minorities of colour, ethnicity and culture, at the very least some of them, in the short run, and superficially. This is the case with 'positive discrimination'. Marx even

argued that what would now be called racism benefited the people of India in the nineteenth century. British rule benefited the indigenous majority, he wrote, even when Britain was 'actuated by the vilest interests, and stupid in her manner of enforcing them'. For, in objective fact, Marx claimed, it brought about a social revolution for the better. This is on the principle, crudely, that you cannot make an omelette without breaking eggs, or as Marx more grandly puts it, *Sollte diese Qual uns quälen / Da sie unsre Lust vermehrt, / Hat nicht Myriaden Seelen / Timur's Herrschaft aufgezehrt?* Should this torture then torment us/ Since it brings us greater pleasure/Were not through the rule of Timur/ Souls devoured without measure? (Goethe, 'Westöstliche Diwan. An Suleika'.) Marx, K., 'The British rule in India', in Marx K. and Engels, F., *Selected Works I*, Moscow: Foreign Languages Publishing House, 1958, p. 351.

5   By the end of the Middle Ages slavery no longer existed in England. Cartwright's ruling of 1569 made it definitely illegal—in his celebrated formulation, 'England has too pure an air for slaves to breathe'. Two centuries later Lord Chief Justice Mansfield ruled that 'no one could be a slave on English soil' (1772). A great popular agitation in the next generation resulted in the abolition of the slave trade in all British possessions in 1806. Slavery was ended in the British Empire when 776,000 slaves were freed on 31 July 1834. We see in the year 2000 lines being quoted and praised as applying currently to England that 'the way you touch my hair/The way you think, the way you stare/It's right there in your history/Just like slavery for me' (Andrea Cork). We can only wonder if the author and her distinguished and influential admirers realise just how far back, in England and the British Empire, the black experience of slavery lies in the past.

6   *Thirty Years of Lynchings 1889-1918*, New York: NAACP, 1919. Nordholt, J.W.S., *The People that Walk in Darkness: a history of the Negro people in America*, New York: Ballantine, 1960, pp. 243-53.

7   Macpherson, W., *The Stephen Lawrence Inquiry*, Cm 4262-I, London: The Stationery Office, February 1999, p. 12.

8   Macpherson, *The Stephen Lawrence Inquiry*, Cm 4262-I, p. 23.

9   Macpherson, *The Stephen Lawrence Inquiry*, Cm 4262-I, p. 23.

10 Holdaway, S., *Recruiting a Multi-Racial Police Force*, London: HMSO, 1991. Holdaway, S., *Inside the British Police*, Oxford: Blackwell, 1993. Holdaway, S., *The Racialisation of British Policing*, London: Macmillan, 1996. Holdaway, S. and Barron A., *Resigners? the Experience of Black and Asian Police Officers*, London: Macmillan, 1997.

11 Holdaway, S, 'Statement to the inquiry', 12 June 1998. Macpherson, *The Stephen Lawrence Inquiry*, Cm 4262-I, p. 28.

12 Macpherson, *The Stephen Lawrence Inquiry*, Cm 4262-I, p. 23.

13 Macpherson, *The Stephen Lawrence Inquiry*, Cm 4262-I, p. 28.

14 Macpherson, *The Stephen Lawrence Inquiry*, Cm 4262-I, p. 28 and p. 185. (Emphasis added.)

15 Tizard, B. and Phoenix, A., *Black, White or Mixed Race? Race and Parentage in the Lives of Young People of Mixed Parentage*, London: Routledge, 1993, p. 33.

16 Macpherson, *The Stephen Lawrence Inquiry*, Cm 4262-I, p. 22.

17 *Policing for a Multi-Ethnic Society: principles, practices and partnership*, Rotterdam Conference, 1996, p. 10. (Emphasis added.) Macpherson, *The Stephen Lawrence Inquiry*, Cm 4262-I, p. 23.

18 Without diminishing for one moment the necessity of applying the principles of politeness rigorously to minorities where it has been neglected, their application, within the constraints of the police officer keeping control of the situation, would be welcomed by many members of the majority community who have also been spoken to with unnecessary roughness by a police officer. The gap between the range of politeness shown by police officers to, say, old ladies found inadvertently driving down a new bus lane and the range of politeness shown to people in a colour, ethnic or cultural minority can be easily exaggerated. (Macpherson sometimes reads as though the norm for a police officer's politeness is how he or she behaves in the presence of a High Court judge or a bishop, and that any deviation from that norm occurs only in the treatment of people from minority groups. Many police officers are as polite as that—in all modern circumstances a surprisingly large number on a surprisingly wide range of occasions. Some are not.)

19 Buchan, J., *The Thirty-Nine Steps* (1915), Bath: Parragon, 1999, p. 144.

20 Macpherson, *The Stephen Lawrence Inquiry*, Cm 4262-I, p. 22.

Chapter 14: The Political Uses of Disruptive and Separatist Anti-Racism

1 Hayek, F.A., *The Intellectuals and Socialism* (1949), London: IEA Health and Welfare Unit, 1998.

2 Marx, K. and Engels, F., 'The Eighteenth Brumaire of Louis Bonaparte', in Marx K. and Engels, F., *Selected Works I*, Moscow: Foreign Languages Publishing House, 1958, p. 259. (Emphasis added.) In the passage quoted Marx is referring specifically to the draft French Constitution of 1848.

3 Macpherson, W., *The Stephen Lawrence Inquiry*, Cm 4262-I, London: The Stationery Office, February 1999, p. 35. (Emphasis added.)

4 Marx, K., 'The Civil War in France' (1870), in Marx and Engels, *Selected Works I*, 1958, p. 485. By contrast, a people reared under the 'new, free social conditions' of communism is able to throw the whole lumber of the state on the scrap heap'. *Ibid.*

5   Marx, K. and Engels, F., 'Manifesto of the Communist Party' (1848), in Marx and Engels, *Selected Works I*, 1958, p. 44.

6   Marx and Engels, 'The Eighteenth Brumaire of Louis Bonaparte' (1852), in Marx and Engels, *Selected Works I*, 1958, p. 295.

7   '*Gens sans feu et sans avue*', people without hearth or home. Marx and Engels, 'The Class Struggles in France 1848-1850' (1850), in Marx and Engels, *Selected Works I*, 1958, p. 295.

8   Macpherson, *The Stephen Lawrence Inquiry*, Cm 4262-I, 1999, p. 35.

9   Pierre-Joseph Proudhon.

10 Wolfe, T., *Radical Chic and Mau-Mauing the Flak Catchers*, London: Cardinal, 1989.

11 Marcuse, H., *One Dimensional Man: studies in the ideology of advanced industrial society*, Boston: Beacon Press, 1964, pp. 256-57.

12 See, for example, Lukács, G., *History and Class Consciousness: studies in Marxist dialectics* (1923), London: Merlin, 1971.

13 Horkheimer, M. and Adorno, T., *Dialectic of Enlightenment*, London: Allen Lane, 1947, pp. xii, 4.

14 The pinnacle they had reached by February 2000 was shown in an interview on BBC Newsnight in connection with the repeal of the law that prohibited the promotion of homosexuality in schools by local authorities, including the prohibition of the promotion of homosexual sexual practices. (No law prohibited any other organisation or private individual from promoting homosexuality.) A London headteacher was the main interviewee. Government guidelines were to be issued subsequent to the repeal of the prohibition, advising her to promote the family of life-long monogamy as the preferred context for childrearing. She said she would not follow them. Every possible arrangement was now the household context of her children. Any of them could be good, any of them could be bad for the child. The 'moral' basis of her stand was that every child was entitled to feel that its domestic arrangements were as good as any other child's, whether they are those of a never-married teenage mother living without a man, their mother and her current boy-friend, their divorced mother or father, a male or female homosexual pair, local authority care, or their married biological parents. It would be unfair to suggest that this blandly smiling headteacher with her air of moral rectitude played any significant role in creating this view. But the example is apposite, and comes immediately to hand.

15 Popper, K., *The Open Society and its Enemies* (1945), London: Routledge and Kegan Paul, 1966.

16 Stark, F. (Hrg.), *Revolution oder Reform? Herbert Marcuse und Karl Popper: eine Konfrontation*, München: Kösel, 1976.

17 'It's in the way you patronise/The way that you avert your eyes/ ... It's in the way you touch my hair/ ... It's when you say 'No offence to you'/ ... It's in the invasion of my space ...' etc. All of these things could be the actions of a racist, but there is nothing in the actions themselves that is peculiar to racism, and as evidence of racism the criterion used to distinguish one from the other would have to be stipulated. Racism is 'in your paper policy/Designed by you, for you, not me', [Racism by Andrea Cork, quoted in Green, D.G. (ed.), *Institutional Racism and the Police: Fact or Fiction?*, London: ISCS, 2000, pp. 8-9). It would be almost impossible to discover any policy on paper of any public body in this country that requires black people to be treated less favourably than white people. That does not matter. 'Paper policy' is nevertheless 'designed' to benefit white people and not black people.

18 That 'the pigsty of parliamentary democracy' is the perfect tool for capitalist oppression is standard Leninism. (Lenin, V.I., 'The State and Revolution' (1917), in *Collected Works II*, Moscow, Foreign Languages Publishing House, 1947, p. 171.) Trotsky called British parliamentary democracy 'the system of institutions and measures whereby the needs and demands of the working masses, who are striving upwards, are neutralized, distorted, rendered harmless, or purely and simply brought to naught'. Trotsky, L., *Where Is Britain Going?* (1925), London: New Park, 1978, p. 49. These ideas, in a kind of 'find: proletariat, replace ethnic minority', have been transferred wholesale into the current confrontational anti-racist rhetoric. 'It's in your false democracy ...' It is 'your' not 'our' democracy. However long we have been here, we are not responsible for it.

19 Trotsky, L., *The Death Agony of Capitalism and the Tasks of the Fourth International: the transitional programme* (1938), London: World Books, c. 1978, p. 20.

20 Trotsky, *Where Is Britain Going?* (1925), 1978, p. 42.

21 Trotsky, *The Death Agony of Capitalism and the Tasks of the Fourth International: the transitional programme* (1938), c. 1978, pp. 26-27 and p. 61.

22 White, W., *A Man Called White*, London: 1949.

23 Trotsky, *The Death Agony of Capitalism and the Tasks of the Fourth International: the transitional programme* (1938), c. 1978, p. 47.

24 Communists must not 'allow themselves to be seduced for a single moment by the hypocritical phrases of the democratic petty bourgeoisie'. 'Communists must drive the proposals of the democrats ... to the extreme ... thus, for example, if the petty bourgeois propose purchase of railways and factories, the workers must demand that these railways and factories shall be simply confiscated by the state without compensation as being the property of reactionaries ... If the democrats propose proportional taxes, the workers must demand progressive taxes; if the democrats put forward a moderately progressive tax, the workers must insist on a tax with rates that rise

so steeply that big capital will be ruined by it.' Marx, K. and Engels, F., 'Address of the Central Committee to the Communist League' (1850), in Marx and Engels, *Selected Works I*, 1958, p. 116.

25 Trotsky, *The Death Agony of Capitalism and the Tasks of the Fourth International: The transitional programme* (1938), c. 1978, p. 23. (Emphasis added.)

26 Trotsky, *The Death Agony of Capitalism and the Tasks of the Fourth International: The transitional programme* (1938), c. 1978,p. 35.

27 Cathcart, B., *The Case of Stephen Lawrence*, London: Penguin Viking, 1999, p. 380. The manifesto of the party reads: 'The Socialist Labour Party ... is a natural home for Socialists and the millions of people throughout England, Scotland and Wales who feel disenfranchised or dispossessed by injustice and inequality ... Our Party was founded by trades unionists, [and] environmental and peace activists who have struggled consistently to ... combat racism, sexism, homophobia and ageism and secure justice for all. We believe in direct action ... against oppression; at the same time, we seek representation for Socialist policies through the ballot box'.

28 'Youth and age', in Palgrave, F.T., *The Golden Treasury of the Best Songs and Poems in the English Language*, London: Collins, 1861, p. 293.

Chapter 15: Stereotypes and Prejudice

1 E.g. Godwin, W., *Enquiry Concerning Political Justice* (3rd edn., 1798), London: Penguin, 1985.

2 Hobbes, T., *Leviathan* (1651), London: Collier-Macmillan, 1962, p. 100.

3 Talmon, J.L., 'Totalitarianism of the right and totalitarianism of the left', *The Origins of Totalitarian Democracy* (1952), London: Mercury, 1961, pp. 6-8.

4 The best account of English football hooliganism from the inside is to be found in a book by an astonished outsider, an American from Baton Rouge, Louisiana. Buford, B., *Among the Thugs*, London: Secker and Warburg, 1991.

5 Dalrymple, T., 'Oh, to be in England: choosing to fail', *City Journal*, Winter 2000, pp. 103-04.

6 'Racism tolerated "because it comes from my mates"', *Daily Telegraph*, 30 November 1999.

7 'Statement of Doreen Lawrence, 8 March 1998', Macpherson, W., *The Stephen Lawrence Inquiry: appendices*, Cm 4262-II (Revised), London: The Stationery Office, February 1999. [No page numbers supplied.] (Emphasis added.)

Chapter 16: Conclusion

1   Cathcart, B., *The Case of Stephen Lawrence*, London: Penguin Viking, 1999, p. 412.

2   BBC2 'Newsnight', 17 November 1999. (Emphasis added.)

3   Johnston, P., 'Fear of defeat in Lords brings race-law U-turn', *Daily Telegraph*, 28 January 2000.

4   Jeremy Vine, 'Newsnight' 4 February 2000.

5   Cathcart, *The Case of Stephen Lawrence*, 1999, p. 416.

6   Talmon, J.L., *The Origins of Totalitarian Democracy* (1952), London: Mercury, 1961, p. 87.

7   Sorel, G., *Reflections on Violence* (1906), Glencoe, Ill: Free Press, 1950.

8   Benda, J., *The Great Betrayal*, London: Routledge and Kegan Paul, 1928. In the original French it is *La Trahison des clercs*—'The treason of the intellectuals'. That is, indeed, the title given to the American edition of Benda's book.

9   Pierson, J., 'Social work and civil society: the mixed legacy of radical anti-oppressive practice', in Philpot, T. (ed.), *Political Correctness and Social Work*, London: IEA Health and Welfare Unit, 1999, p. 51. John Pierson was trained as a social worker in the 1970s, and became senior lecturer in social work and social policy at the Institute of Social Work and Applied Social Studies at the University of Staffordshire. He is co-editor of the Dictionary of Social Work, 1995. His remarks are all the more interesting because his complaint is not against what he refers to as the 'New Left and Marxist' roots of social-work anti-racism, but against the fact that these roots failed to nourish enough New Left growth in social work.

10 Pierson, 'Social work and civil society: the mixed legacy of radical anti-oppressive practice', 1999, p. 54.

11 Pinker, R., 'Social work and adoption: a case of mistaken identities', in Philpot, *Political Correctness and Social Work*, 1999.

12 *Rules and Requirements for the Diploma in Social Work*, Paper 30, London: CCETSW, 1991.

13 *Rules and Requirements for the Diploma in Social Work*, Paper 30, 1991, p. 46. (Emphasis added.)

14 Humphries, B., Pankenia-Wimmer, H., Seale, A. and Stokes I., *Anti-racist Social Work Education: 7. Improving Practice Teaching and Learning—A Training Pack*, Northern Curriculum Development Project on Anti-racist Social Work Education, London: CCETSW, 1993, pp. 25-26.

15 Humphries, *et al.*, *Anti-racist Social Work Education: 7. Improving Practice Teaching and Learning - A Training Pack*, 1993, pp. 32-33.

16 Humphries, *et al.*, *Anti-racist Social Work Education: 7. Improving practice teaching and learning - a training pack*, 1993, p. 41.

17 Washington, B.T., *Up from Slavery* (1901), London: Norton, 1996.

18 Washington, B.T., 'The awakening of the Negro', *Atlantic Monthly*, 78, 1896.

19 du Bois, W.E.B., 'The training of black men', *Atlantic Monthly*, 90, 1902.

20 Burt, T., *Thomas Burt MP, DCL, Pitman and Privy Coucillor: an autobiography* (1924), New York: Garland, 1984. Douglass' inspirational book is *Narrative of the Life of Frederick Douglass, an American Slave, Written by Himself* (1845), Oxford: OUP, 1999. By following the same precepts as those of Frederick Douglass and Booker T. Washington, 'the proverbial and enduring qualities of thrift, hard work and self-sacrifice', (as the Asian English-language tabloid, *Eastern Eye*, put it), the immigrant population from the Indian sub-continent and Uganda had produced many multi-millionaires within the space of a few years. By 1997 Shami Ahmed owned a fortune of £50 million made in the fashion trade. His father was an immigrant from Pakistan, who began by selling cheap garments from a market stall. By using ethnicity constructively, for example through providing food to the British population, a new generation of curry millionaires has appeared. Perween Warsi's fortune was estimated at £35 million in 1997, Kirit and Meena Pathak's at £25 million, and G.K. Noon's at £20 million. Several other Indians have become millionaires through the fashion trade. Reuben Singh, aged only 20 and selling fashion accessories, was worth £27.5 million in 1997, although still a student in Manchester. Tom Singh had a fortune of £115 million. Naresh Patel (£50 million) owned the Colorama photo-processing laboratories and the Europa supermarket chain. Lakshmi Mittal, 46, the Indian-born head of the Ispat international steel empire, had a fortune valued at £1.5 billion. The Hinduja brothers, Srichand and Gopi, who were valued at £1.1 billion, had powerful political contacts. Indians have been created peers by both Conservative and Labour governments in recent years. Lord Paul, chairman of the Caparo steel empire, and Lord Bagri, chairman of the London Metal Exchange were made peers in 1997. Lord Alli is a peer created under Blair's Labour government. G.K. Noon joined the Reform Club in 1997. Beresford, P. and Merchant, K., *Eastern Eye*, February 1997. At the other end of the scale of wealth, in any English town taxi drivers and shopkeepers from the Indian sub-continent can be seen working hard as their way of 'making good', while allegedly many of their young white neighbours are prevented from doing the same by adverse social conditions and because they are excluded from any opportunities for employment by an unjust society.

21 Washington, 'The awakening of the Negro', 1896.

22 X, M., *The Autobiography of Malcolm X*, Harmondsworth: Penguin, 1968. X, M., *By Any Means Necessary*, London: Pathfinder, 1992. X, M., *Final Speeches* (1965), London: Pathfinder, 1992.

23 'Statement of Neville Lawrence, 7 March 1998', Macpherson, W., *The Stephen Lawrence Inquiry: appendices*, Cm 4262-II (Revised), London: The Stationery Office, February 1999. [No page numbers supplied.]

24 'Statement of Neville Lawrence, 7 March 1998', Macpherson, *The Stephen Lawrence Inquiry: appendices*, Cm 4262-II (Revised). [No page numbers supplied.]

Index

Independence

The Institute for the Study of Civil Society is a registered educational charity (No. 1036909). The ISCS is financed from a variety of private sources to avoid over-reliance on any single or small group of donors.

All publications are independently refereed and referees' comments are passed on anonymously to authors. All the Institute's publications seek to further its objective of promoting the advancement of learning. The views expressed are those of the authors, not of the ISCS.